THE CHRISTIA

# *The Christian Youth Manual*

STEVE CHALKE

KINGSWAY PUBLICATIONS
EASTBOURNE

First published 1987
This revised and expanded edition 1992





*Cover photos: Scripture Union, Gordon Gray*
*Cover design by W James Hammond*

ISBN 0 85476 285 X

Printed in Great Britain for
KINGSWAY PUBLICATIONS LTD
1 St Anne's Road, Eastbourne, E Sussex BN21 3UN by
Richard Clay Ltd, Bungay, Suffolk
Typeset by Watermark, Crostwight, Norfolk

# CONTENTS

# PREFACE

'I am told that C.S. Lewis once claimed that almost 90% of the ideas for his writing were not original but borrowed from elsewhere. I take great comfort in such an idea!' That's how the preface to *The Complete Youth Manual*, the forerunner of this book, began. The reason for this was simply that it consisted in large measure of ideas, concepts and information that I had begged, borrowed and stolen from sources far too numerous to remember let alone acknowledge.

You are now holding a copy of *The Christian Youth Manual* – an updated, revised and substantially expanded version of that original book. But, whatever the changes and additions have been, one thing remains exactly the same: Just as much as ever my writing is dependent on all that I am constantly learning from the wide array of youth leaders and teenagers I continue to work alongside.

Though it's impossible to credit everyone who has indirectly contributed to this book, I want to mention some of those who have had a major influence on the development of my understanding of leadership and youth ministry. These include Holmesdale Baptist Church in South London where I grew up and became a Christian; South Ashford Baptist Church where I first led a youth group under the wing of my friend Steve Flashman; Emmanuel Baptist Church in Gravesend, where I worked for a year before going to theological college and where I met David Beer whose friendship and guidance have been a great influence on me, and Tonbridge Baptist Church, where I got the opportunity to experiment with and develop what were, to me, new concepts of youth ministry. I'm also grateful to everyone at Haddon Hall Baptist Church in Bermondsey where I am currently a minister and where I continue to learn more about team leadership and new styles of youth work.

Thanks are also due to Spurgeons College – the principles I learned there are the backbone of the work that I am involved in today, and to everyone at *21CC* and *ALPHA* magazines for their constant encouragement over the material, included in this book, which originally appeared as part of 'Chalke Talk' (a monthly article for youth leaders I have written for them over the past four-and-a-half years).

There is a major emphasis in this book on teamwork. Without a really great team around me at Oasis neither the original writing nor the updating of this book would have been possible or desirable.

Lastly, I've saved my biggest thanks for Cornelia, my wife. Without her constant love and support I'd be sunk!

*Steve Chalke*
*The Oasis Trust*
*December 1991*

# Part One

# PRINCIPLES

# 1
# TEENAGERS – THE MISSING LINK
## *Understanding teenage culture*

> The world is passing through troublesome times. The young people of today think of nothing but themselves. They have no reverence for parents or old age. They are impatient of all restraint. They talk as if they know everything, and what passes for wisdom with us is foolishness to them. As for the girls, they are immodest and unwomanly in speech, behaviour and dress.[1]

Just the kind of sentiment that is expressed countless times each week by everyone from parents to school teachers, magistrates to shopkeepers. It is typical of the kind of complaint heard from many people in the church today.

In fact, this remark was made by Peter the monk, in the year 1274! But he was not the first to notice the downward trend in the behaviour of young people.

> When I look at the younger generation, I despair of the future of civilisation.[2]

That was Aristotle in the year 300 BC.

It is no new thing for those who are older to sit round and bemoan the behaviour of the young. All that is said in many Parochial Church Councils, deacons' and elders' meetings, or muttered by a group of ladies trying to tidy up the mess left in the church kitchen by the youth club the night before, is merely an echo of what has been said by many other voices in times past.

Young people are frequently exhorted to 'act their age', but this is often nothing other than a thinly disguised demand that they behave like mature adults. This, of course, is an impossibility for an adolescent who by definition is not an adult, but is still in the process of maturing. Mentally, physically, emotionally, socially and spiritually he is not yet fully mature.

### What is an adolescent?

The Oxford English Dictionary defines an adolescent as someone who is between the states of childhood and adulthood. James Dobson describes the adolescent years as a 'turbulent voyage'[3] which involves leaving behind the protection of the harbour of childhood and heading for the open sea of adulthood.

It's not easy to be an adolescent; the comforts of childhood are in the process of disappearing but the rewards of adulthood are slow to make themselves available. Adolescents are caught between two ages; they are in transition between two worlds.

When they were children they trusted their parents to make decisions about money, food and accommodation. But now they are beginning to move into the world of the 'grown-up' taking their first faltering steps to adulthood; making their own decisions; earning their own living and gradually becoming independent.

### An inborn desire

It is not just that society expects all this of the adolescent, but, much more than this, there is a natural inborn desire to 'leave the nest'. Girls of this age used to be called 'flappers', a very descriptive term for those 'trying out their own wings'! This process varies with each individual. Some are over-confident and want to launch out too far and too soon, but others tend to be more than cautious process varies with each individual. Some are over-confident and want to launch out too far and too soon, but others tend to be more than cautious and require a gentle push. The desire for privacy and independence is natural and just as strong in the young human as it is in the young bird who desperately wants to leave the nest. God created this desire and we struggle against him if we try to hold it back. Anne Townsend points out in *Families Without Pretending* that adolescence is a time of letting go and she adds that from now on the parents are 'watching and supporting the first tentative steps of a new adult, and...must learn to make a relationship with them on new terms'.[4]

**An explosive mixture**

James Dobson asks, 'How would you like to be thirteen years old again by the wave of a magic wand?' Then he gives the answer 'No thanks!...Everyone in our culture wants to remain young, but not that young! And why not? Because we grown-ups remember our adolescent years as the most stressful and threatening time of life.'[5]

Doctors and sociologists tell us that life contains several crisis points for the adult, such as marriage, having children, moving, changing job, mid-life, retirement and bereavement. But if we take a careful look at the questions and uncertainties faced at these points we soon become aware that most of the same underlying insecurities and doubts occur together during the adolescent years, when there is not as much experience to call on for support. There are the bewildering physical changes, as well as the sexual anxiety and guilt that develop along with the adolescent's new desires. There is self-doubt and feelings of inferiority, the worries about appearance and acceptance by others, and fears about failure and rejection. Then there is the lack of ability to express oneself as clearly as one wishes. All this within the context of the emotional vulnerability these years bring. The adolescent is an explosive mixture of insecurities and self-questioning. But though this has been human experience for centuries, the modern adolescent faces still greater problems.

**The generation gap is created**

F. Musgrove, a British sociologist, states that the adolescent was invented at the same time as the industrial revolution took place:

> Having invented the adolescent, society has been faced with two major problems: how and where to accommodate him in the social structure, and how to make his behaviour accord with the specifications.[6]

What he is saying is simply that the industrial revolution reconstructed society in such a way as to allow much more room for adolescents as a separate group than had ever been the case before.

In many cultures the young person moved much more easily between childhood and adulthood than he does in the West today. The transition took place at puberty, when the boy or girl was initiated into adulthood, leaving childhood behind for ever. In some so-called 'primitive' societies these initiation rites involved the infliction of pain which the boy had to endure with courage and determination. For instance, a boy would go off into the jungle to hunt alone for several days; if he returned alive he was a man, if not, well it didn't matter anyway!

In Roman times, we are told, the transition from childhood to manhood was signalled by the wearing of the toga, whereas in this country, in medieval times, at the age of fourteen a boy might become a squire, his responsibility being to serve a knight by accompanying him into battle and bearing his arms.

In Jewish society, at the age of thirteen a boy would have his barmitzvah and pass into full manhood. In rural societies this was the point when the boy joined his father in working the land or going fishing, and so on. As a child he had learned by watching his father, but now, as he reached the age when he was beginning to want to assert his sense of responsibility, he was given ample opportunity. He became involved in the real responsibilities of life, entering the world of work.

It was not that the youth was pushed without experience into the full responsibility of mature adulthood. At this stage he was still given time and freedom to develop slowly and grow; for example, the medieval boy was a squire, not a knight, or he joined his father on the land in a kind of apprenticeship. Though much is made of the fact that at thirteen a Jewish boy became a man, closer study of the Old Testament reveals that even within this there was some distinction between an adolescent aged thirteen to twenty years and a male of over that age (see Lev 27). A period of adolescence definitely existed, but it came complete with much greater responsibility. It comes as no surprise, then, that some anthropologists say that the adolescents of primitive communities did not suffer the same neurotic 'difficulties' as those of modern industrial societies.

In modern Western society the transfer of responsibility is a much more gradual process. As you grow older you slowly collect more of the rights and responsibilities of adulthood. This starts at the age of ten and continues up to twenty-one years. At ten, young people can be considered responsible for criminal offences. At thirteen they may do light work within certain hours and conditions, if local bye-laws permit it. At fourteen they can be allowed to see a criminal trial or go to a PG film alone. They can also go into a pub but must not buy or drink alcohol. At fifteen they can open a Giro account. At the age of sixteen they can leave school and work a forty-eight hour week. They can hold a licence to drive a motorcycle, buy tobacco and drink wine or beer with a meal on licensed premises. They can consent to medical or surgical treatment. They may get married with parental consent, although this is not necessary in Scotland. Girls can legally consent to sexual intercourse. At seventeen they can go into a betting shop but must not bet; they can become a street trader and hold an ordinary driving licence. At eighteen teenagers have reached the age of majority: their parents no longer legally control them. They may get married without parental consent. They may drink alcohol in a pub, watch adult films, place bets and make legal contracts, for example, enter hire purchase agreements. They can be sent to an ordinary prison in England, be tattooed and can vote. At the age of twenty-one they may stand as a candidate in an election and become an MP, adopt a child, or be sent to an ordinary prison in Scotland.

In this way the process of entering adult life is spread out over no less than eleven years!

**In the goldfish bowl**

Even until quite recently within our own culture, a boy could leave school at fourteen and move straight into an apprenticeship, working alongside, for example, a carpenter, a plumber, an electrician, or a butcher, and there learn his trade 'on the job'. But as our society has developed and become more complex, the educational requirements needed for many jobs have multiplied, so that the adolescent is expected to remain longer within the educational system and today the minimum school leaving age is sixteen. This has led to the assumption that a fairly high level of general education is required for almost all jobs in our society. Today the aspiring electrician will probably stay on longer at school, and be pushed to take GCSEs. From school he may well go on to college or university or at least take some kind of sandwich course before being given any real responsibility.

Adolescents have been contained in a gigantic 'educational goldfish bowl', removed against their natural inclinations from responsibility and involvement in what they feel is real life. Society has turned them into a race apart, segregating them from the serious activities of adulthood. They have energy, drive and enthusiasm, but are not given opportunities for responsibility. They are mentally alert and questioning but are kept from decision-making within society. This has exacerbated the adolescent's natural sense of frustration and inadequacy. The message from society is that adolescents are spare parts, unworthy of responsibility; they have ample time on their hands to brood on their plight.

This gap between the child and the adult, which the modern industrial society has created, has been filled by a cultural explosion: the emergence of the 'teenager'.

**Rock 'n' roll and the teenage explosion**

1953 was an important year. The word 'teenager' was only a few years old, and certainly wasn't the household term it is today. But what happened in 1953? Bill Haley recorded *Crazy Man Crazy*, the first white rock 'n' roll record ever to enter the charts.

If it is true that adolescents are an explosive mixture of emotions and that modern society's segregation of youth is largely responsible for this then it is also true that the emergence of pop music supplied the spark which finally caused that long-threatened explosion to take place. Its arrival also provided the gust of fresh air that fanned the flames of the fire that resulted.

**You've never had it so good**

In the years that followed the second world war, the standard of living in the West slowly rose. By the mid-fifties a time of plenty had arrived in North America, and this spread to Great Britain towards the end of the decade. Harold Macmillan's slogan was 'You've never had it so good'. Yet there was an undercurrent of unrest among the young, a desire for change and action, which the 'luxury' of their segregation from the 'serious' activities of life allowed to develop and spread.

Malcolm Doney, tracing the developments of rock music and

culture, explains that in the years which immediately followed the end of the war, young people were bored and frustrated with the white popular music of the day. It was

> the music of a bygone era...dreamy and escapist...fine for the Mums and Dads. It was the kind of armchair comfort that had helped them through the war.[7]

He is referring, of course, to the big band sound which came with singers such as the young Frank Sinatra. The music was smooth and sophisticated, neat and tidy, with professional polished performances but no sense of reality.

> Seen now through the permanent soft focus of nostalgia it seems pleasant and easy. But for the kids of the fifties it was deadly...they wanted raw excitement – life.[8]

**Rock – the voice of rebellion**

Into this situation stepped tubby Bill Haley and the Comets. The quality of their music was hardly exceptional; what was so riveting was that they had begun to play their own versions of the old rhythm and blues songs which were so popular among the blacks of America. *Crazy Man Crazy* was the first of a string of hits for Haley on both sides of the Atlantic, as was the film *Rock around the Clock*. From then on rock 'n' roll became the teenage music. It was exciting, raw and powerful; it had drive and energy. In place of the well-groomed sophisticated looks of Frank Sinatra came the rock 'n' roll singer, tough, sinister, aggressive and streetwise. Just as rhythm and blues was a musical expression of the frustration, pain and alienation of black people, so now rock 'n' roll was becoming the voice of the young in America and Great Britain, the voice of their rebellion. In 1969 a rock journalist could write,

> Rock music was born of a revolt against the sham of Western

> culture; it was direct and gutsy and spoke to the senses. As such it was profoundly subversive.[9]

### Your mother doesn't like it

Rock music had one other supreme quality which no doubt contributed greatly to its ability to capture the imagination and commitment of so many teenagers. Put simply, parents hated it; they despised it and all those who were responsible for it. To parents it seemed that rock 'n' roll was the music of depravity. It was well-known that its origins were negroid and it was a development of primitive jungle rhythms and therefore linked with voodoo. It was nothing less than satanic, an instrument of the forces of darkness. This was great news for the young because it meant it was theirs, exclusively. Nothing could be better!

> Help save the youth of America. Don't buy negro records...the screaming and idiotic words and savage music of these records are undermining the morals of our white youth in America. Don't let your children buy or listen to these negro records.[10]

Of course, in some church circles this attitude still persists. Rock music is unChristian. In *Solid Rock*, a magazine edited by Tom Morton and produced in 1980, there is an excerpt from a Christian tract entitled *Spellbound* where the comment is made,

> One of the greatest victories in the Occult world was to penetrate the Christian music with their satanic beat. I know of Christian kids who destroyed their rock records, but after listening to Christian rock, the druid beat soon pulled them back into worldly rock music again...then the desire to study the Bible cools off![11]

### The fire spreads

All of this wasn't really Bill Haley's fault and in fact, had it been left to him, rock 'n' roll would probably not have survived. But he was just the forerunner, behind him came other much stronger, far more aggressive and appealing characters.

First, there was Elvis Presley, dark and handsome with a growling voice, the idol of thousands of teenagers in Britain and America. The girls dreamed of being his, and the boys admired his macho image. He was a hero to look up to and imitate. He was, in the words of Malcolm Doney, 'the personification of the mothers' nightmares and the daughters' loves'.[12]

At this stage rock 'n' roll was still almost purely American. There were, of course, our very own British Elvis look-and-sound alikes – Tommy Steele, Adam Faith, Billy Fury, Marty Wilde and, most successfully, Cliff Richard, but it was all a carbon copy of the American situation. It was 1963 before the change came with the arrival of the Beatles who were soon to take over and hold high the torch which Elvis had grown weary, or incapable, of carrying. Shortly after them came the Rolling Stones, the Animals and the others. Now rock 'n' roll was truly British, and increasingly became the focus for many young people in their struggle to express themselves. Geoffrey Cannon talks of 'the magic peculiar to rock music of making you think your own thoughts harder and faster and at the same time, making you feel reasons to be connected with your kin'.[13]

Rock 'n' roll became a kind of glue holding the growing youth culture together.

**Youth culture arrives**

In the post war industrial boom, young people were enjoying their share of the increased wealth. They had greater spending power than ever before and very few responsibilities. They were, in fact, the only age group in society with money to spend on impulse. Manufacturers were presented with a new and untapped market, one that was ripe for exploitation. It has been said that the term 'teenager' was itself invented by advertising men towards the end of the war to give the adolescent market an identity. Adolescents needed their own identity, and for different reasons big business wanted to supply it. John Allan says, 'The advertisers set about prising the money from the kids. The strategy was to make them feel important, special, unique.'[14] What had been missing had been an image around which to build this new identity. Bill Haley and rock 'n' roll arrived on the scene at just the right time and commercial enterprise put all its weight behind both him and his music. Around the music they were to build a whole industry. In the wake of rock 'n' roll came the distinctive clothes, the hair styles, the record players, musical instruments, badges, magazines and books, and even language, all designed exclusively for young people. The youth revolution was on. 'Pop culture' as well as pop music had arrived.

Clifford Hill states: 'The rise of the pop culture in the mid-1950s is generally regarded as the beginning of the social revolution that has been shaking Britain to its foundations...ever since.'[15]

The emergence of the pop industry is one of the most significant developments of this century. It has played a massive part in shaping our whole culture, a part that has only been equalled by the new technology more recently made available with the silicon chip.

### The 'missing link' is found

Modern society had widened the generation gap to an extent unthought of previously, and into that gap had dropped 'the teenager'. Teenagers dressed differently, thought differently and were generally accepted as having their own separate place in society. The 'missing link' between childhood and adult life had been well and truly found!

The whole situation is summed up in an experience I had while visiting a church in the Midlands. 'When I was fifteen, all I wanted to be was like my dad,' the minister explained to me, 'to have a suit like his.' This particular minister had been a young man in the forties with aspirations typical of the youth of his generation. I have travelled widely through this country meeting young people in many situations but have never found one who would still say, 'All I want is a suit like my dad's.' Nothing could be further from the aspirations and hopes of any teenager alive! My dad is a great bloke; I get on very well with him, especially since leaving home! But never in a million years would I want to wear trousers or a jacket that look anything like his. Today adolescents no longer look to their parents for this kind of role model; instead they look to one another, to their own leaders, the pop stars, and others within their own culture.

**When I was young it was different**

Many older Christians have explained to me that in their youth, though they may have found church services boring, uninspiring or irrelevant, there was absolutely no thought in their minds that there could be any other pattern. One elderly lady recently told me, 'We knew we had to grin and bear it.' There was never any hint of rebellion. But things are different now. Adolescents have received an enormous boost of confidence, they demand a voice, they have opinions and views and want to be heard; the teenage movement has seen to that.

Often I have heard leaders and others within the church expressing a sentiment which runs something like: 'When we were young we didn't expect all this. Why should we even think about rearranging the services for the young people? We don't do it for other groups. What about elderly folk or middle aged mums? We don't design things just to suit them, and neither will we for teenagers. The church is a family, they must just fit in and take their place.'

It's true that the church is a family but, as well we know, the family unit too struggles with the problems of the teenager. To bring an adolescent through those difficult years requires wisdom and sensitivity. They have a will of their own; no longer can the law be laid down to them. Teenagers do not want orders but advice, and every parent knows that many times that advice is ignored. The social habits of teenagers are different from those of the adult and some working relationship needs to be found which gives them freedom and yet supplies much needed boundaries. It's no good the church saying, 'Fifty years ago we didn't have all this fuss with teenagers and so we're not going to stand for it today.' For fifty years ago the teenager did not exist!

**Food for thought**

We must sit down and attempt to understand the cultural situation in which our young people find themselves. This task is never easy; it requires our best thinking, our greatest sensitivity, and a good dose of the love of God which will allow us to accept a person as he is.

The problem is that youth culture is changing rapidly. For those of us in our twenties, thirties or forties it's no good saying that we know what it's like. We cannot simply regard today's youth culture as nothing more than a reflection of our own teenage years. Just watch a film on television made ten years ago which reflects life then...it's almost archaic now, not just because of dress, music and language but also, and perhaps most importantly, because of its attitudes and outlook on life.

In the late fifties young people faced a generally optimistic future. Despite the cold war threats of a nuclear catastrophe, most young people applied themselves to schoolwork, honestly believing that an educated person would be a more fulfilled person. They had questions about the future but saw hope.

In the sixties the mood changed as the anti-establishment feeling became much more widespread. There were marches on the streets with slogans and banners. This was the age of flower power. An alternative society was planned where all you needed was love.

In the seventies, the idealism of the sixties was smashed and disillusionment spread. 'The Beatles said all you need is love and then they broke up,' was Larry Norman's comment.[16] A new slogan emerged: 'If it feels good, do it', and the young became known as the 'me generation'. They were inward looking and unconcerned with the outside world.

In the eighties things were different again. We were no longer living in the 'me generation'. Young people faced a very bleak future filled with immense pressures unknown to previous generations, including widespread unemployment, worldwide food and energy shortages, over-population and the global uncertainty caused by the nuclear arms race. Increased crime and broken homes led to confusion, disillusionment, frustration and depression. Observers have dubbed the youth of the eighties the 'anxious generation'.

Now the nineties open up before us, and though it is a little early to attach any labels too firmly to a new generation of young people, it is clear that most of the pressures faced by the young of the eighties still stare them full in the face. There are, of course, encouraging signs that the pace of the nuclear arms race is beginning to slow as relationships between East and West improve. But now frightening new dangers which threaten our future loom on the horizon. The teenagers of the nineties will face life on a planet scarred and spoilt by pollution and misuse of its resources. Issues concerning the environment will dominate the next decade as the problems of world pollution, deforestation, the disappearing ozone layer, the greenhouse effect and global warming make their mark and shape our lives. The teenagers of the nineties are looking just as anxious as their predecessors.

Anxious they may be, but not idle. Increasingly the young people of the eighties, and now in their turn those of the nineties, are attempting to face and tackle the big issues. Band Aid, Live Aid, Sport Aid, School Aid, Comic Relief, all provide glorious examples of this. But today's teenagers are also involved with CND, Greenpeace, and the anti-apartheid movement. There is a growing desire to face the problems of late-twentieth-century life full on, and to find solutions.

This is, of course, a generalisation. Each young person is born an individual and grows up with a unique combination of influences caused by family, school, friends, geographical location and so on. Bromley is geographically very near to Brixton, though culturally young people growing up in the two towns may be influenced very differently, perhaps resulting in somewhat contrasting views of life, of themselves, others and authority. Young people may not have the biblical framework that we would wish, nor a specifically Christian moral code, but we are blind if we write them off as superficial, aggressive, uncaring, or concerned solely with their own pleasure.

Teenagers are exploring the world in which they live. This is a difficult task in which they are searching for advice and guidance (even if it sometimes seems quite the opposite!). But perhaps more than all this they seek acceptance by adults who will take them seriously and grant them responsibility. Is the church prepared to answer the call?

# 2
# IT'S NO FUN BEING A TEENAGER
## *Understanding adolescents*

The exact age spectrum covered by the term 'adolescence' is a matter of some dispute. J. A. Hadfield in his book *Childhood and Adolescence* states that the term is usually taken to cover the ages from twelve to eighteen.[1] Pete Gilbert writing in Youth For Christ's *This Generation Youth Evangelism File* places the boundaries wider at eleven and twenty-one years[2] and Trevor Partridge of Crusade for World Revival says, 'The age span of adolescence is approximately 11 to 22!'[3] Of course, if we are going to identify adolescence with the teenage years, then it runs officially from thirteen to nineteen. But wherever we place the exact limits of adolescence, it is clear that the needs, aspirations and questions of an eleven, twelve or thirteen year old are quite different from those of an eighteen to twenty-two year old.

### Adolescence or adolescents

One of the greatest dangers when dealing with adolescents is to lump them all together as one, believing that their needs are all the same. As we saw earlier, this cannot be done. Teenagers are individuals and cannot be compartmentalised. There are no golden rules that will apply universally to them. It has been pointed out that theory deals with adolescence with a 'ce' whereas the youth leader deals with adolescents with a 'ts' and that makes all the difference! Recognising this, it can still be helpful to realise that adolescence consists of various phases and that it has often been sub-divided into three rather loosely defined age groups. Because generalisations are always dangerous unless handled very carefully, it is important to recognise that individual teenagers may reach various stages in their development earlier or later than others. The three stages of adolescence outlined below help us to have a greater understanding of the young people with whom we work.

**Three stages of adolescence**

*(1) The homosexual stage (11–14 year olds)*

The use of this term has often been misunderstood. The point is simply that during this phase a young person tends to relate far better to his or her own sex than members of the opposite one. These years usually mark the onset of puberty (which we will deal with later) and are also characterised by 'gang activity'. Gangs are normally single sex, exclusively male or female.

Gang formation is a natural impulse although much stronger within boys than girls. Gangs are held together by a common interest in such things as football, cricket, BMX bikes, skateboards, a particular group of girls or kind of music.

Some gangs will exist just for the sake of existing, the common interest being nothing more than the sense of belonging to one another. You will often see a gang wandering the streets on a Saturday afternoon or at some time doing absolutely nothing except belonging. In Tonbridge where I used to work, a gang of youths congregated outside the church building almost every night, and would just sit on the fence for hours doing nothing, except being together. They were never really interested in joining in organised activities but would very much appreciate it if time was taken to chat with them and get to know them. On the occasional evening when I am back at the church building, they are still sitting there although they do seem to have moved about ten yards up the road to a new piece of fence, and new faces have joined the gang while other older ones have disappeared!

There is usually a tremendous loyalty to the gang which extends to each member, quite irrespective of their personal qualities, simply because they are members. The greatest sin is to sneak, to squeal or split on another gang member.

It is too easy for us to dismiss this gang spirit as 'just a childish phase'. In fact sociologists tell us it is a very important part of the development of any young person. Our churches, political parties, clubs, etc, are all developments of the gang spirit. The concept of loyalty acquired during this time is of immense importance later in life.

Most gangs have a leader. He is a very important figure, to whom the other members will often give almost unquestioning obedience. Since a teenager of this age will also tend to hero worship those that he admires, a boy may model his whole personality around that of the gang leader, taking on his characteristics, both good and bad. At the same time he may completely abandon his old identification with his father, whose authority he will now not accept and whose character, which he had previously tried to imitate, he now rejects. The heroes whom he had previously tried to imitate, he now rejects. The heroes whom he admires need not be his own age; they may be adults, pop stars, sports men and women, a particular teacher or youth leader.

*(2) The transitional stage (15–16 year olds)*

This period marks the phase of adolescence between the homosexual stage, where the teenager spends his time with those of the same sex, and the heterosexual stage when the teenager's attention is on the opposite sex. In fact, this stage usually occurs earlier in girls than boys. As the adolescent grows he discovers that the gang does not satisfy his need for an intimate friend, someone of the same sex with whom he can exchange confidences and share problems. He begins to form close relationships which as a rule are totally asexual in nature although of course sex is one of the main topics of conversation because the adolescent's biggest problem is learning to cope with his new and very powerful sexual desires.

About this time many adolescents tend to become very moody. They will often go off by themselves, disappearing for hours, refusing to take part in programmed activities even of the most exciting kind. They may not even show the slightest interest in the gang which used to be so important to them. An adult will often try to chivvy the youth up with a 'Whatever has come over you? Why don't you go out with your friends or at least take an interest in something or other?'

The reply is simply, 'I don't want to. I don't feel like it.'

The desire for a close friend to confide in as well as the brooding and moodiness are both symptoms of the same thing: the fact that at this age the teenager becomes interested in the opposite sex in a much deeper way than before. As the young person begins to discover his desires and emotions in this area one 'crush' follows another. At this stage he will be attracted to older people of the opposite sex, such as the church youth leader! Beware: what seems to be an innocent counselling session is often anything but as far as the counsellee is concerned!

*(3) The heterosexual stage (16–21 year olds)*

This stage actually consists of two different phases because at first young people of both sexes find themselves attached to a number of young people of the opposite sex of the same age. At this time sexual curiosity and the simple desire to attract others are very important driving forces. As well as all this, the adolescent is also experimenting and slowly discovering the qualities which he is looking for in a partner of the opposite sex. As a result young people at this stage will often appear to be rather flirtatious.

By the age of seventeen or eighteen the teenager is generally beginning to move on to the second phase, where he is looking for a steady one-to-one relationship. He is beginning to think about marriage and other life decisions, but because the young person does not have the perspective of experience he thinks about these issues in a rather idealistic, or as Aristotle described it, 'high minded'[4] fashion. Idealism is a strong feature of this stage of adolescence.

**What makes a teenager?**

As we have seen, the teenager is an 'inbetween' person. He is travelling on a perilous journey into adult life away from the shelter and security of childhood. This journey has several stages which test him to his limits but through which he slowly and painfully grows and develops. This growth takes place in every area of teenager life; it involves the whole person: physical, intellectual, social, spiritual, moral and emotional. If we are to understand young people we must carefully look at the effects that this process has on their still-developing personality.

Some will ask 'Why bother with trying to understand teenagers? It's impossible; they don't even understand themselves!' The second part of this statement may well be true. It therefore becomes all the more vital that instead of expressing the attitude displayed in the first part of the sentence, we attempt to get alongside young people and exhibit care and concern as we grapple with the problem of understanding them. This is a difficult task, for the areas of development mentioned above are all inter-related, and bring many pressures to bear on one another. Together they form a bewildering, constantly changing kaleidoscope.

*(1) Physical growth*

Anybody involved in work with teenagers is aware of the rapid physical changes that take place in the early stages of adolescence. Puberty begins with a sudden period of growth in height, so that adults will often remark, 'Haven't you shot up!' It is straight after this 'spurt' of growth that sexual development begins to take place. Puberty begins earlier in females than in males, which generally accounts for girls' smaller stature (they have grown less before their growth 'spurt' starts). In girls puberty starts around the age of eleven whereas in boys it is at about thirteen. However, it can occur earlier, as early as nine or ten in girls, or as late as sixteen, seventeen or eighteen.

For girls this is the time when they experience the start of menstruation (the average age for the first period is twelve and a half), breast development and growth of body hair under arms, on legs and in the pubic region. Many members of both sexes will experience the problem of spots, blackheads and acne.

For boys this is a time of equally rapid change. Their voice breaks, they grow at a dramatically fast rate, their muscles develop and they become much stronger. They also experience the growth of body, facial and pubic hair and sexual organs mature and become larger. Boys will also begin to experience the occasional 'wet dream' or 'nocturnal emission'.

It is also the time when sexual awareness begins, which again is usually earlier in girls than boys. Boys become very interested in girls' bodies, whereas girls are usually more fascinated by the boy himself – his walk, the way he talks and his personality. It is the age of crushes which usually last only a few weeks or so before the next one starts. The teenager falls in and out of love regularly!

These physical changes can be terrifying for young teenagers. Their bodies are doing all sorts of frightening things which nobody has fully prepared them for. They are not sure what is happening, they wonder whether there is something wrong with them and whether, perhaps, they have some kind of disease. For instance, as breasts develop they often become sore and painful. Many a girl secretly wrestles with the fear that she has contracted cancer.

For the girl there is the worry of menstruation: will she bleed to death? Some girls dread their first period. A boy worries about what's happening to him when he has his first 'wet dream', and he is acutely embarrassed when his voice starts cracking and screeching.

For those of both sexes who develop late there is the terrifying question, 'Will I ever mature?' The boy worries because he has not started shaving and has grown no pubic hair. Will he ever be capable of sexual intercourse? And his voice is so high that he sounds more like a girl than a man. The same kind of fears surround the girl who listens to her friends talking about their periods but has not had one herself: 'Is there something wrong with me?' Her friends all look like women, but she doesn't even wear a bra. She thinks, 'Perhaps I'm going to be stuck like this for ever.' For those who develop unusually early there are similar problems, as again they ask the question, 'What's wrong with me? Am I ill?'

Sexual thoughts are uppermost in the adolescent's mind, which as we are often reminded, is the teenager's primary sex organ! It is estimated that the adolescent's thoughts will turn to this subject on average approximately once every fourteen minutes! Will God punish him for his sexual thoughts?

Fantasy plays a significant role in their life, with about 95% of all single males and 40% of all females being involved in masturbation at some time during adolescence. There are some very worrying rumours about this habit: it will make you weak and ill, drive you mad or cause blindness. Very many young people are torn by the agony of guilt over masturbation. They wish they could stop but they can't. What would their parents or friends say if they knew?

Physical appearance is very important to teenagers but it is estimated that over 80% of them are unhappy with their looks. For some reason they feel ugly and unattractive. They are too short, for example, or too tall, or they have spots. As a result they feel that they will never be attractive to the opposite sex. A teenager's feeling of sexual or physical failure is aggravated by the media, which present stereotyped ideas of 'success'. For instance, what is prettiness? Answer, 34–24–34!

If we begin to analyse the feelings that result from the process of physical development, we would have to list such things as anxiety, fear, depression, insecurity, lack of self-esteem, inferiority, inadequacy, shyness, self-doubt and over-sensitivity. All these feelings vie with the excitement and challenge of growing up. The teenager will often compensate for feelings of insecurity with a show of bravado and aggression.

*(2) Intellectual growth*

It is during our teenage years that we really begin fully to develop our ability to think in abstract terms and to tackle philosophical questions. Therefore the teenager will start asking life's difficult questions: 'Who am I?' 'What is the meaning of life?' 'What do I believe, and why?' In his search for answers his thinking will be shaped by the big institutions of our society: the family, education, law and government, and the church, and also by television, radio, pop culture, magazines and peer groups.

Today, we live in a very competitive world which puts enormous pressure on the teenager to succeed academically. Where academic success does not come, a deep sense of inadequacy and failure often sets in. It is also true that one of the greatest causes of failure is the fear of failure. The teenager, looking at all that is demanded of him academically, is very often intimidated, and automatically feels a sense of deep failure.

Many teenagers have a sense of intellectual frustration. They just don't feel clever enough. Their brain will not work fast enough and added to this problem they do not feel able to express themselves clearly. Their command of language is not strong enough and when they try to explain themselves they simply get tied up in knots. Adults tend to walk all over their arguments in minutes, dismissing them as worthless and naive.

*(3) Social development*

Every one of us has a need, to some degree or other, to conform to those around us but during the teenage years this desire is much stronger, heightened by the insecurities which accompany development towards adulthood. The adolescent hates to be different whether in dress, habits, speech, pocket money, or the things he is allowed to do. It is very important that youth leaders and parents take into account this need to conform. To be different can bring humiliation and unpopularity, and the young person will come to despise people who he can see have so little understanding of his needs that they don't see this.

The desire to conform will often push the teenager into actions which his better judgement tells him are wrong; for example, involvement with drugs, glue, drink, sex and the occult. I very much enjoy reggae music nowadays and, in concert, even go as far as performing one or two songs in this style. But as a teenager I belonged to a particular peer group which did not allow such freedom of choice. I hated reggae! We discover a strange paradox within the teenager who, while struggling for independence, individuality and self-expression, will at the same time dress almost identically to his friends and develop an exclusive allegiance to a particular brand of pop music – all in the cause of conformity.

*(4) Spiritual/moral development*

When he asks, 'Who am I?' and, 'What is life's meaning?' the young person is exploring spiritual and moral matters. In my work in schools and colleges up and down the country, I have discovered first hand that there are comparatively few atheists among teenagers. The vast majority of teenagers in the UK believe in God, although they are usually very unclear about what this God is like. Most of those teenagers who do not have a clear belief in God have an open mind on the subject.

Because in adolescence it is natural to examine the beliefs you have been taught as a child, many teenagers will question a belief in God or Christianity which up until this point has been based on parental teaching and example. When the adolescent begins to question it is important that he be taken seriously and given satisfactory answers, rather than being continually fobbed off with the simple reply, 'Have faith!'

As teenagers face these questions they will tend to be very idealistic. This should not be despised by adults. As Hadfield tells us, idealism 'is necessary for the full development of a man as a human being'.[5]

In Athens in classical times, at the age of eighteen the youth was taken to the Grove of Agroulos where he took his oath: 'I will never bring discredit in these arms, nor desert the man next to me in the ranks, but will fight for the sanctities of the common good, both alone and with others.'[6]

Idealism also held a high place during the age of chivalry. When a boy came to the age of fourteen, he might be made a squire and, as we have already pointed out, be appointed to serve a knight. In doing so he was expected to show courage, obedience, helpfulness and self-sacrifice. Then when he reached the age of twenty-one he too became a knight. After spending a night in prayer and confession he took vows: 'To be a brave, loyal, generous, just, and genteel knight, a champion of the Church, a redresser of the wrongs of widows and orphans, and a protector of women.'[7]

Hadfield makes a most important statement when he says:

> Idealism in youth comes at a very significant time...strong sexual desires on the one hand, and idealism on the other...appear to spring from the same common source, namely, the need for someone or something outside of the adolescent to fulfil and complete himself.[8]

The teenager begins to find this fulfilment physically and emotionally through a boy or girlfriend and later husband or wife, without whom he feels incomplete. But fulfilment also comes through idealism, for without aims and purpose the teenager will be left with a feeling of incompleteness. Unfortunately, teenage idealism often leads ultimately to a deep sense of dissatisfaction, self-questioning, inadequacy, inferiority and insecurity, for young people are very conscious of the discrepancy between what they are and what they would like to be.

### *(5) Emotional development*

The adolescent faces great emotional strains in coping with the four areas of development that we have already outlined. But as well as, and as a result of all this, comes the emotional trauma of working out new relationships within the family unit.

The young person striving for independence very often feels as though his parents still regard him as a child. In reality, teenagers need and, in fact, want less independence than they think, while parents generally need to give more independence in the right kind of areas than they imagine to be possible. This tension is a normal part of growing up.

During the teenage years all emotions are more intensely felt. As James Dobson states:

> Fears will be more frightening...pleasures will be more exciting...irritations will be more distressing, and...frustrations will be more intolerable. Every experience will appear king-sized. Their emotions move quickly up and down...they are...human yo-yos.[9]

Adolescents are easily swayed by the emotion of the moment and because they experience their feelings so deeply they tend to be explosive, often regretting their behaviour soon after the event.

It is also important to mention that a major factor in the lives of many young teenagers is the emotional stress and insecurity which is caused by the broken home. It is common knowledge that one in three marriages ends in divorce, while it is estimated that over 50% of those which continue are actually very unhappy, unsatisfying, and often only kept together for financial reasons or through the lack of courage to do anything else about the situation. Because the teenager is getting such a bumpy ride he needs a point of stability. Traditionally this has been provided by the home but where that fails him he urgently needs to find security elsewhere.

### External pressures

We have outlined the five areas of growth within the teenager and the problems they bring. But, as we have already seen, there are externals that further complicate the situation. The teenager, like us all, will feel pressure from outside. Peer groups, family life, education and the media, all squeeze the teenager by putting enormous pressure on internal insecurities.

If we are to understand the young people with whom we work, then we must give them the compassion, love and understanding which they deserve. It is vitally important that we grasp the complexity of the situation in which they find themselves. Life, it seems, is a hurdle course which they are told they must bravely face and run.

### The teenager and the Bible

In his very helpful book, *Christian Youth Work*, Mark Ashton is concerned with what he describes as 'theory and theology'. At one point he states that 'the most serious weakness in the Christian outreach to teenagers today is not a failure to understand our culture, it is a failure to take the Bible sufficiently seriously'.[10]

Too often Christians have approached youth work in a totally secular manner, listening very hard to all that the sociologists and psychologists have to tell them about the make-up of young people, but totally ignoring the biblical doctrine of man and his fallenness. It is nothing less than diabolical when the church is conned by the secular voices which surround it into believing that the world of the Old and New Testaments has no relevance to the problems we face in society today. Just as the Bible has very much to tell us about marriage and divorce, so it has much to say about young people. Nor are we to research the subject of 'understanding youth' with purely secular tools and then apply a veneer of biblical thoughts to what has been a sociological study. The basis from which we start as Christians is quite distinct from that which others may regard as foundational to their thinking. Christian youth work is not a secular cake with biblical icing; instead the basic recipe is filled with biblical ingredients.

**The Bible and the newspaper**

Secular understanding tells us that through sociological insight we can discover the pressures and problems faced by teenagers and then, by seeking to be sensitive, can help them to discover their own path into maturity and fulfilment. But in fact what God says through his word, as revealed in Scripture and ultimately through Jesus Christ, is that real fulfilment can never be achieved in this way. Fulfilment is not just a matter of being right within ourselves but comes as we are also right with those around us, and with God. Human nature is flawed; we are all tainted with original sin. The Bible is clear that each one of us has free will, and has used that freedom to reject God's law. Each one of us has broken the first commandment, which is to 'love the Lord your God with all your heart and soul and mind', and thus we have rebelled against his authority. Each one of us needs to repent of our rebellion against, and apathy towards, God our Creator. True fulfilment and freedom is not the result of achieving everything we want and obtaining all that brings outward success but in fact is the opposite, coming through the surrender of our will and personality to God's will. As the old hymn says, 'Force me to render up my sword and then shall I be free.'

We must not end up in the situation where we come to believe that a teenager's attitudes and behaviour are simply the result of his internal struggles and environmental surroundings. We have been talking about some of the pressures which are brought to bear on any teenager through our culture but the question of exactly how the individual deals with these and develops his behaviour patterns is ultimately one of personal responsibility. It is not good enough to say, 'I am as I am because I was hit on the head with a hammer at the age of three and a half, and fell down a manhole when I was ten!' We are all sinful by nature and choice.

Institutions and other external pressures influence us because they appeal to our own sinful inclinations, and internal crises and traumas simply aid and abet our selfish desires. The Christian youth worker's task is to take eternal biblical truth and apply it to the changing influences of twentieth-century life, to hold the Bible in one hand and the newspaper in the other.

**Abundant life**

The Christian also needs to state the biblical teaching that the teenager, like everybody else, is not to be valued on the basis of what he has achieved or possesses. This is especially important in these days of such high unemployment among the young. Conversation at social gatherings is very often built around a discussion of the roles which the participants play within society. To the question, 'Who are you?' the answer very often comes back, 'Oh, I'm training to be a doctor', or 'a lawyer', or, 'I'm a teacher', etc. But what of those who have no employment? What of those who feel depersonalised by their daily task, or those who feel they cannot succeed in the eyes of the world for one reason or another? What of those who live with the failure of unfulfilled ambition? What happens to the person who makes such proud boasts when, through retirement or illness or redundancy, he is robbed of his role and therefore, it would seem, his reason for existence? As Christians our job is to state clearly that a man or woman's value is not dependent upon the salary and professional position that they manage to command. Our value is quite independent of all of this and is derived from the fact that out of his love God created us as individuals to live for him. It is for this reason that we have real purpose. Even though we have all turned our backs on our Creator, he still offers us true fulfilment through Jesus Christ who claimed, 'I have come in order that you might have life – life in all its fullness' (Jn 10:10, GNB).

# 3
# TO BE OR NOT TO BE
*The place of youth work in the life of the church*

Mark Ashton, Secretary of the Church Youth Fellowships Association, commented on a recent survey about the attitudes of teenagers towards the church: 'If the survey's statistics of decline in Church going during adolescence are anything to go by, there is a drastic failure by the Church to communicate to young people.'[1] But why should the church work with teenagers anyway?

**God's agenda**

On the day of Pentecost Peter stood up and preached to the adults who had gathered together in Jerusalem, with the result that many of them were converted. There's no mention of a fringe meeting for teenagers led by one of the other apostles! Paul on his missionary journeys preached to all sorts of groups in many situations as he took his message into different cultural settings, but never, so far as we know, to adolescents; with the possible exception of Timothy, his work was focused on adults.

It seems to be clear that the early church did not embark on a programme of organised youth work. There were no first-century youth pastors! Jesus took children on his knee and showed a special affection for them but no mention is made of his dealings with youth. It is true that once he had a conversation with a 'rich young man', but we cannot be at all sure what that term implies, and one conversation does not give us grounds for surmising that he was actively involved with work among this age group.

As a result of this 'biblical evidence' it is possible to relegate youth work to a very secondary place in church life, or even to reject altogether any kind of emphasis on evangelism and work among this age group. The claim is sometimes made that this is clearly in line with the teaching and practice of the early church. Youth work, it is said, is just not on God's agenda!

In fairness, this view is perhaps a reaction to the situation that has arisen in many churches where the word 'evangelism' has become almost completely synonymous with children's work and nothing more. Some churches have opted out of responsibility to adults. In fact, some of the church's critics have long accused it of indoctrinating children, because they are immature and cannot argue back, yet of not daring to challenge adults who could easily demolish its arguments.

Although the danger of using an emphasis on children or youth to avoid adult evangelism needs to be recognised, the thinking that attempts to dismiss youth work on biblical grounds is misguided, stemming from a shallow understanding of the New Testament and its cultural background. As we discovered in chapter one, it was only recently that the concept of 'the teenager' arose, so that in New Testament times there was no such thing as an adolescent as we now know it. The early church could not evangelise teenagers or adolescents as a separate group because they did not exist! This does not mean they did not evangelise people of this age, but simply that they were regarded as part of the adult world. In Jewish thinking only two states existed, child and adulthood. Perhaps Paul's comment to the Corinthians suggests this. He states, 'When I was a child, my speech, feelings and thinking were all those of a child; now that I am a man, I have no more use for childish ways' (1 Cor 13:11, GNB). He talks of childhood and then manhood with no mention of adolescence.

When Jesus was twelve years old his parents left him behind in Jerusalem where they had been attending the feast of the Passover. They did not actually miss him until they were well into the journey home; in fact a whole day had elapsed before they began searching for him (Lk 2:41–44). If we are honest we struggle today with what we feel is the irresponsible attitude displayed by Mary and Joseph that could allow them to leave their twelve year old in the city of Jerusalem while they set out on the road back to Nazareth! What we fail to understand is not only the solidarity and sense of corporate responsibility of the community who had all travelled to Jerusalem together but also that at the age of twelve, Jesus was on the very brink of adult life, with his barmitzvah only months away. We have already seen that this did not mean he would be pushed out into the adult world and expected to behave with the full maturity of manhood from the day he was thirteen, but none the less Jesus was afforded a much higher degree of personal responsibility than we would give to a child of the same age.

## The church's mission to youth

Today we are in a completely different cultural setting. The teenager has arrived, and represents a very important and influential element in our society. Because the church has been commissioned by Christ to bring the good news of the gospel to the whole world it has a responsibility to this element of society. There are many who desperately struggle to capture the teenager's attention, time and money. There is a multitude of voices which offer direction and purpose. It is therefore of the greatest importance that as the teenager is bombarded by advice, views and information he be given a good, clear and accurate understanding of what God has to say about his life as revealed through Jesus Christ. In fact, even before the 'teenage awakening' there were those who recognised this need. Hudson Taylor, the founder of the China Inland Mission (now the Overseas Missionary Fellowship), once wrote with great insight,

> If we think that boys and girls in their teens are too young for soul experiences we are indeed mistaken. At no time in life is there greater capacity for devotion if the heart's deepest strings are open to the love of Christ.[2]

Trevor Partridge of Crusade for World Revival states,

> These are the spiritually sensitive years of life, it is during these years that important life changing decisions are made and if the challenge of the gospel is clearly presented, decisions can be reached for Christ. What a tremendous opportunity and challenge we have to present Christ to the youth of our nation.[3]

**The granting of responsibility**

In 1985, Paul Hardcastle had a number one hit single with *Nineteen* commemorating the tenth anniversary of the end of the Vietnam War: 'The average age of a combat soldier was nineteen . . . they saw active service every day for one year . . . they came under fire on every day of that year.'[4]

In wartime the American nation turned to its youth, thrusting them into the firing line, pushing them into responsibility in this awful unwanted task; Great Britain did the same in the Falklands crisis and the Gulf War. But for the most part modern society has segregated its teenagers in the giant educational goldfish bowl we have already talked about, depriving them of responsibility and involvement in 'real' life. It is important that the church responds to them on a different basis, giving to them the opportunity to get their teeth into what they consider a real challenge. Christians are often tempted to complain about the difficulties that modern society presents them with, but here is an opportunity handed to the church as a result of the insensitivity of the secular world. Does the church have the courage and enough understanding of young people to accept it?

Too often the church has judged young people in their late teens – young people who are of the same age as those called upon to fight for their countries – to be more or less totally irresponsible for anything but the most menial tasks. Recently I spoke with a non-Christian professor who was involved in research into some of the religious cults active in our country today. He said that he had come across many young people involved in such movements as the Unification Church (Moonies) and the Church of Jesus Christ of Latter Day Saints (Mormons) who had explained to him that they had been brought up within the traditional Christian church, but had never been given real responsibility or a sense of challenge. Now they had found a cause not only to believe in, but to live for, where they were respected by others and where their involvement was regarded as vitally important. He claimed that it was time that the church once more began to capture the imagination of young people, who, he said, had so much to offer, who were capable of incredible devotion and the possessors of vast resources of energy, drive, vision and enthusiasm.

**The place of youth work in the church**

In a recent survey carried out by the British Council of Churches it was discovered that six out of every ten Christians in this country made their commitment to Christ during their teenage years. When over half of those of us who are Christians made that decision during adolescence, we are foolish not to give very careful thought to the place of youth work within the overall stategy of the local church. Here are people of massive need and also enormous potential! Never could Jesus' statement have been more true: 'I tell you, open your eyes and look at the fields! They are ripe for harvest' (Jn 4:35). If the church fails the young there are many waiting in the wings with very different gospels to proclaim and sell!

**Attitudes to youth work**

We have established that youth work is a valid area of ministry in which the local church should be involved, and we have looked briefly at some of the barriers to communication with young people. But there is more than one motive for work among young people, and not all are good:

*(1) A way to the adults*

During the early part of this century many churches saw children and young people simply as a means to an end, that being to draw adults 'under the sound of the gospel'! It is still a quite commonly held principle that the way to 'reach' adults is firstly to 'win' their children. So, a Sunday school and/or youth fellowship are started on a housing estate with the prayer that one day these activities will give birth to an adult church. Through the young it is hoped to gain access to the homes from which they come and so eventually to win their parents.

Two things need to be said about this policy. Firstly, it does not work. Experience shows that very rarely do adults respond to the gospel because of their children. Roy Joslin in his fascinating book *Urban Harvest*[5] gives many examples of London churches which pursued this policy earlier in the century and are now, humanly speaking, on their last legs.

Secondly, it is devious. Even if this policy did produce results, it would still amount to the exploitation of young people. It is dishonest and degrading because it sees them as nothing more than bait used to hook those for whom we are really fishing.

The church should be involved with the young for their own sake, because it is recognised that they have needs themselves which Jesus Christ wants to meet, and not use them as pawns in a spiritual chess game. The world exploits and uses teenagers to its own end. Let's make sure the church does not adopt this same policy.

*(2) Pew fodder*

Sometimes youth work is undertaken to satisfy the local church's desire to see a 'nice group of young people' out on the Sunday evening. It brings a sense of security to feel that the church is reaching youth. If this motive is analysed it often amounts to little more than the desire to feel 'that all is well in the garden' and to have the church building full Sunday by Sunday. Thus, young people are seen as 'pew fillers' or 'fodder', acceptable to the rest of the congregation as long as they do not step out of line, or make any demands. All they are required to do is sit in neat rows and keep coming. They are again only wanted as a means to an end and not for their own sake.

*(3) The church of tomorrow*

There is yet another common motive for youth work which can be summed up in the statement, 'the young people of today are the church of tomorrow'. Often this statement betrays the fact that young people are simply seen as a means of perpetuating the institution, or, even worse, that they are not actually a real part of the church today.

The church consists of all those who belong to Christ; Christian young people are already part of the church and older church members need to appreciate this fact. Young people are not 'the church of tomorrow', they are very much part of the church family today! Together Christians both young and old should be working to build the church of tomorrow.

**The local church and youth leadership**

Responsibility for youth work has often been conveniently pushed on to the shoulders of anyone willing to accept the challenge. It is time that the 'burden' was put back where it really belongs; with the whole church. But this has tremendous implications for the way in which youth leaders are found and supported.

*(1) Who appoints the youth leaders?*

Very often, though the decision is eventually rubber-stamped by the church, youth leaders are more or less self-appointed and then left to get on with their demanding work without real support from the church. This should never be the case. Youth leaders should be regarded in the same light as anybody else with a responsible teaching role within the church. They should be set apart and commissioned by the church under the direction of the Holy Spirit (see Acts 13:2) in just the same way as Paul and Barnabas were sent off.

If the church has appointed leaders to the task of evangelism and teaching among teenagers it also carries the ultimate responsibility for this work. Responsibility and authority have been delegated to the youth leader who is accountable not only to the Lord but to the local church. This will also mean that he or she should not be carrying the full responsibility for finding co-workers or the headache of financing the group's ongoing life!

It is particularly important that the local church should take upon itself the responsibility prayerfully to set apart and then support its youth leaders in the light of what has already been said in chapter two about how youth workers so often become the heroes of teenagers. The youth leader is not only in a very influential position but also a very vulnerable one.

When the church takes this responsibility it will be forced to face such practical questions as:

'Do we want to work with youth?'

'What is our aim?'

'Where does youth work fit into the strategic outreach of the church?'

'Is it accomplishing its task within the church and the neighbourhood?'

'Are we helping to hammer out a theology that's true to the Bible and relates to today's teenagers?'

'Are our youth leaders properly pastored and encouraged?'

'Do we send our leaders away for training at the fellowship's expense?'

'Do we ask too much of them by expecting them to be actively committed to other areas of the church's work as well?'

Too often lonely youth leaders have laboured on against great odds, with insufficient manpower, few resources, little training and no real support or understanding from their local church, who only seem to show any interest when things go wrong.

*(2) Training for youth leaders*

Just as those called to work in what we recognise as 'foreign mission fields' need to be properly trained for their task, so do the church's youth leaders. Some friends of mine are now working with the Bible and Medical Missionary Fellowship in India for which they had the opportunity of training at All Nations Bible College. Nobody would have expected them to take up their task without the benefit of this training; it was obviously necessary both theologically and practically and their friends generously supported them throughout this time. Yet often when we turn to work in our own country we adopt a completely different set of principles, wanting to see good results, in double quick time, without any real investment in any kind of training. Of course it is not usually possible for a local church youth leader to be given the opportunity of 'full-time' training, or of being employed on this basis, but it is possible to provide the finance and support to enable him to attend weekend conferences and seminars and to purchase resource books and other materials that are helpful. Many youth leaders would never dare even to suggest that their local church finance their attendance at a conference of particular interest and yet for the church to do just this would be a forward looking investment. The best results are usually achieved when those with responsibility have the tools and the know-how to achieve the task.

*(3) Who finances the youth work?*

Many churches channel a great deal of finance into their

Sunday schools which cater, in the main, for younger children, but very often this is nowhere near matched when it comes to a commitment to youth work. If work among youth is seen as an important emphasis within the life of the church then the financial commitment to it must be real.

*(4) Who prays for the youth leaders?*

Youth leaders, just as much as the missionary in a foreign land, are working across cultural frontiers and need the active sacrificial and effective prayer support of their fellowship. If the church were sending missionaries to Zaïre they would pray regularly for them and expect to receive regular prayer sheets. The same should be true of the church's relationship with its youth workers. In return for the prayer support, these leaders have a responsibility to keep the local church fully informed about developments among the young people. In this way the church as a whole can stand alongside the youth worker in his joys as well as his disappointments and heartaches and can begin to understand the tensions between their culture and that of the young people.

**The youth leader's attitude**

It is vitally important that when the youth leader speaks about his young people to other church members he should not be apologetic but speak in order to bring about the same constructive approach to young people that he himself has.

On the other hand, it is just as important to present the best possible image of the church to the young people! Many a youth leader has fallen into the trap of giving voice to his own frustrations in front of the youth group and stirring up within them an unhealthy resentment of the church of which he and they are a part. It is an act of great discipline and maturity to avoid this trap, especially when a clash has occurred and the youth leader feels that his opinion and/or the position of the young people have not been sensitively taken into account.

Even if you have a sense of achievement or relief because you realise your local church has not fallen into the kind of traps outlined here, it is still wise to look carefully at your church and see how the youth ministry within your fellowship can be improved. It is good to make a periodic assessment of our work. There is a time for changing what we are doing, as well as a time for reaffirming our conviction that some things in which we are involved should remain unchanged. Whether we decide to keep things as they are or to make alterations, the important thing is that we know why we have come to these conclusions.

Having set out these principles which are not only biblical, but lift youth work to the place it rightfully deserves within the church, perhaps it is important to comment briefly on an opposite danger which arises for the local fellowship that takes youth work seriously.

## Young, free and beautiful

Today we live in what is without doubt a youth-dominated society. Our magazines, television adverts and the world of entertainment are filled with images of the young. A current television advert for the *Sun* newspaper contains the line, 'The *Sun* is for you because you're young and beautiful.' Youth is the god that our culture worships.

It was recently said that to be old is 'the greatest sin it is possible to commit today'.

But the Bible does not see young people as a more important group than any other in society. Through the Bible we see God's care lovingly expressed for all age groups and learn that he uses all kinds of people to achieve his purposes. For instance, we read that Jeremiah was known to God while he was still in his mother's womb. Later, when he protested at being called by God to be a prophet, his excuse was that he was a mere youth! But the Lord dismissed this objection, making it clear that he was well able to use a youth to do his work. On the other hand, Moses was eighty years of age when God called him, and Abram was seventy-five! Joel's prophecy which was quoted by Peter on the day of Pentecost states, 'In the last days, God says, I will pour out my Spirit on all people. Your sons and daughters will prophesy, your young men will see visions, your old men will dream dreams. Even on my servants, both men and women, I will pour out my Spirit in those days' (Acts 2:17–18). The Bible is full of stories where God chooses to use both young and old alike. Young people are not more exalted in his sight than any other age group. Therefore, while the place of youth work within the church is important, it should never be allowed to become the one dominating factor in the life of the local fellowship. The church is commissioned to reach adults as well, and to bring both young and old into the family.

# 4
# IS IT A BIRD? . . . IS IT A PLANE? . . . NO, IT'S A YOUTH LEADER
*The principles of Christian youth leadership*

Outstanding athletic ability, endless energy, good looks, a wardrobe full of the latest fashions, a body like an Olympic athlete's, street credibility, an answer for every question, a dictionary knowledge of pop music and an outgoing and charismatic personality that draws young people like honey attracts bees . . . and that's by no means the end of what is expected of an effective youth leader. As a result, most of us, recognising only too well our shortcomings, turn away feeling totally inadequate for such a task. We just don't measure up to this picture of a Christian Superman and even those who do get involved often struggle with a sense of, 'I'm not really cut out for all this; but nobody else will do it.'

## The basic mistake

Dr John Mott once said, 'A leader is a man who knows the road, who can keep ahead, and who can pull others after him.'[1] To a large extent the qualities which allow a man or woman to do this are ones that can be learned and practised. People assume you've either got 'leadership ability' or you've not got it! But this is just not true. Youth leadership, like most things in life, needs to be worked at – it's often a case of '90% perspiration and 10% inspiration'. God grants the basic gifts and abilities but it's our responsibility to work at them. It's also important to remember that no one person will ever possess all the attributes that would make the ideal leader (if such a thing exists anyway!). There are very few 'superstar' youth leaders, and even where they do exist they are not always altogether good for the ongoing pattern of youth ministry within a local framework. Without good forward planning, when an attractive leader leaves the town or moves on into some other job the youth group often simply collapses.

**When is a leader not a leader?**

In this chapter we will explore the qualities and disciplines that can, with hard work and thought, be developed within the youth leader. We can begin to do this by examining four things that a leader is not:

*The leader is not a dictator* who gives orders that others carry out. Jesus taught that the leader should be the servant and that he who wants to be greatest should be the least. This was not just his teaching but also his practice (see Jn 13:12–17). From Jesus we learn two fundamental lessons: leadership is about servanthood and it is also about example, as we put into practice the qualities we are teaching others. Therefore, it would not be right to take a discussion of Christian leadership further without briefly mentioning the subject of personal faith and commitment to Jesus himself. It is so easy for us to end up serving an institution, rather than a person. It is too easy for us to be devoted to the church rather than to Jesus. Young people quickly detect the pseudo Christian and we have a responsibility to examine ourselves continually concerning this issue.

*The leader is not a 'yes man'* who simply listens to the opinion of others and acts upon their ideas and initiative. It has been said that 'a committee is an animal with four back legs'. All committees and working groups need leadership. The leader has to achieve a good balance between under- and over-involvement, if the work is really going to benefit.

*The leader is not a one man band* who does absolutely everything by himself, making all the decisions and single-handedly carrying out the task. If the leader is doing his job properly he will be very important to the work but never indispensable. Where the leader does become a one man band it always leads to three problems: firstly, the feeling that he is indispensable, which will bloat his ego; secondly, a group of co-workers and leaders who do not really feel part of a team; thirdly, the inevitable collapse of all his work when he leaves.

Part of any leader's responsibility is to train others to carry on the task when he leaves. The 'lively' youth work that crumbles because its leader leaves or has to spend time away has in fact always been weak. The superstar who holds everything together himself is actually no real leader at all. It is vitally important that leaders build a good support structure which enables responsibility to be shared.

*The leader is not simply a figurehead* who remains at a distance from the group. It is his job to become involved. In Philippians 2:5–11 we read how Jesus did not cling to his equality with God but emptied himself taking the form of a servant. He was 'found among us'. 'The Word became flesh and . . . we have seen his glory' (Jn 1:14). Jesus did not stand at a distance but was totally involved; we do well to follow his example.

## Effective leadership

Good leadership in any area of life depends upon our ability to make the best use of the resources available to us. The most important as well as the most difficult area in which to do this is that of human resources. This is what sometimes gets called 'man management' but it's really just about getting the best out of people. A man is often made a foreman because he's a good craftsman, or a manager because he's a good salesman. Of course, a manager must have the technical competence necessary to achieve the results which are required, but more than this he must also have the understanding and skill needed to get others to work with him. That is what leadership is all about.

There are several methods of getting people to do what you want and so of achieving your goal, but not all are good.

*(1) Coercion*

When I was young I went to a club where I was told that if I became a Christian I could write my name in the leader's leather-bound book. That seemed like a good enough reason for becoming almost anything, and so I made my commitment. It is easy to try and tempt people into following you by offering them what seems to glitter. Many youth groups run on the principle of always being one step ahead of those in the same town, of importing the latest technology and the newest ideas, all designed as incentives to keep the teenagers coming. This policy will never work in the long term, for rather than producing disciples of Jesus it tends to produce 'Christian groupies'.

*(2) Fear*

A second means of motivation has often been fear. Many a youth leader has resorted to putting down those he or she cannot cope with, or to humiliating the teenager who will not toe the line. Obviously this approach is wrong under any circumstances but it is especially harmful with teenagers who already feel insecure and self-conscious without finding themselves a laughing stock in front of their friends. This kind of treatment will only cause deep resentment.

*(3) Inspiration*

It is often said that there are two ways to get a donkey moving: to whip its backside and to dangle a carrot in front of its nose. The inference is that the second method is more commendable than the first. Although this may well be the case, both methods are highly dubious when applied to leadership of young people rather than donkeys! Rather than constantly threatening the youth group and other leaders, or dangling incentives in front of them to prompt them into action, the leader should aim to inspire the rest of the group with his vision and, by involving them in the task, draw out their best energy and efforts because they want to give them.

## Three aspects of youth leadership

Good leadership is the result of the leader constantly and carefully considering three fundamental aspects of his or her task. We will now look at these in turn:

### *(1) Achieving the goal*

To achieve your set goals is not only important for its own sake but also because the whole leadership team and/or youth group can share in the sense of achievement which results. For instance, a couple of years ago I took a group of young people from our youth fellowship to an inner-city church for a week of mission. This church had twelve members, ten of whom were over sixty. There were no teenagers whatsoever and only three children in the Sunday school. Our goal was to see God bring new life to that church and through our hard work and planning to present him with a vehicle he could use for this purpose. During the mission (and afterwards too) many young people and adults became Christians and the church has seen God's Spirit at work in many ways. Within six months there was a Sunday school of fifty and a youth group of eighty, complete with several youth leaders! My whole youth group were able to share in the sense of achievement which resulted; we were living out the things that they had so often sung about and been taught about for years. Therefore they were ready to give themselves to new goals and targets which we went on to set.

### *(2) Developing individuals*

Each individual member of the youth group (including the

co-leaders) has a need for personal development, achievement and growth and the youth leader must always recognise this fact. It is his job to help increase the self-esteem of the teenagers with whom he is working. This consideration is especially important in the light of all we have said in previous chapters about the way in which teenagers often secretly feel about themselves. The youth leader should continually be asking such questions as:

'Does this person have the maximum responsibility and authority I can give to him?'

'Are his achievements acknowledged by me and by the group?'

'Is his creativity encouraged and fostered?'

'Does he know what I think of him?'

'Do I really know him as a person?'

'Do I understand his aspirations and limitations?'

'How much time do I actually spend talking and listening to him?'

In this way, as each individual is cared for and made to feel secure and important, he will give of his best.

*(3) Building a team*

If it is important to achieve your goals and to encourage the development of each individual member, it is also vital that attention be given to producing a good team spirit within the youth group. Only then will it be really healthy. If this need is not recognised and given time and energy, cliques and even hostile competition may begin to develop. Individuals will then be harmed and the goals of the group will become impossible to achieve. The youth leader should therefore be on the look-out for possible causes of disruption as well as asking himself questions such as:

'Do I welcome and encourage new ideas from my co-leaders and from the young people?'

'Do I listen to what others feel about the youth group?'

'Am I sure that my co-leaders and the group members understand our objectives and aims?'

## A balanced approach

These three considerations are very important for every youth leader. He cannot afford to ignore any one of them as they are clearly all interdependent, so that if insufficient consideration (or too much consideration) is given to one area it is bound to have an adverse effect on the other two. For instance, failure to have clear goals and to achieve them will produce low morale among individual co-leaders and eventually among the youth group as a whole. This in turn will destroy the sense of team unity and belonging. In the same way, a failure to allow individuals to grow and develop will inevitably lead to jealousy and resentment which will detract from the ability of the group to work together as a real team. As a result they will not achieve their goals.

*(1) Goal-centred approach*

The kind of youth leader who is most likely to fall into this trap is the real 'go-getter', the visionary, the ball of fire, always armed with new ideas and lots of talk. He runs a full programme of events for the young people who, in reality, are simply asked to attend, smile, watch his latest idea and keep the numbers at the meetings up. But the only real need being met is that of the leader who needs to feel that he is being 'successful' and is 'full of bright ideas'. Actually, morale in the group is probably at a very low ebb, because the members do not feel important. Some are probably continuing to attend simply out of a sense of duty or because their parents force them to. This can apply to co-leaders as well as group members.

*(2) Individual-centred approach*

The kind of leader who runs the greatest risk of falling into this trap is the 'pastor' or 'encourager', for it is possible to become so wrapped up with those you are counselling and caring for that you lose all perspective on the overall situation and you and your group no longer have a sense of direction. All that matters is that the group exists, that the individual young people come and that their pastoral needs are met. The tasks of evangelism, growth and mission are no longer real considerations. Eventually this situation will lead to the youth group meeting simply because they enjoy the company and have a good time; there may be no known reason for its existence beyond this!

*(3) Team-centred approach*

It is possible for the leader to become so involved with developing a sense of teamwork and unity within the youth group that it becomes a clique where everybody is expected to think and do the same. There is no longer any room for real freedom of expression and even the opportunity for honestly and openly talking about needs, doubts and questions disappears. Opinions cannot be voiced if they in any way conflict with those of the 'team'. This situation is bound to have an adverse effect on the ongoing life of the youth group.

## The qualities of a youth leader

We will now examine the qualities and duties which are important to the youth leader as he works in the three spheres of youth leadership outlined above.

*(1) The leader must plan*

I once heard of a leader of whom it was said that if he was locked in a room for three hours with a pen and a blank piece of paper and instructions to write down his thoughts on where his group was headed and why it was going there, he would at the end of the time still have a blank sheet! Often Christian youth work is undertaken without ever facing up to these questions. The leader must think ahead, asking such questions as:

Where is the youth group going?
Why is it going there?
What are we trying to achieve through it?
How are we going to do this?

What is my role?
Why am I involved?
How do I relate to the youth and other leaders?

It is very important that the leader should know what the group's objectives or goals are and that he should communicate these, first to his colleagues and then to the young people as a whole within the group. He may find himself confessing 'We have a youth group because all churches have youth groups!' Or, only slightly better, 'We have a youth group to win people to Christ!' Though this second answer sounds very spiritual it is often nothing more than an excuse not to think through the real issues and to evade questions like, how? Where? Who and why? Of course, organisation can go too far if we come to believe that through it we can ensure God's blessing. Instead, our attitude should be that we want to allow God to work as freely and easily as possible and therefore we plan for this, creating openings and opportunities which he can use in the lives of people both inside and outside the group. (We will deal further with this whole subject in chapter five.)

*(2) The leader must be imaginative and enterprising*

In this way he wins the confidence of those around him. This is not as difficult as one might at first think. As a preacher, I know well the saying, 'All original thought and no plagiarism makes a very dull sermon.'

In other words, be alert, the world is full of good ideas. Look around for them and when you find a good one take it and use it, adapting it to your situation. Also, listen to the ideas and suggestions of your group and co-leaders, carefully think them through and if something seems right, take it on board and use it.

*(3) The leader must delegate*

Very recently I listened to a vicar bemoaning the lack of response on his 'patch' and the impossibility of the task which faced the church. Minutes later he was talking about the problem of working with a curate. In his opinion, curates created far more problems then they ever solved: 'By the time you've told them what to do you may as well have done it yourself.' As far as he was concerned, training them was an intolerable burden! It's too easy for the youth leader to end up with the same attitude. We must take the risk of giving away responsibility and in doing so give space to others to develop.

We have already stated that the one man band style of leadership will ultimately produce very poor results. To achieve the task it is vital that the leader should delegate – delegation releases him for different work and keeps the other leaders as well as the whole group involved. Thus he gets the best out of himself and out of everyone else. But it should be recognised that there is a difference between delegation and abdication! The leader still has to accept final responsibility while realising that those to whom he delegates will probably never do the job exactly as he wants and sometimes not at all. He must give clear details of the job and check up in good time on the progress that is being made. This course of action will bring with it many disappointments. Often the teenager he relies on will let him down so that he will be tempted to say, 'It's easier to do it myself!' It's been said that the youth leader should always 'treat teenagers as adults, expect them to behave like children but continue treating them as adults'.

*(4) The leader must communicate and motivate others*

It is his job to inspire the other leaders and the young people with his vision. It is no good delegating responsibility unless they can see a good reason for the job being done. The leader therefore needs to motivate them. It is important to say things like, 'I need your help,' rather than, 'You do it, not me.' The leader should also enthuse and challenge those around him by a combination of dedication, optimism, imagination and commitment to Christ. His job is to make other people want to work and to grow in their faith, rather than feel they should work because he ordered them to, and if they don't they will feel guilty.

*(5) The leader must give support*

He must encourage and give backing to his co-workers and young people as they take on responsibilities. It is important to remember again how insecure teenagers are; they need a constant supply of encouragement. Encouragement is especially important when things go wrong and the group or an individual faces failure. The leader must then show that he still believes in their ability. This is just as true in the case of disciplinary action.

*(6) The leader must co-ordinate*

It is his job to get the other leaders and the whole group working harmoniously together and build the sense of team unity. He will be able to do this best by his own example. It is obviously no good the leader trying to call the tune if others see him as always doing his own thing with no reference to, or respect for, their views.

*(7) The leader must continually re-evaluate the situation*

How is everything going? Are we still accomplishing our goals? Whenever we stop just to sit and think or plan we are tempted to feel that we are wasting time! We need to learn that time spent planning and re-evaluating the situation is time very well spent, for it saves hours, if not days, weeks and months of otherwise wasted time at a later date.

*(8) The leader must make decisions*

Though it is important that he listens to individuals and to the group as a whole as well as to his assistant leaders, in many situations the leader has to make the final decisions. Perhaps he has to decide between differing opinions put forward by the group, sort out a difficult problem or deal with discouragement and failure. No problems are ever solved by running away from them; they need to be faced squarely. He should not try to avoid this. He must take the initiative and deal with difficult situations in a positive way. Sometimes it is better to make a decision and later to learn you have made a mistake than not to decide anything at all!

*(9) The leader must identify with young people*

This does not mean that he must wear all the latest fashions and listen to every new album that enters the charts. Nor does it mean that he must dye his hair, wear an earring and continually hide his real age. Young people do not want a leader who attempts to copy them and tries to be exactly like them. They need to feel independent and different in some respects – to be some degree removed from their leader. He is not one of the boys; everyone else knows it and no one will respect him if he doesn't recognise it too. In fact, if the leader could become just like one of the young people, he would no longer be able to lead them effectively. But, having stated this, the leader must not stand aloof and apart from his young people. It is important that he should take seriously their points of view and attempt to understand them, that he should spend time familiarising himself with their culture and the influences that bear on their lives.

*(10) The leader must be available*

This is probably the most important quality of the leader. Jesus made himself available to his disciples, sometimes shutting out everything else to be with them. His disciples saw him in action. During his three year ministry they had the opportunity of getting close to him, asking him questions, enjoying his company, and feeling his acceptance of them. In the same way it is important that the youth leader give quality time to his young people, and that he be honest, caring and trustworthy. It does not matter that he does not have the answer to every theological question that is thrown at him – rather than trying to invent an answer quickly, an honest response is much more helpful. Young people will learn much more from watching him and being able to trust him than listening carefully to his official replies to difficult questions.

Jesus had time for people, and this made them feel important and valued. We will never convince anyone that they can trust us if we are not prepared to give time sacrificially to them, and do it without making them feel that we find it frustrating. Through Jesus, God's word 'became flesh', and through each one of us it should become flesh again! We are not called simply to preach the good news but to be the good news. It's no good talking about good news when you are bad news. Today our daily programme is often so busy that we do not have time to spend on people. We can easily reach the point where we see them as an intrusion, robbing us of our valuable time. The youth leader must be available.

# Part Two

# PLANNING

# 5

# $6 \times 12 = 72$

## *How to build a youth leadership team*

Eventually you will give up your position as a youth leader. How do you recruit, train, motivate and build a youth leadership team? How can you delegate jobs, handle conflict and effectively develop the next generation of youth leaders?

Training new leaders is one of the biggest problems facing Christian youth work and the church in general. Experts refer to it as succession planning. Put more simply, it's the answer to the question, 'Who's going to take over when I leave, and what can I do to ensure that they're well equipped to do a good job?'

The sad reality is that many youth groups flounder or even collapse altogether when their leader moves on, because they have been built on the strength of personal charisma, stamina and ability rather than on a carefully developed on-going team leadership policy.

One of the key tasks of any leader is to ensure the stability of the group in the next generation of leadership. We need to commit ourselves to spotting the potential in others, building leadership teams and training those who will lead after we have moved on.

**The Lone Ranger rides again**

Although there are still a lot of Lone Rangers out there, these days most of us are keen to be seen to talk 'team'. The problem is that building a real team is about far more than learning to use the 'in' language. We probably know at least one Lone Ranger who's utterly convinced that he's a team builder, and would be devastated if he ever discovered the truth about himself.

While being intellectually committed to developing the gifts and skills of others, it is deceptively easy to act in a manner which means that those around you see you in a very different light indeed.

These days Lone Rangers are so unpopular as a breed that they often attempt to cover their tracks by masquerading as team builders. Their technique can make them a little difficult to spot at first (although they are soon detected by the trained eye).

The most common method of disguise which Lone Rangers use is to collect a group of volunteers around them whom they then casually refer to as 'my team'. They further add to the attempted deception by handing out responsibilities of various sizes, but are always most careful to avoid giving training, support and feedback, or granting any real authority. Lone Rangers refer to this practice as 'delegation', although most of us would call it 'being dumped in it from a great height'.

A football team may boast a large contingent of extremely expensive and highly-skilled players, but they won't start winning consistently until they learn to be a team. Success is rarely achieved as the outcome of an individual's talents – it's far more often the result of teamwork. Some team members have lots of talent while others are less skilful. It is the coach's job to pool all the talent and train the individuals to play together.

Lone Rangers see themselves as star performers surrounded by an incidental supporting cast. Effective team builders get used to viewing themselves in the role of team coach. A leadership team is far more than a band of subservient helpers grouped round an all-knowing leader – it's an effective working unit in which every member's input is important to its overall success. In a team, each member is motivated to use their individual talents to the best advantage for the whole group.

In football, feedback is immediate. If teamwork is lacking it is obvious, and prompt action is taken to put things right. The coach either gets the individuals concerned to start playing as part of the team, or gets himself some new players!

Unfortunately when it comes to youth work, feedback is not as immediate, dramatic or direct, with the result that serious problems can develop and escape unnoticed for some time. But although the effects of missing teamwork are not as instant, in the long term they are every bit as destructive.

**Six times twelve is seventy-two!**

In Luke 6:10 Jesus, the man most equipped to make a success of Lone Ranger leadership if anyone could, chooses a team of twelve assistant team workers. Many wiser heads would have been quick to point out the rash stupidity of some of his choices: Peter the hothead; Thomas the cynic; Judas the materialist...ridiculous! What is worse is that in Luke 9:1, just three chapters later, Jesus sends his new recruits out in couples to represent him. He sends them with his authority and trusts his reputation to them, but just as the critics predicted, by the end of the same chapter the disciples have proved totally inadequate to the task of healing a boy with an evil spirit, and have entered into an open fight over who was the most promising team member!

That is why Luke 10:1 is so revealing. Having trusted his reputation to the twelve, Jesus now places it in the hands of seventy-two others. He sends them out in his name to heal the sick and preach in every town that he is about to visit. And you don't have to be a great mathematician to work out the training relationship between the original twelve and these latest recruits. All this bizarre leadership technique could be written off as absurd except for one simple fact: it worked!

So how do you go about building a dedicated youth

leadership team in your local church? At this point you may be tempted to say some rude things about how most people in your church are as interested in youth work as the average teenager is in collecting Max Bygraves singles, and how those that are interested exhibit all the vitality, energy and life of a very flat can of Coca Cola. Do not be deterred!

Building and maintaining a leadership team is actually a far easier task than it may at first seem. It is really just a matter of recognising, focusing and constantly using a few simple principles which most people would claim to understand, though rarely practise.

## The ABC guide to building and motivating a leadership team

There are three main principles you need to bear in mind. As the leader it is your task to motivate your assistants by helping them to:

### *a. Value their task*

If those who work with you feel that the job they are doing is important, they are far more likely to be motivated and enthusiastic about their task. You can give your assistant leaders this sense of confidence in various ways.

*Outlining the strategy.* Show them how their individual task fits into the ongoing strategy for the development of the youth group. People who are asked to perform tasks without information and understanding of how what they do is an important part of the overall plan are bound to be less motivated than those who feel well informed.

*Leading by example.* Enthusiasm and apathy are both contagious. In other words, your personal attitude is highly infectious. If you are positive about the group and your responsibilities, others will tend to follow your example.

*Providing feedback.* Without feedback your team members won't know whether they are doing a good, bad or indifferent job. Nobody enjoys working in a vacuum. Monitor your team members' performance and give them regular, honest (but positive) comment on their successes and failure. Without this input they are bound slowly to lose interest and commitment to the group.

*b. Value themselves*

It is very important that the team understand that you are interested in them as people and not just for the job they do. If you value them, they will be able to value themselves. There are three ways in which you can do this.

*Challenge them.* To get the best out of a volunteer, it is essential to make sure they are constantly challenged by their role. Once a person can fulfil their task without it stretching them, they will cease to be excited and motivated by it. Your team members will never give of their best if they are bored.

*Be a talent spotter.* Watch out for gifts and abilities and then make sure to use them. Delegate; it's a risky business but an essential part of building a team that produces future leaders from among its own ranks (more on how to delegate later in this chapter). 'Trust men and they will be true to you,' said Emerson. 'Treat them greatly and they will show themselves to be great.'

*Praise them.* By setting a challenge you can begin to give confidence to those who work with you, but there is a lot more work to do yet. Make sure that you readily recognise your team members' achievements both publicly and privately. Don't make the mistake of damning with faint praise. Be enthusiastic in your acknowledgement of the achievements of others. We all thrive on recognition, and as a result you will find that team members are keen to do even better in future. In George Bernard Shaw's *Pygmalion* Eliza Doolittle explains, 'You see, really and truly...the difference between a lady and a flower girl is not how she behaves, but how she is treated. I shall always be a flower girl to Professor Higgins, because he always treats me as a flower girl, and always will; but I know I can be a lady to you, because you always treat me as a lady, and always will.'

*Be concerned about them.* Remember that your team members

have a life beyond the youth group. Be interested in their wider world. What's happening to them at home and at work? What problems are they facing at the moment? How are they doing spiritually? When are their birthdays? What are their hobbies? Give them your time and prove that you don't take them for granted.

*c. Value the team*

Showing the volunteers who work with you the value of the role they play and giving them confidence in themselves is important, but you still don't have a team. Now you've got everyone pulling their weight, your task is to get them all pulling in the same direction at the same time! It takes conscious effort to develop and maintain a real team. You can achieve it by helping those who work with you to:

*Feel like a team.* Make sure you are always loyal to your team. When individuals fail, don't fall into the trap of running them down publicly or in front of each other. Show your team that you are loyal to them and that they can always rely on your support. As a result, they will find it far easier to support and trust you and one another. Privately you need to talk through failures and mistakes, but this must be done in a positive and constructive manner.

*Think like a team.* Make sure that you schedule regular team meetings, where those who work with you feel free to express their views and opinions. Listen to what they say, even if you disagree. Talk openly and honestly about progress and problems. Ask for their help, advice and ideas, involving them in setting the future goals and strategy of the youth group.

*Work like a team.* Though each team member needs their own clearly defined role within the group, it is important to encourage them to feel responsible for the overall task of the whole group. Always talk about 'our job' rather than 'my job'. Encourage members to work together, to help each other and cover for each other. In this way you will develop into a team rather than a group of individuals working in close proximity.

**How are you doing?**

Think through the following questions and award yourself a score for each one: 3 if you are strong in that area; 2 if you are average; 1 if you are weak; and 0 if, to be honest, you are useless.

1 I am clear about the goals and targets for our youth work. □
2 I am good at communicating these goals with my leadership team. □
3 I place high priority on listening to the ideas and views of team members. □
4 I am willing to change my mind. □
5 I develop our future goals and targets with the help of the leadership team. □
6 We have team meetings regularly to assess our progress. □
7 I provide opportunities for open discussion of problems to encourage solutions to be found. □
8 I understand that conflict is normal and regard it as an opportunity to solve problems through open discussion before it becomes destructive. □
9 I value the people who work with me. □
10 My team members know that I value them. □
11 I readily give praise and recognition both publicly and privately to individuals for their achievements. □
12 I readily give praise and recognition to the team for their achievements. □
13 I write personal notes of appreciation to staff members. □
14 I remember my leadership team members' birthdays. □
15 I am aware of my leadership team members' personal lives beyond the confines of the youth group. □
16 I'm good at spotting talent and ability in others. □
17 I trust and respect my team members. □
18 I find it easy to delegate. □
19 I find it easy to give away authority. □
20 I work hard to provide opportunities that will stretch and challenge leadership team members and help them develop new skills. □
21 I have set goals for each team member's personal growth. □
22 I've discussed these goals with the individuals concerned. □

23 I discuss the personal performance of each of my team members with them at least once a year. ☐
24 I make sure training is available to my team members. ☐
25 I have a good relationship with each team member. ☐
26 My team members can be honest with me. ☐
27 My team members can be honest with each other. ☐
28 I encourage the team to think and act like a team by supporting one another.
29 I have a good track record for keeping volunteer team members. ☐
30 I enjoy working with other people. ☐

TOTAL SCORE: ☐ ☐

Now analyse your score:
*74 +* You are a skilled team builder, though there is always room for improvement and it is wise to hold off patting yourself too firmly on the back until you've got a friend to give you an unbiased independent score!
*60–74* You have great potential, but need to keep working hard to become a really effective team builder.
*40–59* You need to make it a high priority to read, learn and inwardly digest this chapter!
*Less than 40* You are a classic Lone Ranger and are probably a real pain for others to work with. But don't despair: leadership skills can be learned. Remember the famous words of the Sandhurst Commanding Officer who informed one of his recruits, 'You're not a born leader yet, but we're working on it!'

**The art of delegation**

'Don't talk to me about delegation. When it comes down to it, it's a choice between me and me.'

'The fact is, there is no one else capable of taking on my responsibilities.'

'In the end it's always quicker to do it myself.'

'It's no good trusting them, they'll just let me down.'

'If you want a job done properly, do it yourself.'

'The truth is, they don't have the experience or maturity to cope without me.'

'They just aren't capable of making decisions.'

'But what if they make a serious mistake? They'll really land me in it.'

'When they muck it up, I'm the one who ends up carrying the can.'

'If I let go of the reins, the youth group will just fall apart.'

Have you ever caught yourself muttering comments like these under your breath? If so, read on...

**Delegation is essential**

In Luke 9:1 and 10:1 Jesus grants different groups of his followers his own authority, and then sends them out in pairs to preach the good news and heal the sick in his name. In other words, he was willing to take the bold step of placing his reputation and the accomplishment of his mission into the hands of those far less skilled and mature than he was. That meant taking a big risk.

Delegation always involves risk-taking – it will for you just as much as anyone else.

So why bother to delegate?

Because delegation is an essential step for any serious youth leader, for at least two very important reasons.

1. The ongoing task of successfully leading a youth group which meets the needs of its members, impacts those beyond it and works to a long-term strategy can only ever be achieved by a team. Building a team is the only way in which the heavy demands and responsibilities of leadership can be effectively spread and coped with.

2. The skill, ability and maturity of others will only ever be developed as the opportunity to carry responsibility is given to them. It's a real chicken and egg situation. Those who won't delegate will often claim that it is because there is no one trustworthy to delegate to. Until they start taking delegation

seriously, there's not the remotest possibility that they will ever be able to develop a team capable of helping them carry the load. And if you are tempted to complain that there just isn't anyone trustworthy available, it might be worth reflecting on what exactly you would have done with the disciples if they were the material you had to work with!

**Delegation is painful**

If you find it difficult to delegate, you might as well know that you are completely normal! We all find delegation a struggle – for various reasons.

*We have an inbuilt fear of losing control*

The problem is that we tend to get delegating and dumping confused with one another. This leads to lots of problems for us (not to mention those we have left to sink or swim without our help). Good delegation doesn't result in the delegator losing control, but rather gaining it in a far more meaningful way than before. If you don't delegate it is very easy to get bogged down in detail and lose your overall perspective. Delegation allows you to take a step back, and look more objectively and effectively at what is being achieved overall.

*We don't like giving up responsibilities we enjoy*

Human beings are creatures of habit. We all have an inbuilt resistance to change. Even the most adventurous among us enjoys a framework of routine which provides security. Delegation, which always requires us to adapt and change, is therefore bound to make us a little uncomfortable. Be honest and recognise this about yourself. Then remind yourself that it is only as you are willing to let go that you will have the time or opportunity to grow into wider and higher levels of responsibility with which you will soon become as familiar and confident as those tasks you cling to at the moment.

## Delegation is not abdication

As we have already seen, delegation is not a case of finding a convenient person on whom to dump all the mundane jobs that you find boring. Delegation is about giving away to others parts of your job which are stimulating, carry responsibility and authority and provide the opportunity to grow and develop. But if delegation is about giving away responsibility, it is also about retaining accountability. It is still your job to carry the can for the mistakes your team members make and the times when they fail. It is in just the same way that ultimately your local church leadership should carry the can for the work that you do as youth group leader.

Before all this starts sounding too heavy, remember that as your team members grow into their responsibilities and begin to achieve the goals you have set together, you will also enjoy the privilege of being part of their success.

## How to delegate

So having talked yourself into the position where you are prepared to do some serious delegation, what do you do now? Many leaders who try to delegate find themselves continually let down and eventually infected with the 'delegation doesn't work here' syndrome. To delegate successfully there are a number of vital principles you must employ.

*Decide which tasks you will delegate*

Plan carefully the tasks which you are going to delegate. Why are you delegating them? Do they carry real responsibility, job satisfaction and opportunity for those who take them on?

*Decide who you will delegate to*

It is not just a case of thinking through which tasks you plan to delegate; it is equally essential that you carefully consider exactly who will be suitable to take on each responsibility. If you jump in without thinking this issue through, you are likely to end up giving the wrong jobs to the wrong people. How well are the individual's talents and potential skills suited to the task you want to delegate? It's no good making the only tone deaf member of the church your regular worship leader.

*Provide adequate briefing, training and feedback*

This principle is the forgotten key to the art of delegation. Without a clear understanding of specific responsibilities, objectives and standards prior to taking on the task, plus time for training and feedback on performance – especially over the first few months – any attempt to delegate is almost bound to backfire. Make yourself available to those to whom you delegate. Don't expect them to have subconsciously noticed and noted everything you did and the way you did it. Take time to show them how and explain why. Initially delegation is always time consuming, but if proper briefing, training and feedback are given at this stage, you will find that your investment brings long-term rewards.

*Inform other people*

If you have done a job for a long time, make sure that other people in your team, the members of the youth group and the rest of the church are informed of the change. In this way you publicly give your authority to the member of your team that you have delegated responsibility to. This in itself will give them confidence, help them to take their task seriously, and keep the lines of communication with others clear.

*Monitor progress, but don't interfere*

Having given away responsibility, don't keep sticking your nose in. This kind of misguided interference, to check that the job is being done properly, will only breed resentment and demotivation. Learn to walk the delegation tightrope and cope with the difficult balance between over-caring and not caring. Do this by setting up regular report-back sessions. When a job is first delegated these should be frequent, but as confidence and experience grow they can be placed further apart. You may begin by talking over how things are going once every couple of weeks, but as time goes by this could eventually become as infrequent as once a term.

### Burnout

The turnover of youth leaders in our churches across the country is alarmingly high. In this strategic area, where the church needs committed, experienced, consistent and mature leadership, it is often tragic to see the temporary nature of so much that is done. In many churches inexperienced, poorly trained and ill-equipped troops are conscripted for active service. A burst of initial fervour is followed by a premature retirement. Leaders become wounded, exhausted and burned out.

Burnout is the point at which you realise you have an inability to see any joy in your task, and is the inevitable long-term result of a build-up of excessive stress.

The dictionary definition is (1) to become or cause to become worn out or inoperative as a result of heat or friction; (2) a total loss of energy and interest, an inability to function effectively, experienced as a result of excessive demands on one's resources or chronic overwork.

Stress at controlled levels is no problem. It is the strain which too much stress causes that does the lasting damage. A certain amount of stress is actually good – it makes us more dynamic and keeps us on our toes! If we did not have the pressure of deadlines, other people's demands and our own standards, we would not accomplish nearly so much.

The problem comes when stress produces strain, and eventually burnout. We all have different stress thresholds, where the burnout process starts.

### Burnout: the causes

*The endless task*

The youth leader's task is never completed. Just like everyone else involved in ministry in the local church, you can never sit down and say that the job is done. You find yourself faced with a continual round of energy-draining planning, preparation, administration, meetings and pastoral care.

*No tangible results*

It is draining never to have the satisfaction of seeing your task completed, but it is even more frustrating not to be sure of whether your effort is producing any results. Because a youth leader's work is devoted to pastoral care, spiritual growth and building relationships, it is hard to monitor what is actually being achieved.

*The revolving wheel*

Not only is a youth leader's work never finished, it is also repetitive. Your programme varies as new teenagers join and the group changes, but because it is vital to cover the same ground time after time, you can get the feeling of being trapped on a treadmill. You are always covering the same ground but never making any real progress, and often the group never seems to get any larger.

*Dealing with expectations*

The work gets left to you, but it seems as though everyone in the church has lots of ideas about how you should do it and what kind of results you should be getting.

*Life's pressures*

Demanding as working with teenagers is, this is only one small part of your life and of the overall pattern of everyday pressure you face – work, family, parents, wider church responsibilities, health, finance...and so on. Life's pressures crowd in and slowly begin to cause severe strain.

**Burnout: the symptoms**

The symptoms of strain are diverse, but can provide you with the valuable early warning signals which, if you learn to listen to them, will protect you from the danger of burnout. They include: difficulty in sleeping, lack of interest in food, headaches, indigestion, frequent colds or the recurrence of previous infections, night sweats, chronic tiredness, nagging depression, persistent boredom, uncharacteristic outbursts of anger, overeating, feelings of worthlessness, nervousness and hopelessness, loss of concentration, forgetfulness, making mistakes, anxiety, lack of enthusiasm, demotivation, low self-esteem, doubt and loss of the desire to pray and spend time listening to God.

**Burnout: how to beat it**

1. Identify the causes and effects of stress in your life. Be prepared to confront the source of the problem.
2. Know your limits. Don't get trapped into endlessly comparing yourself with others – your stress threshold is not the same as theirs.
3. Take control by managing your time well. Decide what your long- and short-term priorities are.
4. Set measurable, realistic goals for your youth work.
5. Plan your week and day, and don't leave everything until the last minute. Have the courage to make tough decisions about your work load.
6. Set aside regular daily times to pray and listen to God.
7. Pace yourself. Just like a marathon runner, conserve energy and stamina for the long distance ahead. Sprinters look great for 100 metres and then collapse in a heap! Ask your church to set up a support group of people you trust and can talk honestly to about the pressures of youth work.
8. Be strict about having time off for hobbies and to relax. Make time for physical exercise.

# 6
# SETTING SAIL
*How to plan your church's youth programme*

Of all the teenagers who go to church in Great Britain at the age of fourteen, 71% have stopped by the time they reach their twentieth birthday. That is the claim made by Dr Leslie Francis as the result of a survey made across the denominations by the British Council of Churches.[1]

But such findings can come as no real shock to those actively involved in ongoing youth work. Recently I spoke to a Baptist minister who commented on the fact that of the twenty young people who professed Christianity and were baptised by him three years ago, only two now remained in the youth group, and one of these had just married a non-Christian!

So why can't we keep our young people? Or, to put the question more creatively, how can we build into our church life an effective strategy for youth work that will not only see young people won for Christ but also bring about their development into Christian maturity?

**The road to nowhere**

Many youth groups never achieve much because they are not sure what it is they are trying to do. It is just not good enough for us to hold out the vague hope that teenagers will be converted and then grow to be 'good church members'. If we have an aim it must be carefully looked at and a plan of action drawn up. If you set out on a journey not knowing how you are going to travel, or exactly where your destination is, you'll probably never arrive! In the same way there is a need for careful planning of every aspect of the life of your group together with the development of an overall strategy for its growth and witness.

**First things first**

From the most forward-looking churches with all the latest ideas and facilities at their disposal, through to those where youth work consists of a strict diet of Bible study supplemented only by rather sparse helpings of table tennis; from the small fellowship struggling to cope with a handful of difficult teenagers, without adequate leadership; through to the biggest churches with several full-time workers, the first and foremost principle in Christian youth work is one that's as old as the church itself! It has nothing to do with the trappings of modern high-tech evangelism, sophisticated structures of youth leadership and grand youth programmes. It can be summed up in one word: *example*.

It is example, love and genuine Christian commitment evident in the lives of the leaders that makes the difference between a group in which new Christians are regularly born and nurtured into maturity and those which only seem to produce a superficial attachment which melts away with the passing of years (in some cases even months!). This is not to say that love always produces the desired result. It would be naive to believe this. Jesus spoke about this problem in the parable of the sower, pointing out that sometimes God's word is not allowed to grow into maturity within a person's life (Mk 4:19). He warned that many would fall away, unable ultimately to take up their cross and follow him. Love can be rejected. By its very nature it has to give that freedom to those it cares for.

**Christians or church 'groupies'?**

This emphasis on example is not in any way to downgrade detailed planning (which the rest of this chapter looks at closely) or the use of all the resources available. It simply means that without the leader's depth of commitment to Christ (rather than to the church), such things will not produce strong Christians, only church 'groupies' who hang on because they are fascinated by one new idea or gimmick after the other. If we are not careful we simply build a youth group hungry for sensation, for a visit of the latest Christian rock group or most popular Christian speaker. Large numbers can sometimes hide a constantly changing clientele. In these groups, though the size of the overall group is maintained, youngsters simply come in excited for a month or two and then drift away again, only to be replaced by somebody else. When the gimmicks run out, so do the people. Paul said, 'Follow my example, as I follow the example of Christ' (1 Cor 11:1) – and that must be the goal of each youth worker. To quote Lawrence Richards, 'The youth leader is not primarily a talker or organiser. He is a model, a person who by the power of his Christian example motivates dedication to Jesus Christ.'[2]

Mark Ashton states:

> The key to effective Christian youth work is people – people in whose lives Christ is alive, and who will open themselves to young people, not to talk down to them, nor to dominate them with attractive and charismatic personalities, but to show them how to love one another as Christ commanded us. 'Personal work' is fundamental to youth work. We have to build personal relationships. We have to maximize opportunities for life-to-life discipling, where we can live alongside young people and they can absorb the Christian faith from the atmosphere around them.[3]

**Working together – the Youth Council**

In many smaller churches the youth leader is working entirely alone – if this is the case with you, skip on to the next section and save this one for the future!

A church's youth work will flourish best when there is an overall co-ordinating group of leaders who represent the whole spectrum of what's going on within the fellowship, right through from the Bible study to the uniformed organisations, from the young people's fellowship to the Saturday Night Club, the drama group and the football team. This group should meet for discussion and prayer once every month, avoiding the temptation to do so less frequently. It is probably good to have a church leader such as an elder or a deacon sitting on the Youth 'Council' or 'Committee' to ensure that there is good understanding and liaison with the rest of the church. Too many youth groups have suffered from a breakdown of communication between themselves and the rest of the church or at least its leadership. This leader may act as chairman of the group.

The Youth Council's task is to:

(1) Develop an overall strategy for the work, ensuring that the different youth activities in the church complement one another and are working towards the same goals without producing conflict in the lives of the young people themselves. In this way practical acknowledgement is given to the fact that the individual young person is not the property of any one of the youth movements within the church.

(2) Ensure that individual young people do not slip between groups without proper pastoral care and backup.

(3) Keep a diary into which all special youth events must be entered at a monthly meeting before they become a fixed part of the programme. Conflicts may otherwise arise with regard to use of time, too many commitments on too many nights of the week, as well as direct clashes in dates requiring young people to be in two places at once! In my experience of youth work around the country, this practical step would save a lot of unnecessary tension and bad feeling between leaders of different aspects of the church's youth work.

(4) Build a sense of trust and fellowship between the various

youth activities of the church. You cannot really work harmoniously with someone you don't know well and don't spend time with. The meeting gives the leaders an opportunity to get to know one another and develop the relationships on which all effective work must be based.

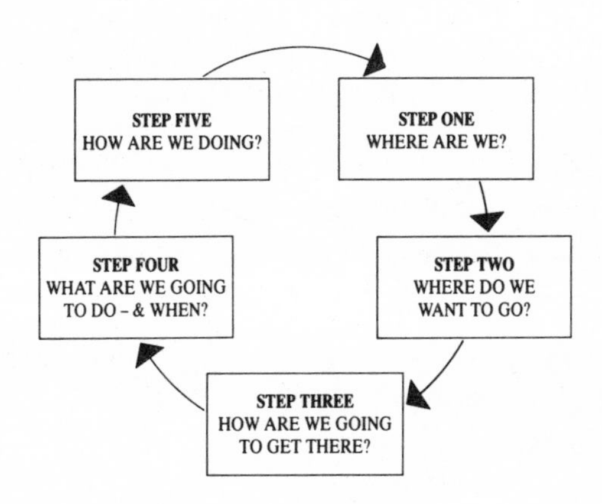


**Five steps to developing an effective youth programme**

At least once a year the Youth Council (and, on a separate occasion, the leaders of each youth activity) should set aside some time, preferably a whole day, when they can retreat together to pray and think over the work for which they are responsible. The group should spend its time looking at the following steps:

*Step one: Where are we? – a diagnostic examination*

Take a good hard look at the strengths, weaknesses and needs of your youth work. Do you have any basic aims? Are they being met? In this way a realistic picture is built up of the present state of your group.

*Step two: Where do we want to go? Setting long-term goals*

In the light of the evidence you have collated, discuss your priorities, setting some long-term goals. Such goals could for instance be to see:

(a) more conversions;

(b) new members added to the group (perhaps – more specifically – doubled in size);

(c) more integration between the different youth groups in the church;

(d) more integration with other age groups within the church;

(e) more development of leadership gifts and qualities among the young people;

(f) a greater depth of commitment to mission and evangelism.

It is possible to tackle too much all at once and, therefore, achieve nothing, so write your goals down in order of priority and concentrate on the top three.

*Step three: How are we going to get there? Setting short-term objectives*

Having set your overall goals and put them in order of priority, you should set about establishing short-term objectives which are designed to answer the question, 'How do we get from where we are to where we want to be?' Objectives are the practical steps that can be taken towards progressively achieving your long-term goals.

For instance, if one of your goals was the development of leadership gifts and qualities among the young people, you could write down a set of objectives such as:

(a) identify those young people with leadership qualities;

(b) select from this list a small group who would most benefit from leadership training at the moment;

(c) make these young people aware of their leadership potential;

(d) set up a relevant youth leadership training course for those concerned

(e) encourage these young people by beginning to hand over authority to them. This involves allowing them to make mistakes without heavily criticising them as a result;

(f) set up a mechanism whereby progress can be monitored, lessons learned, and gifts encouraged further rather than be squashed by negative comment.

*Step four: What are we going to do – and when? Implementing decisions*

Your short-term objectives should now be timetabled and acted upon. For example:

(a) *Within a month* we will draw up a list of those young people that we believe have leadership gifts.

(b) *At next month's* Youth Council meeting we will discuss this list and select a small group to be approached for a training course.

(c) *In two months' time* we aim to have spoken to all of these about the potential we believe they have, and have called them together for an initial meeting.

(d) *In three months' time* we aim to have set up and started a twelve week leadership development course.

(e) *Within four months* we aim to be giving those on the course practical opportunities for expressing their gifts, for example by handing over the leadership of worship or of some teaching. We will include a 'talk back' feature in subsequent meetings to look at the lessons being learned by course members.

(f) *By this time next year* we aim to have moved beyond the training stage to a situation where some of these we now recognise as having leadership potential are actually fulfilling that role within the life of our church.

| Time Scale | Goals |
|---|---|
| 1 Month | Draw up list of potential leaders |
| 2 Months | Hold initial meeting to explain your aim |
| 3 Months | Have leadership course training |
| 4 Months | Create practical opportunities for gaining experience |
| 1 Year | See members of course in leadership roles |

*Step five: How are we doing? Assessing progress*

This important step is often ignored. You should continually evaluate the effectiveness of the methods you have been using and the goals that you have been pursuing.

Because short-term objectives have been set it is easier to monitor your progress towards the overall goal as well as recognise weaknesses and compensate for them. If you acknowledge that you have not achieved some of your short-term objectives or have fallen behind on them, you can reassess the situation and draw up a revised timetable or strategy. This will lead right back into step one, and so round the circle.

## The value of our goals and objectives

When these five steps are followed your youth work is given clear direction, enabling you to chart where you are going and the steps you need to take to get there.

Setting goals and objectives helps us to escape the verbal fog of phrases such as 'our purpose is to give glory to God' or 'to have an effective youth work' or 'to win our town for Christ'! These sound spiritual but they are actually meaningless. They are too vague to give clear direction and simply enable us to evade the real questions we should be answering. Before they mean anything they must be unpacked: 'What do we really mean?' 'What specific objectives can we set down which will result in their being achieved?' 'What practical things can we do and plan over the next year/years which will help us to realise this goal?'

There are two main reasons why people tend to back away from setting goals and objectives in their area of work:

*(1) Fear of failure*

You may be afraid that you will not be able to achieve your goals and so be left with a massive sense of failure. For instance, it's easy to talk about 'winning the town for Christ' but less comfortable to translate that into real terms and set a target of doubling the size of the church in two years! But having clear objectives is not a case of setting cruel task masters but simply of putting down helpful pointers that will assist you in achieving your task. They are there to guide you, not to dictate to you. If an objective is not reached, sit down and reassess the situation by asking the question, 'Why have we failed to reach our target?' Once the cause or causes (there may well be a combination of them) have been identified, set new targets in the light of your findings. Don't feel that you have failed, for if the objective had not been set in the first place you would not now be in this positive position.

*(2) The feeling that planning is not spiritual*

Another reason why some Christians find it difficult to set short-term objectives is the feeling that it's rather unspiritual because such methods are borrowed from the secular world of management! Surely it's not right for God's people to rely on 'worldly' methods when his Spirit should be our real guide and strength? We should be putting our confidence and trust in God rather than twentieth-century management techniques.

To take this view is to misunderstand the real situation, for several reasons:

(a) Perhaps the terminology is new but modern management techniques are simply a way of restating good old common sense principles.

(b) Are we to distrust everything that is not explicitly Christian? Are we not to make use of television, radio, video, telephone, banking and accounting techniques? It is naive to reject all thinking because it is not specifically Christian. We appreciate art that was not created by Christians and in the same way we should appreciate good, clear thinking which enables us to be effective in God's service.

(c) It is not a case of either/or. Our confidence should be firmly placed in God, recognising that we are totally reliant on him. Good planning simply enables us to provide him with the best that we can offer as a vehicle which he can use. God had a very definite plan and purpose in bringing Jesus into the world. He came as the Word made flesh (Jn 1:14) to die so that 'whoever believes in him shall not perish but have eternal life' (Jn 3:16). In Ephesians 1, Paul tells us about God's plan for his people which was established 'before the creation of the world' (v 4). Jesus himself was aware of God's timing and plan within his ministry. On several occasions in John's Gospel he states that his 'time has not yet come' (2:4, see also 7:6, 7:8, 8:20 etc) but in 17:1 he prays, 'Father, the time has come. Glorify your Son.' In the same way we know that Paul had a very definite plan for the evangelisation of the Gentiles and that his ultimate goal was to preach the gospel in Rome (see Rom 1:13).

Far from destroying our faith, setting goals and objectives should actually help it to flourish. It may be difficult to believe that your whole town is going to be won to Christ, but if a target is set of increasing youth group membership by 50% over the next two years, and this happens, it then provides a visible illustration that God is at work. As a result, the group is enthused to believe and pray for more success. Objectives are simply statements of faith (see Phil 3:13–14). We believe that this is what God wants us to do and we trust him to achieve his will through us.

Setting clear goals and objectives also helps you to give your time to those things which are important rather than simply urgent. The way you spend your time should be dictated by the important not the immediate, and this will only happen when, through the process described above, you have determined your priorities.

Having well-defined goals and objectives also helps to build a strong team sense. Without targets to reach it is impossible for there to be a real sense of oneness and belonging. I have spoken to many a minister who feels that the church in which he serves is not giving enough financially or shows little commitment in terms of human resources such as time and talent. Almost without exception, this is simply because the members do not feel a sense of oneness and purpose. They are either unaware of or uninspired by the set of objectives and goals that have been decided upon by the leadership.

**Planning a weekly programme**

Many youth leaders suffer from the 'Help! . . . What can I do this week?' syndrome so that instead of enjoying their work it is full of stress, strain and the kind of anxious feeling that develops in the pit of the stomach when you know you're up against a deadline and you don't have any ideas! Actually there is absolutely no reason why any youth leader should ever be in this position because as a result of working through steps one to five, a programme can be planned well in advance.

Your group's weekly programme should be planned at least one school term ahead to enable you (or someone else) to book visiting speakers, relevant videos etc. Each element of the programme should be chosen because it contributes to the objectives that have been set and therefore fits the term's overall theme, rather than just because it sounds exciting! The impact of such elements is halved if your programme is simply a collection of individual evenings with no direction.

There is no shortage of resources available to help you in planning and for use in your programme. Make yourself aware of these by writing to Scripture Union, Scripture Press and other such groups (addresses are given at the back of this book) and have a long chat to your local Christian Book Centre manager.

Teaching about the Christian life and discipleship will never produce a mature Christian unless it includes the opportunity of involvement. If you are teaching about evangelism your youth group must be allowed to evangelise. If they have talked about sharing their faith with others you should provide the setting which enables them to do just that, perhaps for the first time. Remember your programme must never be sterile, divorced from practice. Biblical teaching must incorporate a healthy emphasis on doing. This book deals with practical ways in which this can be done.

# 7
# BUILDING BRIDGES
*Communicating with young people*

Over two-thirds of teenagers read their horoscopes at least once a week. More than half are no longer virgins by the time they are sixteen years of age, and more than a quarter believe in reincarnation. So states Clive Calver, the General Secretary of the Evangelical Alliance, in a paper on Youth and the Church. There are also the growing problems of teenage drug addiction, glue sniffing, homosexuality, violence, occult involvement, racism, suicide, pregnancy, abortion and unemployment, and so on. In our major cities girls of thirteen, fourteen, fifteen, and upwards are involved in prostitution. Clive goes on to claim that if these things had 'been predicted ten years ago as part of our children's cultural background in the mid nineteen-eighties we would have dismissed them as wild scaremongering'.[1] This is the background against which the church now works here in Great Britain, but how did this situation come about?

### Christian morality abandoned

Since shortly after the turn of the century the church in Great Britain has known a pattern of decline. Though we have now reached the stage where many parents of teenagers have themselves no concept of biblical moral absolutes, the teenager is still told by his or her parents that to sleep with their boy or girlfriend, for instance, is morally wrong. But when they enquire, 'Why?' the answer comes back, 'Because I say it is.' There is no longer any absolute authority beyond that of the parent; it is simply a matter of what society feels is right. Therefore the teenager quite rightly asks (or thinks), 'Why should I behave in a way that you claim is right when there is no ultimate reasoning behind it?' He then pushes ahead with his own course of action, rejecting what he sees as parental hypocrisy, and abandoning any moral boundaries not pleasing to his desires. But though teenagers reject Christian morality, they desperately need a code of moral absolutes within which to operate. Like all of us, they actually need boundaries and limits if they are to reach personal fulfilment. What is the church doing to provide this much-needed framework for life?

**Boring...boring!**

In the course of the schools work in which I am involved around the country, I often say to teenagers: 'Think about church. Now can you give me one descriptive word to sum up your thoughts?' Without doubt or hesitation the reply is always, 'Boring'! Even variations on this – such as dull, drab, irrelevant and old-fashioned – are rarely mentioned. There is no doubt that young people could use all of these words to describe the church but 'boring' is the word which it seems is always on the tip of their tongues. Among today's teenagers there is without doubt a new openness to the spiritual dimension of life. There is even an interest in Jesus as an historical figure and spiritual leader, but sadly there is no interest whatsoever in the church.

If we are to do anything constructive about this we need to understand why adolescents in general have reached this devastating conclusion!

**A teenage creed**

Every group in society holds a wide range of opinions, ideas, prejudices, suspicions and beliefs. These are built on information received from the institutions and influences which surround them. Earlier we looked at those which have the greatest influence on the lives of teenagers: pop culture, peer group pressure, family beliefs, education and the church itself. All these have worked together to convince the young that the church is quite irrelevant to them.

The basic problem which the church faces when dealing with young people is not hostility but sheer apathy and indifference. 'You don't need to go to church to be a Christian', is probably the nearest thing that the average teenager has to a creed. What goes on in church is seen as out of date, dull and lifeless. The liturgy is confusing, the buildings are cold, hymns are old-fashioned, prayers are long and boring, surpassed in tedium only by the sermons which are all too often totally unintelligible and seen as unrelated to life in the real world.

**Have faith, young man**

It's too easy for the church to blame the present situation on the young themselves. During the course of this century, there has been a massive failure to relate our beliefs to contemporary culture and the issues that confront us in the twentieth century so that the Christian faith has become something which is held in a vacuum. As a child and later a young adolescent Christian, I was for ever being told by the church to 'have faith' and, by implication, to 'stop asking such awkward questions'! This approach to the young will just not do. Our Christian faith is rational, and has real answers for and insights into our world situation. If young people regard the church as irrelevant it is not primarily the fault of the media, nor of the Bishop of Durham and his supporters. In fact, however way out some of David Jenkins' statements may be, and at odds with what the

Bible clearly states, it is probably true that he has attracted more attention to Jesus as a person than the evangelical church has for years!

Those people who do go to church are commonly regarded by teenagers as hypocrites because in the minds of most people the statement, 'I'm a church-going Christian' means, 'I'm a very good person...and I think a lot of myself.' Attendance is also associated with being snobbish and intellectual. As Tony Dann of British Youth For Christ points out, 'The gap between most young people and the Church is vast.'[2]

In our schools, religious education no longer consists solely of biblical study; today, the phenomenology of religion and the study of ethics take up most of the syllabus. Assemblies are no longer a daily occurrence and when they do take place they often have little or no Christian content. Another problem is that in cases where there is 'Christian' content, it is often presented out of a sense of duty. In many cases those taking part have no faith themselves and therefore the content is bound to be dull and dry, if not totally misleading!

Added to this developing picture, parents no longer send their children to Sunday school. In fact there are many young people in our country today who have never been inside a church building, and have never received any Christian teaching in their home. The result of all this is that very few young people have any real understanding of Christian teaching.

**Jesus Christ and Peter Pan**

While most young people have an inborn belief in God and the supernatural and are inquisitive about the spiritual side of life, they believe in Jesus only at the level of the fairy story. The common understanding is that he probably never really lived and that if he did there is now very little we can know about him. The Bible is seen as unreliable and inaccurate, written long after the events described. On top of all this, it has been changed and distorted through the centuries, and is corrupted with each new translation. Teenagers banish Christ to the realms of Peter Pan, Father Christmas or Alice in Wonderland. In fact, the only contact many young people have with Christianity is as it is portrayed on the television in the Sunday service, *Songs of Praise* or, more often, the half hour situation comedy where the vicar is always portrayed as a lovable but rather forgetful old fool who has been caught in a sort of time warp and really belongs somewhere back in the 1950s. (Having said all this, it needs to be recognised that once the historical facts have been presented to teenagers, then an openness to Jesus often appears.)

**No real answers**

Teenage idealism often leads young people to begin to think out the great issues of life such as race, ecology, the nuclear debate, politics, the peace movement and religion itself. As they work through these questions their idealistic principles tend to push them to rather black and white answers. In 1984 Leslie Francis published a report called *Teenagers and the Church* in which a number of issues were listed that young people wanted the opportunity to talk about in church but had not been able so to do. Over half of the sixteen to twenty year olds interviewed wanted to hear about personal relationships, sex, marriage, homosexuality, racism, law and order, the third world, work, the environment, unemployment and pop music. Just under half wanted to talk about the occult, cults, prayer, the Bible, television and politics.[3] These findings indicate just how big the gap is within the churches between what many young people want to explore and what the adults are prepared to talk through with them. So the little contact that most teenagers have with Christianity and the church convinces them that it is muddled and has nothing real to say to today's world. It seems to exist within a vacuum, with a lot more to say about our heritage and tradition than the difficult business of twentieth-century life.

## The non-book culture

There is a further problem. The experts tell us that we now live in a non-literary society. It is not that we are illiterate but that most of us just do not read, except when we have to. This situation is in great measure due to the influence of television. (It seems that every few months we hear a new set of alarming figures concerning the huge number of hours of television watched by the average man, woman, girl, boy or family pet!) A survey which was carried out recently among lawyers discovered that even in this 'intellectual' group in our society there were few who read anything beyond that which their profession demanded. Teenagers are used to the fast moving images and rapidly changing pictures that television brings. Even radio is no longer listened to seriously, but has become what is often referred to as 'wallpaper', simply a type of background noise which blocks out the silence! This situation presents a serious problem for the church which has traditionally communicated mainly through the book and the lecture (better known as the sermon!). Even when a young person is interested in the message of Christianity, unless he knows someone on the inside, he may be unable to decipher it and will finally give up in frustration.

## Bridging the gap and communication with youth

Rob White, the National Director of British Youth For Christ, states that there are three areas where the gap with the youth of our country must be bridged by the church if we are going to communicate effectively with them.

### *(1) Bridging the generation gap*

The late US senator, Robert Kennedy, once said, 'The gap between generations will never be closed, it must be spanned.'[4] If the generation gap is to be spanned by the church it is imperative that we begin to understand how today's youth feel, for it is not age which separates adults from teenagers, but misunderstanding.

As we have seen, teenagers tend to have a deep sense of insecurity, inadequacy and a lack of self-esteem. They feel that they are unimportant to adults and that their ideas and opinions do not matter. It is the task of the church to overcome this problem.

If the feelings of young people about themselves could be summed up in a word it would have to be 'insecurity'. What is needed most in our churches is not so much sophisticated and hi-tech youth programmes (though they can have their place) but love, care, understanding and, most of all, acceptance. We must never totally segregate youth from other age groups within the church. Though it is important to provide special programmes for the various age groups, it is unbiblical to section off young people altogether. The Bible states that the church is a family, and Rob White reminds us: 'For the Church to survive it needs to learn to relate to young people and find ways of developing as an all aged family.'[5]

The church should be giving young people a sense of security and importance by showing that it places great value on them, and the only way in which it can ultimately do this is by giving them real responsibility. In my experience most church leadership teams are very slow to give responsibility to young people. The excuse is made that 'they will make mistakes', and that 'they lack experience'! Of course, both of these statements are true, but they are also true of most existing church leaders themselves! It is far too easy to be fooled by our own propaganda into not seeing ourselves for what we are, or, to be more accurate, are not!

In family life children are given responsibility, and through the teenage years this privilege grows, so that by the time the child reaches the age of eighteen he is accepted as a fully fledged adult. Our churches on the other hand often treat eighteen year olds as almost totally unreliable and untrustworthy. We are told they are treated in this fashion because they are irresponsible, but what comes first, the chicken or the egg?

When I was in my teens, I played bass guitar in a band called

Manna which was led by Steve Flashman. At the time I was fifteen, sixteen and seventeen and Steve was already training at Spurgeons College in South London to be a Baptist minister. He was a gifted communicator with a call from God to preach, yet very often he would give me the privilege and responsibility of preaching. It was not that Steve did not want to do the job, for it was his motivation and vision that had created the group and had given us so many evangelistic opportunities in the first place. I knew that he was really trusting me, when so many budding ministers would have held tightly on to the reins and the opportunity to preach for themselves. Today I believe I owe much of my call and vision to that trust and responsibility.

We must also make sure that the responsibility we give is genuine responsibility. Teenagers soon know when what they are told is 'real responsibility sharing' and 'giving them an opportunity' is, in reality, nothing more than using them to do the jobs that nobody else wants!

*(2) Bridging the credibility gap*

We have seen that most young people have little or no real knowledge of the gospel and the church, and are not about to come to us and beg to have their ignorance and prejudice dispelled. The Nationwide Initiative For Evangelism Assembly at Nottingham University in 1981 produced a report on Pop Culture in which they commented that 'young people do not consider the Christian Church possesses relevance to their deep needs'.[6] The report continues:

> We recognised that in relation to young people in a pop culture:
>
> (a) we ourselves and the Churches have failed to communicate and share because of our negative attitudes, even to the extent of seeing youth as a problem, finding their music loud and offensive
> (b) we have not been accepting, nor have we listened to their questions or heard their cries
> (c) the churches have failed to understand that the 'pop' culture is a

valid expression of life and cannot simply be explained away as youth's escape from life

(d) we have not provided an atmosphere or place which can receive the respect of young people and does not cause them to 'lose face' with their peers

(e) we have not within the Christian Church made young people feel they are a valuable and intrinsic part of the Family.

The church has got to go out into the world and begin to share its faith in God where the people are. This is no new idea – far from it; it is simply a working out of the New Testament principle of incarnation. 'The Word became flesh and lived for a while among us' (Jn 1:14). In New Testament times evangelism was something that tended to happen on the outside of the church rather than inside it. When the church met together it was basically for worship, teaching and fellowship.

Today we like evangelism to happen within the church in a neat and tidy fashion. The evangelist stands up to speak at the gospel rally, concert or service while the audience sits in well-ordered rows and submissively listens to his message, at the end of which they make their response to the 'appeal' and become tame Christians. This is what we call 'outreach'.

I have discovered that I am acutely embarrassed when an audience is disruptive and refuses to be polite. In fact, when we meet this kind of response we tend to feel a sense of failure and react by getting very uptight and angry with our audiences. We quickly become insecure about what we are doing, and in an attempt to avoid this feeling we complain about their lack of manners and openness to Christ and spiritual things. But Paul was used to being barracked, and taunted by hecklers. He was used to debate and open, often aggressive, questioning. It is only when we allow people to respond and ask genuine questions, and when we are prepared to accept their honest response to us, that we can begin to appreciate the thinking of the secular world around us and build credibility bridges with our society. This kind of evangelism is not neat and tidy; it is very costly in terms of time and pride. It also requires genuine love for non-Christian young people, for what they are rather than what we want them to be.

The Greek verb meaning 'to preach' (*kerussein*) also means 'to proclaim', or 'to announce' and, as David Watson points out, 'The basic idea behind these words is that of a herald who delivers a message that has been given to him by the King.'[7] The herald's job was simply to stand on the street corners and make sure that everybody heard the message which he had been entrusted to bring by the king. How both he and the message were received was not his concern; his duty was over once he had made the king's mind clear and understandable to all. If he carried out this duty faithfully but then found the message was not obeyed he was not held responsible. But if he failed in his duty to stand in the public places and make the message clear, then the people's disobedience was his responsibility. We are called to 'herald' the gospel – to proclaim it openly. It is our job to make sure that our listeners understand the message, and this means we must give opportunity for questioning, debate and open disagreement. We must step out from our ivory towers.

Our churches need to become more involved in the local community in schools and colleges. Perhaps one thing that should be especially mentioned here is the subject of local church involvement in school Christian Unions. The church fails itself if it does not recognise its responsibility to see that young teenage Christians are supported in their working environment throughout the week. It is very short-sighted when a local church congratulates itself on the size of its Sunday evening youth fellowship while making no real attempt to support its young people throughout the week in their school environment. Many young Christians live double lives, boldly proclaiming Jesus at the weekends but petrified of making a public stand at school during the week.

I well remember the occasion when a stranger straight off the street came to me for counselling one day in Tonbridge. As I sat and talked with him I discovered the school he attended, where he was in the upper sixth year. One of the Christians from our youth group went to the same school and so I mentioned that I knew him.

'How do you know him?' was the surprised reaction. I explained that he was a Christian and came to the church.

'Oh no, you must have got the wrong one...no not him.'

That was an interesting comment because until that time I had regarded the individual concerned as a very consistent Christian! I am still sure he was very sincere but simply lacked confidence and became overwhelmed while at school, unable to apply his faith in a lonely non-Christian environment.

The best evangelists among young people are young people themselves. Therefore, the church can most effectively bridge the credibility gap with the young by enabling and equipping the existing young Christians to be heralds. Time and money invested by a local church in the support of a school Christian Union is time and money very well spent.

Again, as teenagers are converted through local schools' missions and other evangelistic activities it will become clear that the discipling of young people who already have a Christian friend, who has previously been witnessing to them, is a very much simpler task than working with people who have no natural Christian link. In fact, in my experience most teenagers who become Christians and then stick are those who already have a Christian friend.

*(3) Bridging the culture gap*

I have been involved in many missions among young people up and down the country. Never has one which has been well organised and prayed over been unsuccessful in terms of seeing multitudes of teenagers becoming Christians. The problem that we face in this country is not making Christians but making disciples. Young people are spiritually hungry and readily respond to the gospel when we present it to them in clear and down-to-earth terms. The breakdown occurs when we try to integrate the new converts into the church, for it is this which they see as irrelevant.

Many young people who are totally committed to Christ have explained to me that they would never bring their friends to a church service. They may even feel that when one of their friends is very interested in Christianity and Jesus he must be protected from the church! Though it is difficult to generalise concerning either youth culture or church culture, the fact is that there is little point of contact between the two. Our job is to bridge that gap.

During the World Cup in 1986, France played a tense quarter final with Brazil. Unfortunately, I was unable to watch the match on television as I was driving home at the time. I decided to listen to the game on Radio Two only to find out, to my horror, that it was not being broadcast by them or by any English speaking station. As I flicked through the medium wave in desperation I at last found a station that was carrying a commentary on the match, the only problem being that it was broadcasting in French! Try as I might I could not understand a word of what was being said nor even, to my total frustration, pick up the gist of what was happening from the noise of the crowd or the level of excitement of the commentators. Occasionally I heard the name of the French hero Platinée mentioned but in what context it was impossible to tell. By the time I reached my home in Tonbridge half time had been reached and I was pretty sure that the score was at least two all. You can understand my surprise when on eagerly switching on the television set I discovered that no goals had been scored at all during the first half. In fact, the best that had happened was that Brazil had missed a penalty!

The point is clear. Although I had a burning interest in the subject of the commentary and was listening very hard, I could not gather the tiniest morsel of useful information except the name that I already recognised (at least I knew Platinée was playing!). Consequently the conclusion I reached about the game was far different from the message that the commentators were attempting to put across. Many teenagers find themselves in exactly this position. They have a deep interest in Christianity and a desire to understand its truths. But the language that we use is as foreign to them as the football commentator's French was to me. Occasionally they hear the name of the hero, Jesus Christ, but are quite unable to discover the content of the message.

Perhaps there are those who feel that this kind of analogy is going too far and that I am being too negative about the church; it is very difficult for us to understand exactly how confusing and alien we can sound to the outsider. The religious terminology which we often fondly call 'the language of Zion', along with our styles of music, dress and preaching are all exceptionally difficult for young people to cope with. On top of this there is our very confusing attitude to things like discos, the pub, pop music, smoking, dress and hairstyles. We need to think hard and build carefully bridges that will cross this cultural gap. It is a long leap from youth culture to church culture but there are very many stepping stones which we can make use of.

# 8
# IT'S NOT WHAT YOU SAY, IT'S THE WAY THAT YOU SAY IT
## *Developing your communication skills*

'He was born with a silver spoon in his mouth,' we complain as we look on jealously at the visiting speaker who has just held the youth group spell-bound for forty minutes.

Some people are naturals – they seem capable of stringing words together with sickening ease while the rest of us are left to stumble over our sentences and struggle for all we're worth to hold anyone's attention for anything longer than a few minutes at a time.

### Pass the silver spoon

The problem is that we can't leave it all to the experts. Every youth leader needs to be able to communicate clearly in order to present the truth of the gospel, and teach in a relevant way, as well as lead the group effectively.

So let's take a practical, down-to-earth look at communication skills and techniques. And remember that whether it's at home, college, work or out with friends, there is no area of life in which good communication skills are not important.

And if you are already a good communicator, even a silver spoon owner, there's always room for improvement, because learning to communicate effectively is a lifetime's task.

### The fine art of communication

Communication is an art, not a science. Every science is ruled by cast iron, rigid laws. Maths, for instance, is governed by laws of addition, subtraction, multiplication, division, squares, square roots and so on. No room is left for interpretation, innovation, flair or style, and nor should it be. Two plus two is always four; not four-and-a-half or even four-and-a-little-bit.

The laws of any science are mechanical and must be applied exactly and precisely in every case. There is no room for manoeuvre. Communication is different. It is an art. Though it has basic principles these are not rigid in the same way as those of maths and physics.

Think of the three most powerful and compelling speakers that you have ever listened to. They were all different, unique. Although they all employed the same basic principles of communication they used them differently, relying on some more than others in order to build on their own strengths and minimise their weaknesses.

Communication is like playing the piano. Although there are certain fundamental principles and disciplines which must be understood, within that framework there are thousands of variations and plenty of scope for personality, interpretation and style.

Playing the right notes, in the right order and at the right time doesn't necessarily produce great music! Genius is about touch, feel, sensitivity and interpretation.

### Are you receiving me?

There are three basic groups of skills which you use every time you communicate with your youth group, or anyone else.

*1. Verbal*

These skills cover the words that you use; the content of your message; your vocabulary; what you actually say.

*2. Vocal*

This group of skills determines the way you say what you have to say. They relate to the way you project your voice, its resonance, and the excitement and enthusiasm your voice communicates.

*3. Visual*

This third group of skills relates to what your face and body communicate about what you say. That's the silent message you send to your hearers. The way you move, your expression, what you wear, the way you look, stand, etc; the energy and confidence you convey – or not, as the case may be – are all part of the communication package.

Your communication is most effective when the verbal, vocal and visual aspects of your communication technique are all working well and in harmony. The credibility of your message is determined not only by the quality of your verbal presentation (your words) but by whether the vocal and visual aspects of your message are consistent with what you say.

The greater the harmony between the three the higher the credibility of your message. And the less these three work together the bigger your problem. Perhaps what is most alarming is the fact that research and common-sense both tell us that when the verbal, vocal and visual elements are inconsistent, it is the verbal message which gets lost. However carefully you choose the words you use, you won't communicate clearly until you get the other parts right.

Poorly developed vocal and visual skills will effectively block your verbal message and prevent it from getting through to your hearers.

For instance, the verbal statement, 'I'm really excited about the youth group getting involved in this new project' is completely undermined by a youth leader who utters these words in a halting monotone while shuffling nervously from foot to foot and staring at the floor as he clasps his hands tightly in front of him.

Think of each presentation you give as being like a song. The lyrics (verbal message) must fit the tune (vocal message) and image of the singer (visual message).

Imagine Motorhead, dressed in leather and denim, playing at 50,000 decibels through a 6 mega-watt sound rig at Wembley Arena, screaming out the lyrics to 'Tie a yellow ribbon round the old oak tree'. Somehow it doesn't work! And when that happens it is always the tune and image that win, while the lyrics get lost. The way you express an idea is as important as the idea itself.

## Getting it right

How exactly can you recognise and then improve weak and ineffective areas in your communication technique? Experts tell us that there are four levels to learning and developing any new skill. These apply to all behaviour patterns and therefore are obviously relevant to improving your verbal, vocal and visual communication skills.

Let's take the example of the youth leader who, because of nervousness, speaks in a boring monotone voice whenever he is addressing a group. These are the four levels through which he needs to progress:

### *Unconscious incompetence*

'We don't know that we don't know.' At this stage the youth leader has no idea of his problem. No one has ever dared mention the monotonous tone of his voice and he has never conducted any self-assessment exercise.

*Conscious incompetence*

'We know that we don't know.' For the first time our youth leader has woken up to the situation and acknowledges that he has a voice problem which is effectively blocking his communication.

*Conscious competence*

'We work at what we don't know.' Our youth leader begins to make a continuous conscious effort to correct his problem and introduce variety of tone into his voice. He is slowly training himself to adopt new vocal skills.

*Unconscious competence*

'We don't have to think about knowing what we know.' Using a variety of vocal tones and strengths has now become second nature to our group leader. He no longer has to concentrate on the sound of his voice. His talks are now far more engaging and easy to follow. He is now free to begin working on other aspects of his verbal, vocal and visual communication techniques.

How do you discover just how effective your communication is? Try some of the following.

- Record yourself next time you lead the youth meeting – and listen to the tape later. It's a brave thing to do but it is constructive and great for hints on your verbal and vocal styles.
- If at all possible get a friend to video you speaking. You obviously need to choose the meeting carefully, but watching yourself a few times will do wonders for your assessment of the visual aspects of your communication style. Perhaps you've never realised that no one can see your face under your trendy haircut, or that when you emphasise a point you look as though you're conducting the Royal Philharmonic Orchestra! After all, what you see is what they get!
- Ask a good friend to give you some honest feedback on your presentation style. (Only ask someone you really respect

and trust!) Suggest they tell you what you get right as well as things that need work. The object is constructive criticism, not a demolition job.

- Watch other speakers, and assess for yourself what it is about them that makes them easy or hard to listen to, and what you can learn from the way they communicate.
- List three communication habits you want to change – and start practising.

**The seven pillars of good communication**

Let's examine seven basic behavioural skills which apply equally whether your audience is one, one hundred or a thousand people. They form the foundation on which good vocal and visual communication is built.

*1. Eye communication*

Good eye contact is the most essential skill in your communication style. The three 'I's of eye contact are:

- intimacy
- intimidation
- involvement

If your goal is intimacy or intimidation then extended periods of eye contact are appropriate. Lovers will gaze longingly into one another's eyes for what seems like hours without feeling threatened by each other because of the intimacy they share.

A boxer will stare into the eyes of his opponent as the two men face each other at close quarters before the start of the fight in order to intimidate his rival.

But the vast majority of communication situations call for involvement not intimacy or intimidation. When we talk to another person and are relaxed, enthusiastic and confident we naturally tend to hold eye contact with them for periods of five to ten seconds before looking away momentarily.

The goal of good eye communication is to make this a habit so that even when under pressure and speaking to a crowd, we naturally maintain this confident and relaxed eye pattern.

To fail to make good eye contact (to gaze out of a window, at the floor or at your feet while listening or talking) or not to hold it long enough, always gives the impression of nervousness, distance, awkwardness or disinterest.

### *2. Posture and movement*

There are a number of reasons why people don't stand upright. For instance, a teenager who is very tall will often develop a stoop so as not to stand out from the crowd. He may never grow out of the habit which started through adolescent self-consciousness.

For others, their bad posture is a result of earlier laziness or a deliberate teenage attempt to appear disinterested and fed up, which has once again become a habit.

Whatever the reason for the habit's formation, the effect is unfortunately the same. Bad posture gives the impression of a lack of confidence and low self-esteem, even when they are not the reasons for it. Stand tall and don't slump.

Likewise, someone who stands rooted to the spot while speaking gives listeners the feeling that he is ill-at-ease and nervous. Confident movement conveys the sense that a speaker is relaxed and in control and also adds energy to his communication technique.

Don't try to imitate anyone else; you will only end up looking awkward and plastic. Be yourself, but aim to stand upright and be fluid as you speak, rather than appearing wooden or locked into rigid positions.

### *3. Facial expressions and gestures*

Facial expression is once again very important to your communication style. It conveys to others an impression of whether you are open and knowable or closed and distant. It is doubly important because people spend more time looking at your face than any other part of your body.

The problem is that most people think they smile for most of the time – but they are wrong! Psychologists tell us that actually one third of us have faces which tend to look rather serious and intense even when we think we're smiling.

Although fake and false smiles don't work (they look plastic and don't last), it is possible to practise the art of allowing the smile that you feel inside to surface, even when under pressure.

He who smiles is perceived as open and friendly, relaxed and comfortable. He who doesn't, isn't!

It is essential too to make sure our gestures (hand and arm expressions) are also saying the right things to those we are communicating with.

We all have nervous gestures, things we tend to do with our hands when we are speaking and don't have anything to hold on to. Sometimes these habits can be quite embarrassing for us, not to mention our audiences. Our goal should be to be in control of our gestures so that they naturally and clearly emphasise the point we are making as we speak, before our hands and arms fall comfortably to rest at our sides.

### *4. Dress and appearance*

Experts say that when we meet someone new, we form an immediate vivid impression of them during the first five seconds. It then takes a further five minutes to add another 50% to the mental picture that has been built up in the opening seconds of our encounter.

Because this initial impression is based entirely on what we see, it is obvious that, for that reason alone (and there are many others), what we wear and the way we look are very important.

Our clothing and its smell, our weight, face and hairstyle all communicate a great deal about us. They have implications, not only for the way others perceive us, but for their initial impression of how we feel about ourselves.

This is not a middle-class excuse for worshipping new clothes and expensive hair-dos. It is simply a statement about basic personal care and cleanliness.

*5. Voice and vocal variety*

Your voice can be a vehicle on which your message is delivered, or a barrier which effectively prevents any real communication from taking place. The key to achieving the first situation, instead of falling into the second, is good use of vocal variety. As we saw with our nervous youth leader, a monotone delivery makes it very hard, if not impossible, to hold the attention of others for any significant period of time. Variety of tone creates interest and keeps your audience involved.

Your voice should convey the excitement, enthusiasm, pain, concern or other emotion that you feel. It is also important to create variety in the volume of your voice.

Lloyd George, the famed speaker, once gave some advice to the young Harold Macmillan about how to make a speech.

> Say just one thing, but say it many times. Say it with passion, say it with tears, say it with anger, say it with love, say it with longing. Whisper it, shout it, say it with your voice, say it with your eyes, say it with your hands, but just say one thing.

*6. Non-words, pauses and language*

How many times have you listened to someone speak and attempted to count the number of times they say 'you know' or 'sort of'?

Non-words are all those um's, er's, ah's, well's, OK's, just's and really's that we get into the habit of using but which we don't need, add nothing to our message and are distracting and irritating to our listeners.

In fact, most non-words are simply used as pause fillers. Get used to pausing instead of using your non-word. You can pause naturally for three or four seconds even in the middle of a sentence.

When you first try this it will seem like an embarrassing eternity, but if you subsequently listen to yourself on tape you will be aware of how naturally you come across. Pauses can in fact be used as a very powerful part of speech.

Beware of using jargon. Most people use some jargon language, but Christians seem to be especially prone to this complaint!

Jargon is a way of communicating in shorthand to insiders who understand the code. But our task is to make sure that no one is excluded; we can't be sure how much or how little people understand. Don't use 'in' language.

We communicate most effectively when we are able to choose the right words at the right time. Work at increasing your vocabulary by actively incorporating new words into your use of language. Choose a new word each day and force yourself to use it. Set a target of a minimum of six times. The words don't have to be long or intellectual – just new to your usage.

*7. Listener involvement*

A good communicator is attempting to do far more than simply pass on information at an intellectual level. The aim of all good communication is to involve the audience fully.

The more involved they are, the harder it is for them to become distracted. Therefore the use of good stories, humour, questions, challenging statements, dramatic quotes and feedback as well as visual aids like overhead projectors, flip charts, videos, etc are all important.

A famous Hollywood director once said that the art of making a good film was to start with explosion and then slowly work up to a climax!

Spend some time on each of these points, and remember – practice makes permanent!

# 9
# UNACCUSTOMED AS I AM
## *The Art of Public Speaking*

Why do some youth leaders go weak at the knees and get a sudden attack of palpitations every time they look at a microphone, while others insist on behaving like budding Tony Campolos just waiting for the world to wake up and recognise their talent? Everyone falls into one of four basic categories when it comes to public speaking. Which one best describes you?

- Avoider *'Not on your life, I'd rather volunteer to be trampled by a raging herd of demented elephants.'* You go to great lengths to avoid public speaking, the thought of which terrifies you. Occasionally you get trapped, but in general you manage to find excuses.
- Resistor *'I'll do it if I have to, but without being over modest I'm completely and utterly incompetent. I am to public speaking what dry rot is to carpentry.'* You are a reluctant speaker, but because you recognise that public speaking is sometimes important you will speak (without much enthusiasm) when really necessary.
- Acceptor *'It's my responsibility so I'll do it. I'm OK. In fact, occasionally I surprise myself and end up having a great time.'* You've learned to cope with the pressures of public speaking and actually quite enjoy yourself sometimes.

- Seeker *'I love it. Eat your heart out, Billy Graham – here I come.'* You find speaking stimulating, and thrive on the opportunities you get of motivating, inspiring and teaching others.

Are you an Avoider, a Resistor, an Acceptor or a Seeker? The surprising thing is that these categories refer not to actual ability but rather to attitude (in other words, perceived ability).

Most people who describe themselves as Avoiders or Resistors would be quite surprised if they watched a video of themselves speaking; not by how badly they performed, but by how well they did!

Generally we tend to be in a higher speaking category than we perceive. But beware: it must be said that there are a few Seekers around whose actual skills don't quite match their egos!

Just how good a public speaker are you? Does your youth group look forward to what you have to say, or have they had to learn to suffer in silence? Dare to find out by completing the self-assessment questionnaire at the end of this chapter.

**Into the unknown**

You get up to speak to your youth group and it feels like the bottom is about to fall out of your stomach. You're sweating like an unfit, heavyweight boxer, and your heart's beating so hard you're sure it's making a last-minute attempt to smash its way through your rib cage and escape before you make a complete fool of yourself.

Don't worry! At least 95% of all those who speak in public suffer from associated stress or anxiety of one kind or another. But there are several steps you can take to help yourself cope more effectively.

The easiest way to reduce tension is to prepare what you are going to say properly and well in advance. Lack of preparation and organisation is the single major cause of anxiety for speakers.

To be well prepared and the owner of a good set of notes is

bound to have the result of helping you be more confident and relaxed as you speak. It means that your energy will be channelled into communicating with your audience instead of worrying about the content of what you are going to say.

**I love it when a plan comes together**

The problem is often not that speakers don't prepare, but that they don't understand how to do so effectively. So what are the principles of good preparation?

*Don't panic*

It's easy to be panicked into beginning your preparation with the wrong question in mind. Don't make the fatal error of starting by trying to answer the question, 'What on earth can I say to hold my group's attention?'

Avoid the pressure to believe that a good talk is simply a collection of snappy, entertaining, humorous stories and punchlines.

Instead, deal with the primary issue of deciding your aim and objective by asking, 'What do I want to teach and what attitudes or behaviour do I want to change?'

*Pin-point your objective*

To establish your objective get a piece of A4 paper and at the top write down, in one simple sentence, what you want your talk to accomplish. You may have decided to look at:

- a subject – worship, prayer, the Holy Spirit
- an issue – unemployment, abortion, the environment
- a passage of Scripture
- a Bible character – David, Peter, Ruth

But establishing your objective is something far more specific than simply choosing a subject.

What is the purpose of this presentation? How does this teaching apply to my own group? What do I want them to do about it? What attitudes and behaviour is the Bible challenging?

If you can't state your aim clearly in one sentence it's too complicated! At the end of the evening your youth group should be able to go away and, if asked, be able to sum up your theme in a phrase or sentence.

If you have communicated effectively their phrase should be very similar to the one you started with. If you didn't have one in the first place they have absolutely no chance of remembering or acting on it.

*Assess your youth group profile*

Your next job is accurately to assess your youth group's needs. It is no good simply lifting material from elsewhere and transplanting it into your presentation. It will need adaptation. Your job is to tailor it to suit your youth group's needs.

A suit may be cut from the finest cloth and have 'Pierre Cardin' printed on the label inside, but that doesn't mean it will fit. What are your group's specific needs, values, expectations, limitations? Ask yourself two questions:

1. Generally – how do they feel and think about themselves, you, the world and Christianity? What you say must be culturally relevant and accessible to them. Your job is to start where they are and build from there.
2. Specifically – how good is their knowledge of your chosen subject? It's no good giving a degree level lecture to GCSE students or vice versa. Don't use abbreviations, technical terms or other jargon that your audience won't understand.

*Establish your main points*

Build what you are going to say from the centre out, not the outside in. In other words, your target is first to establish the main points of your message or presentation.

On your piece of A4 paper start to scribble down all the related ideas you can think of underneath your objective. Generate as many ideas as possible. Write down everything. Don't attempt to edit.

It is at this point that you should make use of books,

commentaries, cassettes, magazines or any other resources that are appropriate.

Having gathered sufficient material, begin to look at how the ideas you have collected relate to each other. You will discover that there is a series of main points emerging.

Draw them out and write them down. You should aim to identify between two and five (at the most). These main points will now form the structural backbone of your message.

*Develop supporting ideas*

Having established your main structure it is now important to relate your other material to it. Where there is material which does not readily fit into your structure in a natural way, drop it, or shelve it for next time.

*Topping and tailing*

This is the point at which you should add your introduction, conclusion and other illustrations which all play vital roles in your presentation.

It is only now that you have fully developed the 'meat' of what you are going to say that you can really do this effectively. Until now you didn't know accurately what it was that you wanted to illustrate.

Your introduction serves a very important function. You need to grab your group's attention and whet their appetite for your subject. Work hard at it rather than making the mistake of trying to stand up and get away with slowly drifting into your message.

Good devices to help create arresting introductions include humour, anecdotes, rhetorical questions and shocking statements.

Your conclusion is equally important. Too many presentations just peter out or grind to an embarrassing halt. Your conclusion may be a powerful story or quote with a punch or some other device. But whatever form it takes its job is to bring your audience back to your central objective and call them to action.

**How to use 'keyword' notes**

You don't have to be an expert chef to appreciate that although a meal may be absolutely packed with protein, vitamins, fibre and health, its fate depends far more on how the ingredients are presented than their combined nutritional value.

If the meal fails the looks and taste test, its dietary qualities, however significant, are unlikely to prevent it ending up in the dustbin. To put it in the immortal words of those three well-known twentieth-century philosophers Bananarama, 'It ain't what you do it's the way that you do it.'

And when it comes to preparing and presenting a talk the same rules apply. Bluntly, your Bible studies may well be among the most profound and theologically correct given by any human since Jesus himself, but if you don't work hard to make them appetising nobody is listening.

Quality content is of course essential – junk food does nobody much good. But ask yourself for a moment whether as you struggle to present sound truth your youth group are struggling equally hard not to end up sound asleep! Do you present your material in a way which maximises or minimises its impact?

**Unaccustomed as I am...**

When was the last time you watched a speech on TV from a politician, preacher or some other public speaker, who came across with all the energy, charisma and vitality of a dead gerbil? Why was it? Nine out of ten cases of instant viewer boredom are generated by speakers who use scripts or full notes which they are then unable to break free from.

Instead of building rapport and talking with their audience they end up being trapped into reading to them. It must be said that though not always the case, being tied to a script or notes has several very common and equally devastating effects.

- Monotone delivery. Using a script is one of the biggest causes of monotone delivery. It not only has the effect of robbing your voice of variety of tone, but also variety of volume, speed of delivery and emotion. Without these vital qualities it becomes impossible to hold the attention of others for any significant period of time.

- No eye contact. Good eye contact is essential to effective communication. Failure to achieve this creates an impression of distance, disinterest and awkwardness. Obviously using a script or full notes has the effect of removing or lessening your ability to engage your audience in any meaningful eye contact.
- Limited facial expression and other gestures. These too are bound to decrease in direct proportion to the amount of time you have to spend looking down at a script.
- Unscripted spontaneity. The fourth and fatal weakness of the scripted talk method is that reckless moment of enthusiastic abandon, when a speaker moves away from his prepared script and then, running out of steam looks down to find his place – and can't! All he sees on the page is a mass of confusing words, none of which seem to relate to what he is now engaged in. Panic sets in and chaos follows. 'Beam me up, Scottie.'

**What are effective notes?**

- They are *brief* enough to prevent you from getting locked into them, and therefore give you the freedom to communicate with your audience in an animated and natural way.
- They set out *key words* and phrases containing your main points, ideas and illustrations. You can then use these as triggers or cues to recall your material.
- They are *clearly printed* (whenever possible) on one side of A5 or A4 paper which, while you are speaking, can be positioned on a lectern or table or in your Bible without having to be picked up, turned over or fiddled about with.
- They are *printed large* enough to be easily seen and read as you glance down at them. Don't cram too many words on a line or too many lines close together.
- They should use a *clear coding system* to make their content

assessable at a glance. For instance, print your main points in block capitals and then outline them with a highlighter pen, present your sub-points in lower case (you might also choose to use a second highlighter colour for them) and box your illustrations and quotes. Down the right hand side of your page indicate the positioning, using a number and title, of any OHP transparencies or any other visual aids you intend to make use of.

## The finishing touches

Effective use of keyword notes depends on how familiar you are with your material. Practise it using them several times until you are confident you know it well and your ideas flow freely. Your goal is to reach the point where you rely on your notes as little as possible, which will enable you to concentrate on your audience and the task of communicating with them. Make sure you do at least one full stand-up rehearsal when you run right through your material out loud.

If you have been in the habit of using a script or full set of notes and feel dependent on them, don't attempt to make the switch to the keyword system straight away or all in one go. Instead work hard to cut down your notes step by step rather than trying to change your whole approach in one fell swoop.

## Ten commandments for using visual aids

There is a very misleading idea around that using OHP transparencies, flipcharts, whiteboards, handouts or other forms of visual aid as part of a talk or Bible study is the 100 per cent guaranteed, failproof method of automatically doubling the effectiveness of your message.

The truth is that well-presented visual aids will add to your communication style as they stimulate your youth group's interest and serve to focus their attention. But badly prepared visual aids will only detract from the effectiveness of your message. Far from solving your communication problems, they will multiply them!

For effective preparation and use of visual aids there are ten important principles which form an essential guide for all those who want their visual aids to work for them, not against them. Because the most common form of visual aid is the overhead projector (OHP) transparency, we will concentrate on this, although most of the principles outlined also have wider applications.

*1. Keep your visual aids simple*

Don't fall into the trap of cramming your overhead or other visual aid with too much detail. To do so will confuse rather than impress your audience and is bound to result in them quickly losing interest. Added to this, presenting detailed information means using lots of words, which in turn necessitates small print – often impossible to read from a distance!

For maximum effect the contents of your transparencies should be set out in as concise and simple a form as possible. Overheads should be used to summarise briefly the content of your talk. The aim is to focus visually and reinforce your main ideas, not to restate your case in a detailed way. The more simply information is displayed the easier it is to retain. Only use essential key words and phrases.

As a rule of thumb, overheads should never have more than thirty-six words (excluding the title) on a maximum of six lines.

*2. Present your material as visually as possible*

Think carefully about the best way of presenting your material. Aim to use graphics and diagrams instead of, or in support of, words whenever possible. Once again avoid the trap of being too elaborate and complicated. The visual impact of your message will be greatly enhanced by this simple but very effective technique.

*3. Do not use your visual aid to make more than one point*

Each overhead should deal with a single issue. It's far more effective to use a number of transparencies to make consecutive points than to try and condense all you want to say on one sheet. Added to this, the impact of your message will be significantly reduced if you 'leak' or reveal your main points to the audience before you get to them. Don't allow your visual aids to steal your thunder.

*4. Produce your visual aids to a high standard*

So, your overheads are concise, simple and make good use of diagrams. But are they attractive? There are several useful tips you can follow to ensure that they are. Always print clearly; do not use joined lettering. Make sure your lettering is large enough to be seen in the room you are planning to use for your presentation.

Don't scribble out your transparencies in a hurry – take time to be neat and tidy. Use a piece of lined paper as a backing sheet while preparing your overheads to ensure your information is presented in straight lines. Only write and draw in colours which can be seen easily from a distance.

*5. Do not rely on your visual aids to carry your message*

Visual aids should be seen for what they are – simple aids to assist your communication technique. Their function is to reinforce your message rather than make your point for you. Remember that your overall effectiveness relies on your total communication style. In the final analysis it is this which makes the difference between an effective and ineffective presentation.

*6. Do not crowd your presentation with too many visual aids*

Using too many overheads will simply have the effect of overwhelming your presentation. Every time you use an overhead you divide your audience's attention between yourself and it. The more transparencies you use, the greater the amount of time they spend looking at a screen instead of at you, which effectively breaks down your opportunity to build a rapport with them through good eye contact and the use of other gestures.

Add to this the constant interruptions created by having to keep on fiddling around with positioning the overheads on the projector, and you have managed to create a major communication barrier!

*7. Do not compete with visual aids*

The art of using visual aids is that of learning to direct your audience's attention where you want it when you want it. But as we've already said, when you use an overhead your youth group's attention is divided between it and you. Don't make the mistake of competing with your own visual aids throughout your talk.

When you have made the point you want to with your projector, win back your group's attention by turning the projector off and taking a step towards them. Don't speak until you have re-established eye contact with them. If you have to write on the overhead, stop talking while you write.

When you need to give a long explanation of a transparency, switch off the projector. On the other hand, don't keep flicking your projector on and off so that it becomes distracting.

*8. Position your OHP correctly*

Take care to place your OHP and screen correctly. Wrongly placed it will seriously detract from your ability to hold your audience's attention. Don't set your screen either directly behind you, or square with your audience to your side. Doing so will mean that you have to compete for attention with it.

Instead, place it at a 45° angle to your audience, slightly to one side of the centre of the room. This enables you to occupy the central position and so more easily focus your group's attention on the material displayed or yourself, as you choose.

*9. Address your audience, not the OHP screen*

A major problem that often arises is that speakers get trapped into talking to their screen rather than their audience. Remember to face your audience even when using a transparency, and though you may glance occasionally at the screen, keep eye contact with them.

*10. Arrive early to check your equipment*

Even the most effective set of multi-coloured, three-dimensional, scratch-and-sniff overheads ever produced is useless if the projector on which the overheads are going to be shown is not working, or lost, or both!

Make sure you arrive early enough to find, check, set up and focus the equipment needed. Obviously, in the case of an OHP or any other projection equipment, spare fuses and bulbs will always be kept in stock...

## How good are you at public speaking?

| | Always | Some-times | Never |
|---|---|---|---|
| When preparing a Bible study or other talk: | 10 | 5 | 0 |
| 1. Do you identify your basic objective before planning the content of your presentation? | | | |
| 2. Do you analyse the opinions, needs and limitations of your group before starting to plan the structure of your presentation? | | | |
| 3. Do you finalise your main points before building the rest of your presentation round them? | | | |
| 4. Do you work hard at your introduction in order to catch the full attention of your group from the outset? | | | |
| 5. Do you think through the conclusion of your presentation? | | | |
| 6. Does your conclusion sum up what you have said and call your group to action? | | | |
| 7. Do you make good use of illustrative stories, quotes, questions and humour? | | | |
| 8. Are your visual aids neat, simple and easy to understand? | | | |

# Part Three

# PROBLEMS

# 10
# TO CONFRONT OR NOT TO CONFRONT
## *Handling disagreement and conflict*

'I've never been spoken to like that before...what are you going to do about it?'

'Call yourself a Christian youth worker? You're nothing but a thoroughly bad influence on all those impressionable teenagers.'

'I just can't cope with working with him any more.'

'He's a liar. He stole it. I saw him.'

'She never listens to anyone. Call this a team? It's a joke.'

'Our young people are ruining our church. Why don't you teach them a bit more reverence and respect?'

'The vicar's going to hear about this. You won't get away with it. I want this youth club shut.'

Tension, anger and disagreement – sad realities from which even the most spiritual among us are never immune. Every Christian youth leader has to cope with the seemingly continual upsets between young people and their parents, young people and other church members and even, every now and then, young people and the church leaders! On top of this, problems regularly arise between the members of the group itself.

Then there are the tensions between you and the other members of the church or its leaders, the almost regular criticisms from parents, and your ongoing problems with your fellow youth leaders and some of the young people in the group.

Although when trouble raises its ugly head you sometimes find yourself as a spectator with a ringside seat, more often you are inside the ropes with the unpleasant job of refereeing the big bout, or even worse, an unwilling contestant being forced to defend yourself as best you can while trying to resist the temptation to hit back!

**To confront or not to confront**

Learning to confront and handle disagreement constructively is a difficult but essential skill for any leader. Unfortunately it is one that Christians have often been very poor at. A significant reason for this is perhaps the feeling that to acknowledge our difficulties would be to admit our failure to be what we preach about being. The situation is not eased by worship song lines such as 'Bind us together, Lord' and 'Let there be love shared among us, let there be love in our eyes', which have left some Christians naively believing that if we were 'truly' spiritual, disagreement and tension would simply vanish.

The church's response to disagreement in its ranks has too often been to push it under the carpet and pray for it to disappear. However, any reading of the New Testament which is more than skin deep reveals plenty of tension in the life of the early church. Two obvious examples of this are Paul's disputes with Barnabas and with Peter, though even a superficial reading of the epistles reveals many more.

The youth leader who through weakness or 'niceness' fails to confront and deal with disagreement, is simply storing up big future trouble. Unresolved disagreement or ill-feeling is always destructive.

**Four principles for managing disagreement**

*1. Anticipate problems*

Wherever possible your aim should be to deal with disagreement before it boils over and develops into open or heated conflict. In order to do this you must:

- Be alert to the current feelings and opinions of others. Make it a priority to keep in touch with what those around you are thinking.
- Avoid the temptation to 'opt out' and let things drift when you are aware of disagreements or clashing opinions.

*2. Clarify issues*

In order to deal with a developing disagreement, you first need to diagnose the real situation effectively. Never assume that you know all the facts, or that your initial view of the core issues is accurate. Get honest feedback from others involved. Their perspective may be very different from yours and could introduce you to valuable insights and information you would otherwise have been totally unaware of. In order to do this it is essential that you:

- *Focus on issues, not personalities*. Don't be drawn into shifting the focus of attention from the issues to the personalities involved. Never fall into the trap of making derogatory or demeaning comments about others. These dangers are especially accute if you are personally involved in the dispute! Always do your best to protect the dignity of everyone involved, and resist the temptation to put others down even when you regard their views as stubborn or stupid. Unless proved otherwise, assume that each person involved is expressing a genuine concern from their point of view. Your task is to do all you can to re-establish strained and broken relationships and build up all the individuals' true understanding of themselves and their sense of self-worth.

- *Listen with empathy.* Attempt to put yourself in the shoes of each person involved in the disagreement and see things from their perspective. Your attitude and behaviour will determine how much you are told and how receptively you are listened to. If you appear judgemental or condemning, all you will end up doing is getting the shutters pulled down on yourself. Always remember that the most powerful key to influencing the attitude and behaviour of others is the way that you relate to them, not the strength of your argument. If you are involved in the argument yourself, you often won't get any critical feedback of your attitude or views freely volunteered. This means that in order to learn of and understand views that differ from your own you must demonstrate openness and actually ask for feedback. And you must never react negatively when you receive it!

### *Identify the stakeholders*

A stakeholder is someone who has an important stake in the issue under consideration. This, of course, might include you. But the list of stakeholders is made up not only of the main characters in the disagreement, but should also include everyone who is going to be concerned with its outcome, both those who have to implement decisions and those who have to live with them.

### *Assess the sources of disagreement*

Why does the issue being disputed exist?

- Does it exist because of inaccurate or incomplete information held by some or all stakeholders involved? If so, how can you ensure that the situation is effectively remedied as soon as possible?
- Does it exist because those involved hold to differing methods, goals, aims or principles? If so, is there a higher level at which all the stakeholders share a common vision? If

common ground on which agreement already exists can be identified, it can then be used as a foundation on which a way forward can be built.

- Does it exist because of different perceptions of the present situation? If so, remember that what one person sees as a challenge or opportunity, another may regard as a problem or threat.
- Does it exist as a result of the lingering resentment left over from previous unresolved conflicts? People who have felt betrayed, put down or neglected often act in punishing ways to even up the score. When disagreements stem from old wounds they can be difficult to diagnose, because those involved rarely acknowledge the real problem and are sometimes almost unaware of it themselves. Is there a way in which these can be uncovered, faced and dealt with? Remember that someone who is antagonistic towards another individual may simply be working out their resentment or negative feelings towards the whole group or church.

Working through these four principles will enable you to begin to gain a more objective understanding and assessment of the root causes and central issues behind any disagreement you are faced with.

**How good are you at handling disagreements?**

For each of the following questions, place a tick in the column which best describes your approach. Be totally honest – there's no one to fool but yourself!

| | Always | Sometimes | Never |
|---|---|---|---|
| 1. I make sure I let my emotions cool down before taking action over any disagreement. | | | |
| 2. I am careful not to assume that I know all the facts or that my initial view is necessarily accurate. | | | |
| 3. I take time to collect a good level of background information from all those involved in any disagreement. | | | |
| 4. I take time to listen to the views of others, and demonstrate openness rather than appearing judgemental or condemning when they present opinions that differ from my own. | | | |
| 5. Before deciding on a course of action, I endeavour to discover the root causes rather than just the circumstances of the disagreement. | | | |
| 6. When I have gathered the relevant information and thought through the issues involved, I decide on a course of positive action. | | | |
| 7. When faced with tension or disagreement, I actively avoid the temptation to 'opt out' and let things drift. | | | |
| 8. I am careful to focus on issues and actively avoid the trap of shifting my attention to the personalities involved. | | | |
| 9. My goal in taking action is to re-establish strained and broken relationships and build up all the individuals involved in any dispute. | | | |
| 10. I am aware that the most powerful key to influencing the attitude of others is the way I relate to them, not the strength of my arguments. My action reflects this. | | | |
| Number of ticks in each column:<br>Number of points: | | | |

For each tick in the Always column give yourself 4 points, for each Sometimes 2 points, and for each Never 0 points.

If you scored between 30 and 40 points you are either an archangel or have a very serious self-awareness problem and need to see a qualified counsellor as soon as possible!

If you scored between 20 and 30 you are a naturally gifted and sensitive person, willing to listen, with the courage to be decisive and speak the truth. You know that although it may be painful, true depth to a relationship comes through honesty.

If you scored between 10 and 20, then you've got a lot of hard thinking to do about the way you handle conflict. You want to be nice and not upset anyone, so you suffer in silence. You may see this attitude as humility, but really you have muddled humility with a lack of honesty and courage.

If you scored between 2 and 10, you have not learned to speak truth and honesty in love, so when you are confronted with conflict you bottle up your feelings. This is dangerous: bottled emotions have a habit of exploding at just the wrong time, and can land you in a lot of trouble.

If you scored between 0 and 2, the most positive thing that can be said is that you haven't read this chapter carefully enough. And don't even think of applying for a job as an arbitrator!

**Choosing your response**

Every professional golfer has a full set of clubs at his disposal. His task is to choose the most appropriate one for each shot and so produce his best game. He only selects a club after thinking through the kind of shot he wants to make, and would be a fool if he always chose the same one just because it was his favourite!

Equally, to deal effectively with disagreement and prevent destructive conflict, a skilled leader needs a whole range of problem-solving approaches in his repertoire. Like the golfer choosing the right club, so the skill of any leader is to choose the appropriate course of action for each problem. The leader who makes the claim, 'This is how I always deal with disagreements...' is a loser. Whether the style of confrontation is aggressive, apologetic or non-existent, he is no different from the golfer who always insists on playing his shot with a number 9 iron whether it's a six-inch putt or a 300-yard drive!

Your task, as a good leader, is to become familiar with as wide a variety of approaches to dealing with conflict as possible, and then develop the ability to choose and use the right one at the right time. There is no one universally applicable approach that is always guaranteed to do the job.

Make sure you choose the course of action, rather than being forced into one or simply allowing a situation to happen to you and get out of control.

### Getting it right

In order to choose your course of action, the basic question you must always ask is: how flexible should I be in dealing with this problem or disagreement? Some situations need extreme firmness, while others require a softer, more accommodating approach. The methods of dealing with disagreement and conflict fall into three basic categories.

*Soft*

This includes non-resistance, which involves choosing to accept the other party's views and opinions; maintenance, which allows the status quo to continue to exist; and co-existence, which accepts that two opinions can live alongside each other. Maintenance, which may at first be mistaken for weakness or giving in, may actually be the best way forward in some circumstances. For instance, you may have higher-priority issues to deal with, or need more time to collect information, build rapport, let emotions cool or allow recent changes to stabilise before taking another stance.

*Flexible*

This includes approaches such as bargaining, collaboration and consensus, and involves co-operation between all parties who give and take on all sides. All those involved in the disagreement commit themselves to sit down and listen to each other, so that through frank and honest discussion they can jointly develop an acceptable solution or way forward. Collaboration is the way forward when issues being faced are so central that the total commitment of all parties involved to the selected course of action is important for a successful outcome. In reality such a course of action can only be taken if all participants in the discussion are trustworthy, capable and willing to communicate with each other – and have got adequate time for discussion.

*Hard*

This approach is one of domination, where an attempt is made unilaterally to use power and influence to gain complete compliance to a strongly held view or opinion. Domination can sometimes be appropriate when speed of action is absolutely essential, but using it unwisely can be destructive.

**The 'have a word' checklist**

How do you choose the right course of action? Is the correct approach hard or soft? How firm or flexible should you aim to be? Here's what you do:

- Assess the situation under the four principles set out above and choose your initial course of action.
- Check that you have made a wise choice by answering the following three questions. Put a tick in the correct box:

| | Yes | Probably | Probably not |
|---|---|---|---|
| 1. Will my chosen course of action clearly advance the youth group's agreed goals? | ☐ | ☐ | ☐ |

| | Yes | Probably | Probably not |
|---|---|---|---|
| 2. Will my chosen course of action clearly be acceptable to others involved? | ☐ | ☐ | ☐ |
| 3. Will my chosen course of action clearly result in greater benefits and fewer draw-backs than any alternative possibilities? | ☐ | ☐ | ☐ |

If all three of your ticks are in the 'yes' column, you should feel confident to pursue the course of action you have in mind.

If you have any ticks at all in the 'probably' column, you should give the pros and cons of your proposed course of action further serious thought and carefully consider a more flexible approach before making a final decision on the way forward.

If you have any ticks in the 'probably not' column, do not proceed. Rethink your approach urgently. The cost of your proposed action is likely to be considerable, either in terms of scarred or lost relationships and/or your goals for your youth work.

# 11
# UNHAPPY FAMILIES
## *Handling teenager/parent relationships*

To say that the task of responsible youth leadership is demanding has to be one of the greatest understatements ever made. Among the most difficult situations you face are those occasions when you find yourself wedged in the middle of strained or broken relationships.

You seem to be the jam in the sandwich as you stand between teenagers and their parents; teenagers and their school; teenagers and the rest of the church; teenagers and society as a whole; in some senses even between teenagers and God.

This is not to mention the times when you find yourself keeping the peace among the group members themselves! All this on top of your responsibilities to family, work, other church commitments and friends, and perhaps finding a few minutes a month to relax!

In this chapter we're going to look at some of the common problems that arise within parent/teenager relationships. It is so easy for youth leaders inadvertently to add fuel to an already established fire unless they have a good understanding of why both parties hold certain attitudes. In order to do this we are going to look at how that household game King of the Castle is played. This is a unique, real-life game for parents and teenagers, originally known as Unhappy Families. Both parents and teenagers automatically assume that they have the winning hand, and realise too late that they are all losers.

### King of the Castle rule book

Let's look at some of the most important rules which govern this game.

1. Parents and teenagers must always play against each other.
2. Never admit that you are wrong, even when you know you are.
3. Never admit that the other side is right, even when it's obvious they are.
4. Cheat whenever you can.
5. If the other side scores any points, make sure they think you haven't noticed.
6. Act like you're winning, even when you know you're losing.
7. Bribe and manipulate the other side whenever you can.
8. Always exaggerate.
9. Make sure you impose on the other side a set of rules different from the ones you intend to play by yourself.
10. Try not to listen to what the other side is saying. This could cost you the game – or much worse than that – lead to it being cancelled!

### Teenage trump cards

There are various trump cards that teenagers throw at their parents in order to be King of the Castle. What are the issues that lie behind them?

*'You don't own me.'*

This is a very popular card. But why does it get played so often? It's easy for parents to fall into the trap of believing that their children belong to them. But there are some very obvious and natural reasons why this happens.

- They did produce the child in the first place!
- Through the years of childhood, parents do carry the full load of responsibility for the child's safety and growth. The child would be helpless without them.
- Children are very demanding, and as a result the home, future plans, savings, holidays, and even the day-to-day timetable all focus on their needs. Parents do give up their time, freedom and resources to take care of 'their' children.

*'You treat me as if I'm still a child.'*

Everybody accepts that a young bird or animal must leave the nest or den. But parents are slower to accept that there is a natural 'growing away' from the home which is part of the maturing process and which is going on within their own children.

It's very important for adolescents to be allowed to assert their own individuality and freedom. For parents it is hard to accept that if the young are let go they will usually return of their own accord. If they are firmly bound to the home by too many rules and regulations they will either break away in resentment, often never returning, or they may live for ever in an immature world where, even as adults, they remain incapable of making decisions for themselves.

It's right that there should be a level of protectiveness without which adolescents would be vulnerable and exploitable. But to be over-protective for too long creates the very weaknesses that the parent is struggling to overcome.

The only way in which parents can teach responsibility to teenagers is gradually to let them make more and more important decisions for themselves.

*'You don't trust me.'*

It's very easy for parents to misread the growing-up process as rebellion, ingratitude, selfishness or rejection, and therefore to struggle to withhold trust. The problem parents face is finding the right pace at which to grant freedom. How quickly should the reins be loosened?

Unfortunately there is no universal answer, as each young person is different. Some are far too eager to be free of all accountability to parents, and need to be held back, whereas others actually need to be prodded to take the first steps beyond the den.

What teenagers usually fail to grasp is that, although often poorly expressed, their parents' desire is normally to shield and protect them and sometimes even to prevent them repeating some of their own mistakes. Parents quickly spot their own failings in their children; indeed they often imagine them even when they don't exist.

*'You always think you're right.'*

This is a major card which both sides use from time to time. What often lies behind the parents' attitude is the feeling that 'I've lived longer therefore I know more', based on the belief that experience is the only real source of wisdom.

When teenagers play this card it is often in response to statements from parents such as 'It's right because I say it's right,' or 'You'll do it because I say so,' with no attempt to explain why. Parents can, while claiming authority that belongs to age, allow their attitude to sink to the level where it is no more than unreasoned tyranny.

Christian parents can sometimes be especially prone to this. They can fall into the trap of always reinforcing their views with statements like 'If you were a Christian you wouldn't behave like that' and 'Do you think Jesus would be proud of you?'

*'Why don't you mind your own business?'*

Having acknowledged a teenager's need for independence, it must be remembered that parents are still ultimately responsible (officially until the age of eighteen, but emotionally far beyond that). There are cases where family bonding breaks down altogether due to accident, failure, unemployment, loss of health and so on. But it is usually the parents' budget that must somehow meet the economic consequences while they also cope with all the other pressures the situation creates.

Parents usually stand by their children. Emotionally, physically and financially they are responsible. Teenagers sometimes argue that they don't want their parents to feel this way, or that they resent their involvement. But this is like saying an irresponsible parent is the best parent!

If parents totally relinquish their responsibility, all it achieves is to shift the responsibility on to society as a whole. In other words, other people's parents!

### Parents' trump cards

Now what about the other side of the coin? Let's look at some of the big cards parents bombard their teenage children with when the accusations fly across the living room war zone.

*'Why don't you grow up?'*

Teenagers are adolescents and by definition are not fully mature yet. So to expect them to consistently behave as though they were adults is to ask the impossible.

The term adolescent means 'in between'. Adolescence has been described as a turbulent and dangerous voyage. It involves leaving behind the protection of the harbour of childhood and heading for the distant shore of adult life.

Younger children trust their parents to make all life's big decisions for them (money, food, clothing, the future, and so on). Teenagers are beginning to move out of this insular world and to take their first faltering steps towards adult life and independence. Sometimes they will fall over!

*'Why don't you take life a bit more seriously?'*

The ancient Greeks used to say that the problems of youth were the same as those of a charioteer who, at one and the same time, was both struggling to urge forward his galloping horses, and yet desperately attempting to control and direct their charging power. It's a case of raw energy versus discipline.

It would be wrong to see adolescence as simply a difficult and depressing stage through which everyone must travel. Often it is also one of the most exciting experiences that life brings.

Unfortunately the struggle to harness the energy and enthusiasm in the most creative and constructive way tends to take a bit of time to get right!

*'You always argue about everything.'*

Emotionally teenagers are fighting a civil war with themselves. On one hand they have a sense of inadequacy and insecurity which creates the need to be loved, supported and accepted by adults, especially their parents. On the other hand there is the natural desire to be assertive, independent and different.

This struggle often shows itself in fits of rebellion, aggression, or stubbornness at home. To pit yourself against your parents is both daring and at the same time safe. You still 'belong' even if things go drastically wrong.

Teenagers have also begun to spend much more time outside the home and are being introduced to other homes and family set-ups. They will meet other parents and see different codes of behaviour and discipline in action.

For the first time they begin to look critically at their parents and the standards they have always known and somehow assumed were universal. This can lead to a new appreciation of the privileges which, up until now, they have taken for granted. But it usually leads to criticism of conditions at home!

*'You'll do as I say.'*

Teenagers' developing sense of independence means that they will begin to question their parents' beliefs and expect them to be ready to explain their views and opinions honestly. For parents to say that things are done this way 'because I say so' will only build resentment.

The childhood philosophy of 'Mother knows best' will no longer do. It is easy for parents to forget that they went through the same stage themselves. They can therefore mistake it for rebellion or disrespect, rather than recognise it as the honest search for what is right and why.

Though teenage criticism is often tactless and self-opinionated, the challenge itself is wholly natural and justified. Teenagers are not looking for clever or infallible answers from their parents, but simply the patience to explain their reasoning and listen to other points of view.

Without explanation, demands and prohibitions are bound to heat up considerably the battle to be King of the Castle. If handled well, this aspect of adolescence can open up a new and honest friendship between parents and teenagers which was never possible before.

*'You're not going out looking like that!'*

One feature of King of the Castle which often infuriates the young, is the triviality of the issues that parents choose to argue about: hairstyles, taste in music, earrings, clothes.

Many stages that teenagers would otherwise rapidly grow through and forget are given a ridiculous level of importance as they become the battleground on which the young feel compelled to show their strength.

Meanwhile, having lost all credibility over pointless debates, parents feel hurt and outraged at their inability to discuss with their children the serious issues of sex, drink, faith and so on, where guidance and help is actually desperately needed.

On these big issues teenagers will actually be grateful (though they may never openly admit it to their parents) for firm, reasoned guidelines and clear limits which breed a sense of security into their lives.

*'You treat this house like a hotel.'*

Teenagers have begun to form a whole new circle of relationships outside the home and are also looking for a far greater degree of privacy than ever before.

Their desire for independence means they need to feel that they are no longer owned or controlled by their parents. As a result, parents can feel abandoned as they mistake their child's behaviour patterns for open rejection.

They can be deeply hurt by their child's straying affection, as all sorts of outsiders begin to command more authority, respect and attention than they think they do. This can even include the local youth leader!

This situation is made worse by the fact that, on the one hand, teenagers tend to develop hero figures, while on the other, they are as subtle as bricks when it comes to stating how they feel!

**The umpire's role**

Although not always appointed (because it is entirely up to the players to decide whether they want one or not), the umpire – who is always unofficial – can play a very important role in the outcome of the game.

Often youth leaders have the privilege of doing the honours. However, the job is made considerably harder when, as often happens, one side recognises the appointment but the other ignores or even resents it. You may find the following rules useful.

1. Wherever possible listen to both sides of King of the Castle and get a chance to think the whole situation through before passing comment.
2. Never assume you understand any game of King of the Castle without asking lots of questions first. Opening questions like how? what? where? and when? are best because they unearth the real issues and feelings involved.
3. Don't break confidences. You will end up watching the end of the game from the terraces.
4. Never be tempted to quote one game to illustrate another. Teenagers are very good at working out puzzles, and nobody likes the thought that they might end up as your next illustration.
5. Never belittle problems that are shared with you. Remember

that every family will have some level of conflict – so don't over-react.

6. Don't behave in a superior way. You may be umpire this week, but remind yourself how often you've been a player.

7. Although your advice may be asked, it will often be resented by one or both sides. It is very common for umpires to get a rough deal – so be warned!

8. It is your job to help parents and teenagers understand each other so that they can sort out their own conflicts. Advise them, but don't try to play for them.

9. The Bible has plenty to say about family life, so make sure you tackle the issues involved in King of the Castle regularly as part of your youth group programne.

10. Remember that you can be sacked at any point in the game and sometimes no doubt will be. Reinstatements are also regular occurrences.

# 12
# THE DEMON DRINK
*Teenagers and alcohol abuse*

What has inspired songs and poems in every generation? Is part of many royal and state occasions? Is used to mark births, marriages and deaths? Will bring sadness and ruin to hundreds of individuals and families this month?

Despite current licensing laws it is claimed that as many as sixty per cent of teenagers under eighteen are likely to have bought alcohol illegally in a pub or off-licence and that only sixteen per cent regard drinking as being in any way dangerous to their health.

As a result, alcohol, which like tobacco enjoys the privilege of being socially acceptable as well as legal, is the drug which poses by far the greatest threat to the youth in this country.

## One for the road

Alcohol is the most common drug used by teenagers in the UK today. But how much do you know about its use, abuse and effects? Find out by answering the following ten questions. Tick the boxes of the figures you think are correct. The right answers appear at the end of the chapter.

1. How many people die from alcoholism each year in Europe?
a. 100,000 ☐ b. 600,000 ☐ c. 1,000,000 ☐ d. 2,000,000 ☐
2. How much does the British public spend on alcohol every day?
a. £5 million ☐ b. £14 million ☐ c. £26 million ☐
d. £33 million ☐
3. One of the following has double the alcoholic content of the others? Which one is it?
a. 1 measure spirits ☐ b. 1 pint beer ☐
c. 1 glass wine ☐ d. half a pint of cider ☐
4. What percentage of the adult male population of Great Britain have been drunk in the last three months?
a. 50% ☐ b. 25% ☐ c. 15% ☐ d. 10% ☐
5. What percentage of the adult female population of Great Britain have been drunk in the last three months?
a. 50% ☐ b. 25% ☐ c. 15% ☐ d. 10% ☐
6. One of the following age groups drinks almost 50% more alcohol than the national average. Which one is it?
a. 18–24 years ☐ b. 25–34 years ☐ c. 45–54 years ☐
d. 55–64 years ☐
7. Alcohol is involved in what percentage of accidents in the home?
a. 30% ☐ b. 40% ☐ c. 50% ☐ d. 60% ☐
8. What percentage of drivers killed in road accidents are above the legal blood/alcohol limit?
a. 25% ☐ b. 33% ☐ c. 66% ☐ d. 75% ☐
9. What percentage of drivers killed at night are above the legal alcohol limit in their blood?
a. 25% ☐ b. 33% ☐ c. 66% ☐ d. 75% ☐
10. What percentage of drivers killed on Saturday night have excess alcohol in their blood?
a. 25% ☐ b. 33% ☐ c. 66% ☐ d. 75% ☐

**Young, free and alcoholic?**

According to recent statistical research in the UK, one in every ten people that drink alcohol socially will eventually become alcoholic. And the facts also show that the popular teenage theory – 'I'm too young to be alcoholic' – is very far from being true.

While for some alcoholism is a condition that develops over time, for others it is an instant problem, served up with their first ever drink.

But we must beware of falling into the trap of believing that alcoholism is the only problem caused by excessive drinking. You don't have to be an alcoholic to get banned from driving for being drunk at the wheel of a car. It's not only alcoholics who find themselves pregnant after a drunken party. Many people killed in drink-driving accidents are only occasional drinkers – some have never drunk a drop before in their entire lives!

## On the bottle

Why is drinking a growing teenage problem? There are a variety of pressures on young people in our culture which influence them in this area. We will look at some of the most important.

### *Accessibility*

Although the law states that it is only at the age of eighteen that a teenager can legally purchase alcohol in a pub or off-licence, it is estimated that up to ninety-five percent of all seventeen-year-olds drink regularly. The licensing laws restrict where alcohol can be sold and consumed, where it can be sold and consumed and to whom it can be sold, but they do not cover the issue of who is actually allowed to possess and drink it. The present licensing laws state:

- It is an offence to give alcohol to a child under five.
- Children under the age of fourteen are not allowed to enter the bar area of a pub (ie the place where drinks are bought and consumed).
- Children of any age can enter parts of licensed premises

other than the bar (ie beer gardens) and can be bought alcohol to drink if they are over five years old.

- At the age of fourteen young people can enter the bar of licensed premises and be bought a drink by an adult. They cannot buy alcohol for themselves.
- At the age of sixteen teenagers may purchase alcohol (except spirits) with a meal served at the bar of a pub.
- At the age of eighteen a teenager can legally purchase alcohol on licensed premises.
- It is an offence to be drunk in a public place or to be drunk and disorderly.
- It is an offence to drive while unfit to do so because of the effects of alcohol in the blood.

These restrictions are very difficult to enforce and as a result it is estimated that around sixty per cent of thirteen- to seventeen-year-olds are likely to have bought alcohol in a pub or off-licence at some point.

*Advertising*

A great deal of money is spent on advertising alcohol in magazines, newspapers, at the cinema, through sports sponsorships and on radio and television. Its effectiveness is clearly seen in that we instantly recognise the slogans and can name the products without a great deal of brain-stretching activity.

These adverts often make very good use of humour while the qualities claimed for the drinks are in some cases, to put it modestly, nothing short of supernatural!

But then again, adverts that told the truth with scripts like: 'I bet he drinks Heineburg Red Label X. He's got bloodshot eyes, a beer gut, stomach ulcers and was banned from driving last week'; or 'Any time, any place, anywhere...you can make a complete and utter fool of yourself', are hardly likely to sell a lot of drinks!

There are, in fact, a number of restrictions relating to the advertising of alcoholic products on television. The advertising must not:

- be directed at teenagers
- encourage the excessive use of alcohol
- link drinking with driving
- advertise spirits.

But it is at least open to debate as to how effectively the spirit of the first two points of this code are adhered to.

*Peer group pressure*

I bought my first pint at the age of fourteen. I didn't want to do it, because if my dad had found out he would have killed me! I risked my neck simply because the desire to conform to my friends' behaviour weighed even more heavily than my dad's threats.

*Social acceptability*

While preparing this chapter I read through ten books and booklets (both Christian and secular) on drug abuse, only two of which had any reference to alcohol at all. Alcohol has become a socially acceptable and even status-providing drug. Curiosity tells the young that a substance to which society pays so much attention must be worth trying.

One recent survey revealed that around half the teenagers under eighteen who drink regularly were given their first drink by their parents at home. A teenager might be forgiven for believing that learning to drink is part of learning to be an adult.

**More than meets the eye**

Most people view alcohol simply as something that makes them feel relaxed and uninhibited. The reason for this is that alcohol is a narcotic acting on the brain and the central nervous system rather like a general anaesthetic. It numbs them!

Although moderate use of alcohol presents no serious long-term problems for a healthy individual, regular heavy drinking (four or more pints a day for men and three-and-a-half or more for women) increases the drinker's chance of suffering lasting physical or mental damage.

Besides alcoholism itself – the state of physical or psychological dependence on alcohol – other problems include liver diseases such as hepatitis and cirrhosis, stomach ulcers, heart disorders, brain damage, high blood pressure and even some cancers. Death is also sometimes caused through suicide or accidents in the home or on the road.

Teenagers will often claim that they can control their drinking and know exactly how much they can take. The truth is that this is impossible.

Exactly how much effect a drink has depends on a whole number of factors, including: strength (roughly half a pint of beer or cider = one measure of spirits = one glass of wine); its mix (different combinations of drinks will have different effects on different individuals); speed at which it is drunk; amount of food in the stomach; drinker's body-weight; drinker's health; amount of sleep the drinker has had recently; time that has elapsed since the previous drink; drinker's mood and emotions; company the drinker is in; and the drinker's tolerance level (ie how much he is used to drinking).

**What the Bible says**

At a recent international conference for church leaders, a group of German pastors was deeply shocked by what they saw as the North American delegation's 'worldly and liberal' attitude to the issue of women in ministry. In fact, so distressed were they that later, as they sat in a local bar lamenting what they had heard, tears of grief ran down their cigars and straight into their pints!

Not all Christians see eye to eye on the subject of alcohol. Christians who had a heavy drinking habit before their conversion often choose to make a radical break with their former lifestyle by giving up alcohol altogether. They see this as an essential part of their Christian witness. Other Christians can be found many a lunchtime or evening in the local pub, sharing a pint and sometimes their faith with friends.

### To drink or not to drink?

Let's take a look at eight major biblical principles which should help to shape our personal response.

*1. Alcohol is a gift from God*

According to Psalm 104:14–15 the Lord makes plants grow 'for man to cultivate, bringing forth food from the earth' and 'wine that gladdens the heart of man'. In Deuteronomy 14:22–27 Moses tells the people of Israel to set aside one tenth of all the annual produce – including grain, oil, new-born animals and wine – for a huge feast to be held in the Lord's presence!

And the advice of Proverbs 3:9–10 is: 'Honour the Lord with your wealth, with the firstfruits of all your crops. Then your barns will be filled to overflowing, and your vats will brim with new wine.'

In the light of this hard biblical evidence it is impossible to maintain the view that alcohol is 'the devil's brew' or in any way inherently evil. The line of argument that when God gave alcohol to 'gladden the heart' he only meant it to be used as a chest rub is hard to substantiate!

In John 2:1–6 Jesus turns water into wine at the marriage feast in Cana. Although this act must be balanced by the fact that in New Testament times it was not possible to distil alcohol in the same way as we do today (which meant that its alcoholic content could not reach the level of today's drinks), and that it was often the Jewish custom to dilute wine by mixing it with water, it was still wine, not gallons of grape juice, that Jesus produced.

*2. Jesus drank and mixed with heavy drinkers*

Jesus was once mistaken for a 'glutton and a drunkard'. This was because he came 'eating and drinking' and spent much of his time with people of whom the term 'drunkard' would be an accurate description (see Matthew 11:18–19). It is impossible to develop a philosophy of withdrawal from the secular world and non-Christian influences through a study of the life of Jesus.

### *3. Alcohol abuse is dangerous*

Proverbs 23:29–35 outlines some of the effects of over-consumption of alcohol:

- bloodshot eyes
- physical injury
- misery and self-pity
- inability to see or think straight
- habit-forming tendencies.

Proverbs 20:1 warns that 'wine is a mocker and beer a brawler; whoever is led astray by them is not wise', while Isaiah 5:11–14 makes it clear that one of the causes of Israel's downfall as a nation was its drink problem.

### *4. Drunkenness is condemned*

'Do not get drunk with wine' (Eph 5:18). 'Let us behave decently...not in orgies and drunkenness' (Rom 13:13). 'Do you not know that the wicked will not inherit the kingdom of God? Do not be deceived; neither the sexually immoral nor idolaters nor adulterers...nor drunkards...will inherit the kingdom of God' (1 Cor 6:9–10).

In Galatians 5:19–25 Paul argues that getting drunk is part of the old non-Christian lifestyle and then comments: 'Those who belong to Christ Jesus have crucified the sinful nature with its passions and desires.'

### *5. Some are called to abstain from drink*

The Bible makes it clear that those who want to serve God must place their responsibilities above their own desires. Because drinking impairs judgement the Bible commands certain groups to steer clear of it.

Proverbs 31:4–5 states that it is 'not for kings to drink wine, nor for rulers to crave beer, lest they drink and forget what the law decrees and deprive all the oppressed of their rights'.

Leviticus 10:9–11 instructs the priests to avoid drinking when they have spiritual responsibilities. 'You and your sons are not to drink wine or any other fermented drink whenever you go into the tent of meeting or you will die...you must distinguish between the holy and the common.'

*6. We must take care of our bodies*

'Do you not know that your body is a temple of the Holy Spirit?' (1 Cor 6:19).

'I urge you...to offer your bodies as living sacrifices, holy and pleasing to God – this is your spiritual act of worship' (Rom 12:1).

Any habit which spoils or destroys your body and health is obviously out of line with God's will. So we must be honest with ourselves about our weaknesses and avoid putting ourselves in vulnerable situations. If you know that after the first drink you can't resist the second and third, stay clear altogether.

*7. We are responsible for others*

The Bible makes it clear that although I may have freedom to drink, I have an overriding responsibility for others. 'Make up your mind not to put any stumbling block or obstacle in your brother's way...it is better not to eat meat or drink wine or do anything else that will cause your brother to fall' (Rom 14:13,21). Youth leaders are in a frontline position on this one.

*8. We must keep the law*

Christians are to respect and obey the laws of the land. 'Everyone must submit himself to the governing authorities, for there is no authority except that which God has established...consequently he who rebels against authority is rebelling against what God has instituted' (Rom 13:1–2). Titus 3:1 and 1 Peter 2:13 make similar points.

**Non-alcoholic bars**

Non-alcoholic bars are more than just the latest Christian fad. They can be used to provide a positive alternative to pubs and clubs and to promote the wider acceptance of non-alcoholic drinks. With the growing concern among the young for the environment and their own bodies (by keeping fit and eating in a healthy way), non-alcoholic drinks are becoming increasingly popular.

There are now many varieties of non-alcoholic drink including alcohol-free lagers, beers, wines and drinks with the flavour of spirits such as whisky or gin. Fruit juice-based non-alcoholic cocktails are also very popular.

Most of these drinks, or their ingredients, can be found in health food shops and a growing number of department stores, delicatessens, off-licences and supermarkets.

The labels used to identify these drinks are usually 'non-alcoholic', 'alcohol-free' or sometimes 'low alcohol'. It is important to remember that some 'low alcohol' drinks contain enough alcohol to place them in the 'licensed' category, which means it is illegal to sell them from unlicensed premises or to under-age youths.

The law in Great Britain says that if a drink contains over 1% of alcohol (approximately 2% proof), a licence is required for its sale. The best way of telling what drinks are suitable for your purpose is to ask whether they can be sold without a licence at the store where you buy them.

For further information on how to set up a non-alcoholic bar, and a copy of their pamphlet *Cocktails*, contact South West Herts Youth For Christ, Room 302, YMCA, Charter House, Charter Place, Watford, Herts WD1 2RT (Tel 0923 244350).

Details of other non-alcoholic drinks can be obtained from the following:

Leisure Drinks Ltd
24 Willow Road
Trent Lane
Castle Donnington, Derby DE7 2ND

General Trading Co Ltd
144 Sloane Street
London SW1X 9BC

The Cocktail Shop
30 Neal Street
Covent Garden, London WC2

Two books with good chapters on alcohol are *Drugs and Young People* by Grahame Knox (published by Kingsway) and *The Time of Your Life* by A MacDonald and Tony Campolo (published by IVP).

## Help

If you need further information, advice or help concerning young people known to you, contact the local branch of Alcoholics Anonymous – their number is in the phone book.

If there is no local service write to: Alcoholics Anonymous, PO Box 1, Stonebow House, Stonebow, York YO1 2NJ (Tel 0904 644026). Another useful specialist agency is Al Anon, 61 Great Dover Street, London SE1 4YF (Tel 071-403 0888). They are part of AA but work specifically with friends and family affected by someone else's drinking. Alateen, 61 Great Dover Street, London SE1 4YF (Tel 071-403 0888) is also part of AA and works specifically with teenagers affected by someone else's drinking. The UK Band of Hope, 25f Copperfield Street, London SE1 0EN (Tel 071-928 0848) provides a very good alcohol and drugs preventative education service. Lots of relevant material is available from them.

Finally, for help for sixteen- to twenty-five-year-olds there is the National Association of Young People's Counselling and Advisory Services, 17–23 Albion Street, Leicester LE1 6GD (Tel 0533 558763).

Answers to the quiz at the beginning of this chapter:
1. c; 2. d; 3. b; 4. a; 5. c; 6. a; 7. d; 8. b; 9. c; 10. b.
(Figures taken from the pamphlet *Drug Misuse*, issued by the Department of Health and Social Security; *Drugs and Young People* by Grahame Knox, published by Kingsway, and *Trend* magazine, published by UK Band of Hope.)

# 13
# CHILDREN AT RISK
*Dealing with the victims of child abuse*

Child abuse is a very serious issue which all youth workers will find themselves facing probably sooner rather than later, if not already. It is an issue which increasingly occupies space in our national newspapers and one that recently-published figures confirm already poses a social problem of massive proportions.

In the year ending March 1989, 40,000 children and teenagers were on the official child abuse register. Latest estimates show that over one and a half million children and teenagers in the UK are now suffering emotional, physical or sexual cruelty.

The accuracy of this figure, published by Childline, is difficult to substantiate, simply because the only cases that have come to light are those which are reported to the authorities. What can be said, however, is that child abuse is a serious, extensive and growing problem.

**Waking up to a problem**

Child abuse is not new. It is simply that our society has taken a long time to wake up to the problem.

In the London of the nineteenth century, an estimated eighty per cent of illegitimate children who were put out to nurse died because unscrupulous 'nurses' did away with the babies once their fees had been paid. In 1868, Dr Athol Johnson of the London Hospital for Sick Children, drew attention to repeated fractures in children. The popular theory at the time was that most of the deformities were caused by rickets.

Unbelievably, it was not until the early 1950s that research in America began to recognise that many of these injuries were not the result of accidents. Furthermore, it was shown that when the children involved were removed from their home environment for periods varying from a week to several months, 'surprisingly' no new injuries developed.

The British Association for the Study and Prevention of Child Abuse and Neglect claim that it was not until the early 1970s that our society as a whole really began to wake up to the reality of the widespread physical abuse of children.

> The issue around child abuse, and particularly sexual abuse, is that it is something that most people don't want to know is around. The danger is that you not only separate yourself from it, but you condemn the people who have not managed to keep it quiet. (Daphne Stathan, Director of the Institute for Social Work.)

But if we are slow to face up to the reality of the physical abuse of children we have been even slower to develop an awareness of the extent of child sexual abuse. Often, even in the rare case when children or teenage victims do find the courage to talk about their experiences, they are not believed or are made to feel dirty and second rate – reactions which only compound their problem still further.

All this poses an urgent problem for those of us who are involved in Christian youth work. There is a high probability that young people in your group have been physically, emotionally or sexually abused. So it's no good trying to play the ostrich, sticking our heads in the sand and keeping the topic of conversation centred on what Paul said to the Corinthian church about meat offered to idols!

If our work with young people is to bear the hallmark of

God's character then we must tackle the problems that have brought pain into their lives. Not only will the problem of child abuse not go away, but it is on the increase. We must think through our response and think it through now.

### What causes it?

It is as important for the responsible youth leader to understand why child abuse, in its various forms, takes place as it is to be familiar with how to make a mature, sensitive and helpful response to the victim when it happens.

It is essential to grasp that the abuser, as well as the victim, is in desperate need of help, care and counsel. There are a whole number of factors and circumstances that may have driven the abuser to this behaviour. These include: poverty, unemployment, social isolation, family communication problems and, in some cases, home overcrowding. Other causes may include mental health problems, alcoholism, the serious disabling illness of a spouse, marital conflict, separation or bereavement.

Some families are inward-looking and isolated so that the members find it difficult or impossible to form a deep relationship outside. A parent/child sexual relationship can even be a distorted search for caring and warmth which the needy adult (and sometimes the child) longs for.

Physical abuse is often the result of severe stress, especially seen in mothers with several young children below school age. Often, sexual abuse is the result of a vicious circle where the abuser was himself a victim in his childhood and carries a resulting immaturity or inadequacy in his character.

### A family affair

The problem is simply that very few children or teenagers will volunteer any information about their suffering, and therefore most cases go unreported and untreated. What makes the pain even more difficult to bear is that the majority of these 'private' crimes are committed not by strangers but by members of the immediate family.

Recent research shows that the average age of a sexual abuser is 35.3 years and that 79% are male. The same research goes on to reveal that 77.4% of cases involve parents, 16.3% other relatives and only 6.3% people outside the family.

Often the victim is sworn to secrecy: 'You won't tell anyone, will you? It's our secret.' Sometimes bribery, threats of rejection or of violence (or more violence) are involved. There is also the fear of the prosecution of the abuser if any help is sought. When your father rapes you it is difficult to assess your loyalties – to him, to your mother and the rest of the family, or to yourself. More often than not, victims feel trapped in a secret prison from which they can find no escape.

## Scars that won't heal

> Up until this moment I have never mentioned my life to anybody, not to my doctors, social workers, or even my mum. At the age of twelve I was abused by my father – I still have nightmares about him. The scars will never heal. I have no friends, never had a boyfriend, I wish I had died at the age of fifteen. I still panic and run if I see a man resembling my father. I feel so lonely and isolated.
>
> I was never frightened of walking home alone in the dark, of being raped or mugged. I knew what was waiting for me at home was infinitely worse than that.
>
> Yes, talking about it does help. Talking makes me cry, which is a relief. The problem is that no one wants to listen.

## What is child abuse?

There are several different but equally damaging forms of child abuse. It is very difficult to define precisely its parameters though it is generally agreed that it broadly consists of four overlapping areas:

*Physical injury*

This is the non-accidental use of force or a deliberate act of omission aimed at hurting, injuring or destroying a child. The immediate difficulty which this widely-accepted definition presents is that it technically includes corporal punishment within the home.

*Physical neglect*

This is the failure of a parent to safeguard the health, safety and wellbeing of a child. It includes nutritional neglect, and failure to provide medical care or to protect the child from physical or social danger.

*Emotional abuse*

This is the most difficult category to define, but among its causes are lack of:

- physical care and protection
- affection and approval
- stimulation and teaching
- discipline and control
- opportunity and encouragement to gradually achieve independence.

*Sexual exploitation and abuse*

This covers a broad range of sexual activities from involving a child in incest or other forms of sexual intercourse to fondling and mutual masturbation. It also includes involving a child in any other pornographic activity.

**How to recognise the victims**

As those who work with young people we need to know how to pick up the sometimes veiled signals that abuse victims send out, and to know what to do when we're asked for help.

Sarah is fourteen years old. She has been a regular and

popular member of the youth group for the past year, but over the last few months has been behaving in a rather uncharacteristic manner. She has started smoking, is looking very pale, seems to have lost interest in her appearance, and wants absolutely nothing to do with the opposite sex.

She is becoming increasingly introverted and even appears to be slightly hostile to some of the other members of the group, especially anyone in authority.

Things come to a head one night when Sarah gets very angry with another member of the youth group who passes a harmless comment. You step in to try to defuse the situation, at which point she breaks down in floods of tears, rushes out of the hall and disappears down the street before anyone can stop her.

Later, when she finally returns, you manage to get her to sit down to chat privately about her behaviour. She's still sobbing and carefully avoids making any eye contact with you by burying her face in her hair and her hands.

She explains that she hasn't been able to sleep lately and is worried about her exams which are coming up in the next few weeks.

It is almost an hour before Sarah's real problem finally begins to surface – incest. She claims that throughout her childhood her father has periodically fondled her and that three months ago, while her mother was out of the house, he raped her.

It only happened once, but he made her promise never to tell anyone. If she did he said he would 'knock her brains out'. Now he rarely speaks to her although he sits and stares at her if they are ever in the same room together. This makes her feel very uncomfortable.

To make matters worse her mum and dad are not getting on well with each other. Her mum is very depressed. Sarah is convinced that she is to blame and she feels very guilty about it.

**The secret prison**

Sarah's story is unusual...not because of what happened to her but simply because she found the courage to tell somebody about it. It is estimated (Baker and Duncan) that 12% of girls and 8% of boys are sexually abused at some point.

The result of this is that it is quite likely that you have come across young people who have been sexually abused, although it is equally unlikely that they will ever find the courage to tell you about it.

Most abuse victims feel that they are permanently locked in a private world of pain, isolation and guilt – a world in which they have been trapped by the person who abused them with words like, 'This is our secret...don't ever tell anyone.'

So what can you do to set the victims of sexual abuse free from the prison that holds them? The first thing is to gain a good grasp of the causes of the problem, as outlined above. Then begin to develop the sensitivity to recognise the outward signs, the behaviour patterns which have been described as 'a silent scream for help'. Do remember, though, that there are all sorts of reasons why young people will display some of the following behaviour patterns which have nothing whatever to do with sexual abuse. (Genuine victims are desperate to find someone who believes them, but occasionally a young person may invent a story to get attention.)

*Lack of trust and acceptance*

Since victims feel that their trust has been betrayed they now feel unable to trust others. As a result they begin to withdraw from existing close relationships while at the same time carefully avoiding forming new ones.

A victim will often develop an intense dislike of being touched. (Strangely, behaviour patterns tend to be extreme, and as one victim shows a dislike of being touched, so another may exhibit a contrasting craving for touch: the extreme may be the clue.)

*Lack of self-esteem*

Victims tend to develop a very poor self-image which shows in various ways including:

- lack of care over dress and appearance, or an incredible over-concern with hygiene and cleanliness.
- anti-social behaviour. This may be loud and bizarre or withdrawn and depressive. Even a normally extrovert teenager may withdraw for part of the day to be alone. Both behaviour patterns are in fact a desperate cry for affection and attention.
- self-destructive habits and behaviour patterns. These include the use of drugs, alcohol dependence, suicide attempts, self-mutilation and either under- or over-eating.

*Abnormal sexual behaviour patterns*

Victims of sexual abuse tend to develop one of two opposite and extreme sexual stances:

- Addiction. The victim has been awakened to a world of adult sexuality – a world which they now find it difficult to leave behind. They may now also believe that this is the right way to act towards someone of the opposite sex. For these reasons a pattern of promiscuous behaviour develops.
- Aversion. As a result of their experience some victims find themselves unwilling and/or unable to form legitimate relationships with the opposite sex.

The problem in both cases is that the victim now finds it difficult to establish a relationship which combines attachment – closeness and warmth – with sexuality.

*Hostility and aggression towards authority figures*

The victim has been let down by those who are supposed to care and protect. This often produces a negative attitude towards all those in authority.

*Learning problems at school*

The victim often becomes preoccupied with adult sexuality and the ability to concentrate and to study drops markedly.

*Physical symptoms*

A victim of sexual abuse may suffer abnormal pain, bleeding, headaches, sleeplessness and bruises in the genital areas.

*Spiritual symptoms*

Victims often suffer from extreme feelings of guilt and an inability to receive forgiveness or accept God as Father.

*Abusive family cycle*

Victims of abuse, when raising their own children, often adopt the same parental patterns they once experienced.

**What help can I give?**

*1. Don't jump to conclusions*

Don't play the evangelical dumbo! Allow the victim to talk to you rather than talking at them. Listen hard and long before you offer advice.

*2. Don't be naive*

Don't assume you can handle the situation alone. Consult those in your church with experience or contact Childline, the NSPCC or another specialist care organisation for advice. Don't trust the shallow promise of an abuser that 'I'll never do it again'. Remember, we are talking about a criminal action.

*3. Don't counsel members of the opposite sex*

The reasons are obvious.

*4. Remember that both the victim and the abuser need help*

Abuse is often a compulsive behaviour pattern.

*5. Don't become just another person in on the abuse secret*

The victim needs the assurance that you are on their side and that you won't do anything behind their back, but you need their active understanding and involvement in telling the local authorities. This is also the best way of ensuring the abuse stops.

*6. Provide security*

Abuse victims need to feel that they can trust you. Make time to talk with them and listen to them on a regular basis. Get alongside the victim as a friend instead of trying to play the part of the professional counsellor.

Remember that it is best not to touch a sexual abuse victim, at least to start with, because this can cause a 'flashback'.

*7. Affirm the victim*

Victims of sexual abuse suffer from low self-esteem and are often riddled with a sense of guilt. Provide constant affirmation and care in order to help them slowly develop a positive attitude about their life, family and future.

*8. Offer friendship*

Offer real friendship without always seeking to centre the conversation on the subject of abuse. Help them by showing that you think of them first as a person – not a case. Spend time with the victim doing ordinary things and talking about other subjects. Help the victim to feel included and cared for even when their behaviour is distrustful. Accept them for what they are, not what you think they should be.

**Helpful books**

*Child Sexual Abuse: A Hope for Healing* by Maxine Hancock and Karen Burton Mains, published by Highland.
*The Battle for Your Child* by David Porter, published by Kingsway.
*Hands Off* by Roger Day, published by Harvestime.
*A Silence to Be Broken* by Earl D. Wilson, published by IVP.

*Healing Victims of Sexual Abuse* by Paula Sandford, published by Victory House.
*Abuse within the Family* by Jenny Robertson, published by Creative Publishing.
*There is an Answer to Child Abuse*, published by New Frontiers.

**Training courses**

Specialist courses are held from time to time for those who need training in this area. For further information contact:

CWR
Waverley Abbey House
Waverley Lane,
Farnham
Surrey
GU9 8EP (Tel 02518 3695)

Ellel Grange
Ellel
Near Lancaster
LA2 0HN (Tel 0524 751651)
and at Glyndley Manor
Stone Cross
Eastbourne
E Sussex

**For further advice and help**

Contact your local GP, or phone one of the national agencies:
KIDSCAPE (they produce a useful resource pack) Tel 071-488 0488
CHILDLINE Tel 0800 1111
NSPCC Tel 071-242 1626
CHILDWATCH Tel 0482 25552

# 14
# DANGEROUS LIAISONS
## *HIV, AIDS and Teenagers*

> It is a fact that 15–19 year olds are currently most at risk from HIV infection.... After all the Government campaigns, information and advertising, ignorance about the transmission of HIV is still rife. – Dr Patrick Dixon.

> AIDS recognizes no boundaries of race, sex, class or age. No one is immune and no one will remain untouched in the years to come as AIDS threatens entire communities and changes the patterns of daily life for everyone. – World Health Organisation.

> Ultimately AIDS will mark the end of the sexual revolution. There is no question about that. The question is how long will it take for us to get that information across to everyone and how many tens of millions of young productive lives will be lost unnecessarily because of AIDS? – Dr Michael L.Wilder.

Sadly, certain elements of the national press and media are very naïve or irresponsible over their approach to AIDS and sexuality. On one hand sex is portrayed in countless films, videos, adverts, songs, magazines and newspapers as life's ultimate experience, one without any consequences; on the other, the same voices lament the tragedy of wasted lives through casual sex, HIV, AIDS and other sexually transmitted diseases. This absurd double standard can occasionally even be exhibited on facing pages of the same magazine. Bombarded by these conflicting and confusing messages, the reality is that most teenagers' first sexual encounters are unplanned, unprotected, unfulfilling and highly dangerous. The untold or unheard truth is that sex without consequences does not exist and that irresponsible sex can be devastating and deadly.

**The church's task**

A recent television documentary 'AIDS: What do we tell our children?' reached the conclusion that while teenagers require information, 'the vital issues are all too often conveniently ignored by educators, parents and church leaders.... We've got to start talking frankly about one of our most basic human instincts. We have to teach kids how to cope with sex.'

Every local church youth leader has a responsibility to the teenagers in their group to tackle this issue now. But the issue of AIDS cannot be addressed as though it existed in a vacuum. The church has two important tasks:

- To inform teenagers about the facts surrounding HIV and AIDS
- To set the issue of AIDS in the context of our overall sexuality and what God has to say through the Bible about it. Teenagers have a right to know that the answer to the AIDS problem is not to never be caught without a condom.

The church does not even find itself in the position of a lone wolf any more on this subject. Our message is not very different from others who are facing up to the crisis that looms, larger and larger, just ahead of us. The World Health Organisation states:

> The most effective way to prevent transmission of the virus (HIV) is to abstain from sexual intercourse or for two uninfected partners to remain faithful to one another.... Until medical research finds a

cure for AIDS or a vaccine to prevent infection, we must rely on changes in personal behaviour to prevent the spread of HIV. Information and education are therefore vital in the fight against AIDS.

## The facts

- Some estimates claim that worldwide more children may already be dying as a result of AIDS than of famine.
- By 1991 it was estimated that 8–10 million men, women and children worldwide were infected with HIV, and that over 1.5 million of them had gone on to develop AIDS. One million were dead.
- Every day, around 5,000 people are newly infected with HIV.
- By the year 2000 it is estimated there will be 40,000,000 HIV carriers worldwide.
- By the year 2015 it is estimated there will be 70 million HIV carriers in Africa alone.
- Each year UK hospitals treat more than 500,000 new cases of sexually transmitted diseases (STDs). These include gonorrhoea, syphilis, herpes, genital warts, chlamydia and now HIV. At present there is no cure or vaccine for HIV.
- In Great Britain almost 50% of young people have full sex before the age of sixteen.
- A national survey of church youth groups in 1991 showed that one in four of this group have had sex by the time they are eighteen. One in ten do so under the age of sixteen.
- Nearly 50% of the 1,000 girls questioned in a survey in 1991 said that they had holiday sex with a man they did not know previously, many of them shortly after meeting. Of those, 60% did not use a condom.
- By the year 2000, 80% of those with HIV worldwide will be heterosexual.
- The ultimate risk group, in terms of HIV infection, is that of the newly sexually active adolescent.

Statistics from ACET, Agape, World Health Organisation, *Cosmopolitan* and MARC Europe.

**What is AIDS?**

AIDS is short for Acquired Immune Deficiency Syndrome and is caused by the virus known as HIV (Human Immunodeficiency Virus). HIV is an unusual virus for two reason:

- A person can be infected with it for several years and remain perfectly healthy, during which time they can transmit it to many other people. In fact many carriers do not even know they are infected.
- Normally when you catch a virus, such as a common cold, certain white blood cells (which are a key part of the body's immune system) produce antibodies which attack and kill it. But when HIV gets into the blood it begins to destroy these vital T-Cells, leaving the body open to other infections.

Once inside, HIV slowly begins to multiply. At first the antibodies reduce the amount of HIV, but they cannot remove it completely. This is because HIV has the ability to hide inside blood cells where it cannot be found. An AIDS test can detect the presence of HIV antibodies in the blood which indicate infection with the virus itself (HIV+).

Around the time that antibodies are first produced, some people may experience a flu-like illness (fever, headache, tiredness) which disappears after a few days. After this initial minor illness there is often a period of several years when the infected person looks and feels well. But during this time the virus continues to attack the immune system. Eventually the system is seriously weakened and obvious health problems begin to develop.

Some of the problems which people with HIV develop are described as 'opportunistic' diseases. This is because they are caused by micro-organisms which are commonly found all around us – in water, food and the air – but which only cause ill-health in people with a damaged immune system.

Eventually, when a person's immunity is very heavily damaged, he or she will develop more serious illnesses. Many patients develop particular forms of cancer. They may also get serious infections of the skin, lungs, digestive system and central nervous system. At this point they are diagnosed as having AIDS. AIDS is therefore the end-stage of infection with HIV. In adults, full blown AIDS takes an average of ten years to develop, though it may do so more rapidly. From what we know about the condition at present most people infected with HIV will eventually go on to develop full blown AIDS.

**How people become infected**

HIV is transmitted in four ways:

*1. Through intimate sexual contact or sex with an infected partner*

HIV is found in the blood and sexual fluids of an infected person. If an infected man has vaginal intercourse with a woman then semen carrying the virus can pass into the woman's bloodstream through a cut or sore inside her body. Infected vaginal fluids can also pass from a woman into a man's bloodstream through a cut or sore on the penis.

If a couple have anal sex, the risk of infection is greater than with vaginal intercourse. The lining of the rectum is more delicate than the lining of the vagina and is more likely to be damaged during intercourse.

Oral sex obviously also carries the risk of infection. Infected sexual fluid can get into the mouth and from there find its way into the bloodstream if there are sores or cuts anywhere in the mouth or throat.

There is also a small risk of infection through mutual masturbation (eg if you have a cut or sore on your hand).

*2. Through infected blood*

Since 1985 all donated blood in Great Britain has been tested for HIV. Before then it was possible to become infected through receiving infected blood, but now the chances of this happening are extremely remote. It is also completely safe to donate blood because a new needle is used every time.

*3. Through injecting drugs*

Drug users sharing equipment including syringes and needles are at great risk. HIV may be present even if a syringe has been 'flushed out', especially if any blood inside has dried.

*4. From mother to baby*

An infected mother can pass on HIV to her baby before, during, or shortly after birth. Research shows that it may be possible for a mother to pass HIV on to her child through breast-feeding. If this is the case it means it may be much easier to pass on the virus than was previously thought.

It is also important to know how HIV is *not* transmitted.
- HIV is a virus which does not survive easily outside the body.
- It is not spread by casual contact at work or school, by shaking hands, touching or hugging.
- You cannot be infected with HIV by touching or sharing objects used by an infected person – cups, cutlery, glasses, food, clothes, towels, toilet seats and door knobs.
- HIV cannot be passed on by sneezing or coughing.
- Swimming pools are safe too.
- HIV is not known to be passed on through tears or sweat.
- You cannot be infected with HIV by mosquitoes and other insects.

All this means that there is no danger of becoming infected through ordinary social contact with someone who has HIV or AIDS.

**Resources for you and your youth group**

*Consequences* A great discussion starter/case study to use with your youth group and get them openly thinking and talking about some of the issues that HIV/AIDS pose. See page 179.
*Who do you listen to? Sex in the age of AIDS* (Josh McDowell). Made in the USA, a brand new 37-minute video available from International Films. Aimed at teenagers and part of the 'Why

Wait?' project. Suffers a little from the long trip across the Pond, but tackles the issue of AIDS in the wider context of sexuality very well. For sale or hire. Phone 081-991 9191.
*AIDS and You* Dr Patrick Dixon of ACET takes a good look at the problem of AIDS, its causes and what the Bible has to say about some of the answers. Published by Kingsway. A good resource for all youth leaders.
*Sex, lies and some videos* One-day conferences for church and youth leaders on how to help young people handle sexuality. Speakers: Dr Patrick Dixon and Steve Chalke. Organised by Brainstormers. Dates: 21st March, Cardiff; 6th June, Manchester; 11th July, Solihull; 5th September, Glasgow; 12th September, London. For further details phone 081-942 9761.

**AIDS and ACET**

ACET (AIDS Care Education and Training) is a Christian agency which has become the largest independent provider of practical home care to people with HIV/AIDS in the UK. In the last twelve months it has cared for one in five of all those who have died of AIDS in the UK.

ACET's goals are to:

- Equip the church to make an effective Christian response to AIDS, respecting its historic teachings and providing unconditional care.
- Provide practical care and support to men, women and children with AIDS, irrespective of race, religion, lifestyle, sexual orientation or any other factors.
- Reduce the number of new HIV infections by giving young people the facts about AIDS

ACET can help you with:

- Speakers for youth meetings, services, seminars and workshops.
- Speakers and resources for local schools. ACET is the largest provider of AIDS lessons in schools in Great Britain and has recently launched a teacher pack and video aimed at

thirteen to sixteen year olds for use in the classroom.

- Information, newsletters and advice.

For more information contact:

ACET
PO Box 1323
London
W5 5TF
Tel: 081-840 7879

**The consequences**

This idea is designed to get your youth group talking and thinking about HIV and AIDS. Use it as a discussion starter and as a way of examining the issues we face when thinking through the right response to those with HIV.

Read the following case study aloud to your group or copy it out on sheets of A4 paper and pass it out to them.

Eleanor is sixteen and has been a member of your youth group for the last three years. Six months ago she started going out with Alex who became a Christian last year through a youth mission in the town. Alex, who is eighteen, is now a very committed Christian who is growing spiritually. Unfortunately he is not that popular with some of the other members of the group who still see him as an outsider.

A month or so ago, Alex was ill with a chest infection for a couple of weeks but is now well again. Last Tuesday your youth leader asked him and Eleanor to lead the worship at the youth Bible study. After several worship songs Eleanor read a passage from the New Testament about honesty and openness and then Alex explained that he has recently received the results of a test which confirmed that he is HIV positive.

A silence descends over the group as Eleanor and Alex go on to explain that they are in love and the Lord has told them to get engaged.

Divide your young people up into groups of five or six and ask them to discuss the following questions. Ask one member of each group to be prepared to report back their answers. Allow at least fifteen minutes for discussion.

1. Do you think Eleanor and Alex were right to tell the whole group about Alex's illness?
2. Do you think it is right for Alex and Eleanor to get engaged? Why or why not?
3. What effect do you think their news will have on the church and parents of youth group members?
4. Do you think that Alex should be held responsible for his situation?
5. What can the youth group do practically to support Alex and Eleanor?
6. Next Sunday, at the Communion Service, would you drink from the same cup as Alex has just used? Why or why not?

Note for question 4 (only to be explained during report-back session). Of the 16,248 people known to be HIV+ in Great Britain at the end of 1991, 2,658 were haemophiliacs infected through bad blood.

Now get your groups to report back to each other. Finish the evening off by using some of the information or ideas from this chapter.

# Part Four

# PROJECTS

# 15
# TAKING AIM
*General rules for planning a project*

**Take one**

'We're really sorry that more people didn't come; we certainly tried our best...I personally wrote to over thirty churches...but it was a wonderful evening and I'm sure it has proved most beneficial in the lives of those that were present.' How many times each week is this kind of comment heard on the lips of the organiser of one type of Christian event or the other?

**Take two**

The visiting group and evangelist arrive for a week's schools mission only to find that very little has been organised for them to do. In the case of the few opportunities that do materialise, teachers are badly informed about who they are and what is going to happen. At the end of the week the organisers can only afford to give them 'a little something towards' their expenses, though they wish it could have been more.

**Take three**

A disillusioned youth leader wearily makes his way up to the speaker or singer at the end of a 'disappointing' evangelistic evening with a washed-out look all over his face which says more than mere words ever could. Though the hall was full, there was little or no response to the appeal.

### Stop and think

In each of these cases what was lacking was good planning and clear thinking. The result is that either the organiser, or those taking part, or both are left disillusioned and dejected. For instance in 'Take Three' what the leader had not realised was that the performer was well known to at least 95% of the audience who had travelled from churches throughout the district to be present because the event had been advertised in the Christian press. (You may have Billy Graham on your stage with support from Luis Palau, having specially flown them both in from America, but if you don't have any 'fish in the pond', even the world's greatest fishermen will be unsuccessful in their attempts to fill the nets!) After the event many an organiser is left asking the question, 'Was it really worth it all?' and some even ultimately end up blaming God for his apparent failure to honour the hard work that has been done in his name. On the other hand, there are performers and speakers who have grown embittered because of the sense of being let down, used, and abused time after time. I have known several organisers and performers who have grown so negative in their attitude that they have finally withdrawn from any real involvement of this kind altogether. However, with thought and good preparation things can be very different.

### Setting your sights

Below are several questions which should be answered when you first set out to plan any kind of event or project. They are outlined here, but should be regarded as an integral part of each of the following chapters. At first they may appear to be in a rather strange order, for they ask that you decide both your aim and target group before deciding what the actual event should be. So often things tend to happen the other way round: we decide to have a concert and only then try and come up with a reason for it. No project should ever be undertaken for the sake of it, or simply because it's a good idea. Strong Christian youth work is the result of having a good clear strategy that uses its resources carefully and therefore powerfully. Each project you run should contribute towards achieving the goals and aims that your youth group has set itself. Therefore the projects outlined here, in section four of this book, will always have the greatest impact when they are planned as the result of developing the kind of strategy that is explained in section one. Remember, activity is not the same thing as direction.

*(1) What is your aim?*

Whether organising a youth service or town wide mission, it is essential to be able to state your aim clearly and simply. It is a good exercise to get out a piece of paper and then jot down ideas until you reach the point where in one phrase or sentence you can sum up what the proposed project is designed to achieve. Sometimes organisers will say, 'Our project is far too complex to be described in this superficial kind of way,' but actually however broad the aim it should be possible to focus and summarise it in a few words. If we are not careful we can simply end up making excuses for muddled and woolly thinking. So first decide whether your project is designed for:

(a) Evangelism

(b) Pre-evangelism

(c) Ministry to Christians

(d) Worship

(e) Entertainment/fellowship

(f) Other

In fact often the proposed project will cover a combination of any or even all of these areas but will still have a particular emphasis in one direction or the other.

*(2) What is your target group?*

First, what age group are you aiming at?

(a) Younger teens

(b) Older teens

(c) A combination of (a) and (b)

(d) Older teens and twenties

(e) An event run by youth but aimed at an older age group

Secondly, what is the spiritual status of your target group?

(a) All Christians

(b) All non-Christians (are they churched or non-churched?)

(c) A mixed audience (what percentages?)

Thirdly, where will your target group be drawn from?

(a) One school

(b) Several schools

(c) One area of the town, town wide, further afield

(d) A local church or churches

(e) Some other contact point

Finally are there any other distinctive characteristics about the target group?

You may feel that some of these details are laborious and unnecessary. In fact, they are very important because they help you pinpoint your purpose and therefore plan the most effective project possible from every point of view. For instance, the effect of your publicity will be maximised if prepared carefully in the light of these questions.

*(3) What kind of project do you need?*

Only after the first two questions have been answered are you in the best position to deal with this one. As stated earlier, someone may have the bright idea of running a huge concert starring one of the better known Christian bands or of inviting their favourite speaker into the town for one night or even a whole week. Or the church may suddenly decide it is about time they had a mission and did some evangelism. The problem in each of these cases is that the motivation may well be nothing more than the desire to run an event. If we are honest, one of the chief reasons for a lot of Christian activity is that it makes us feel good. So first decide on your aim and target.

In reality, this whole process may take place in the mind of a good youth leader almost at a subconscious level. He spends a lot of time thinking over issues relating to the group and then suddenly has the idea of running a particular project. In these cases it is still necessary to go back and answer questions one and two at a conscious level, checking that you really have faced all the important issues.

Having made these three fundamental decisions, you are now in a position to move on to the detailed planning of your event. The specific issues that you will need to deal with are outlined in the following chapters, but here we will briefly look at one last universal problem...money.

**Finance – working out a budget**

As soon as you have decided what you want to do, it is essential that you sit down and answer these two questions:

(1) How much money do you have to spend and where will it be generated from?

(2) What are the costs that you face?

To answer these effectively it is important to draw up a projected budget. This should include all expenses, under such headings as:

(a) Administration

(b) Publicity

(c) The hire of a venue

(d) Artist's and speaker's expenses, fees and gifts

(e) Hire of equipment

(f) Follow up material

(g) Hospitality for visitors

(h) Refreshments

Then your income should be projected under the headings:

(a) Ticket or programme money

(b) Sale of refreshments, books, records etc

(c) Church and other support

(d) Gifts and donations

(e) Other income

So many projects fail simply because this kind of planning is never done. 'We'll just muddle through', is an attitude which is not only dishonouring to God, but also to all others involved, especially those who are financially reliant on you (professional groups or speakers etc). Make sure your project is different!

**How long does it take to organise an event?**

Any event worth putting on will take a significant amount of time to organise. It has been said that the minimum amount of time for something which is located in your church building should be three months, that something in an independent venue within your community should be six months and anything bigger, for instance town wide, should be at least one year. Though this is a good general rule, in my experience some of the events and projects that have been most valuable have only taken place at short notice, but of course, in these cases the need for effective planning is even more necessary.

Each of the following chapters represents a project that I have personally been involved in planning and organising at a local level. They also reflect experience that I have been able to build up as I have travelled around the country working with other churches at 'the performing end' of things. Each chapter will examine the particular questions that need to be faced when organising the kind of project outlined as well as presenting (where relevant) a step by step check list for you to work through.

# 16
# THE YOUTH SERVICE

After three hours we remember 70% of what we hear but after three days only 10%; and we remember 72% of what we see after three hours but only 20% after three days. On the other hand, we remember 85% of what we hear and see after three hours, still retaining 65% of it after three days. But best of all, if we *do* something we remember 95% of it after three hours and 85% after three days.

Sadly, much Christian teaching takes place at a hearing level only and, therefore, it is not surprising that it often seems so ineffective. It is clear that we ought to be concentrating our teaching efforts not only on *hearing* but also on *seeing* and most importantly on *doing* to achieve the best long-term results. This is exactly what Jesus did, for besides the fact that he was often visual in his teaching methods, the disciples also had the opportunity of seeing the gospel at work and of taking on the responsibility of doing as they were sent out by him. They were actively involved in the work, which meant that Jesus' message became deeply rooted into their lives. Jesus did not ask Peter whether he could intellectually grasp the principle that he was the world's Messiah, but instead challenged him to follow him and become a fisher of men. This was action rather than talk.

In the New Testament, being a Christian was something that you did.

I remember 'very tactfully' telling the minister of my home church, when I was about sixteen, what an absolutely awful job he was doing and how, in my opinion, the worship services were about as exciting as 'getting a string vest as a Christmas present'. Part of a teenager's make-up is to be idealistic and outspoken. Not only is this character trait quite natural but it is also a necessary part of growing up. Teenagers will therefore often be critical of the Sunday service. The most positive way to cope with this situation is from time to time to allow them to take part in leading and planning worship, thus giving them the opportunity to learn by doing. As they begin to understand the thinking behind public worship, they will begin to see why it is conducted in the way it is. The repeated experience of leading worship will also gradually change teenagers' understanding and concept of the role of the congregation in worship. It will help them to understand that the 'church service' is not like a double decker bus where two men, the driver and conductor, seem to do everything while everybody else sits watching, but that the congregation's preparation for worship and participation in it is very important.

**How do you run a youth service?**

*First things first*

You should first go to the minister, vicar, elder or other church leader(s) to explain your idea and the thinking behind it. You should ask whether it would be possible for the young people to lead a service, perhaps on a regular basis every two or three months, so that they can begin to understand a little more of what worship is about.

*Brainstorming*

Having obtained the permission of the church leaders to lead a youth service, sit down with the young people themselves and explain the privilege that has been given to them. Then ask for their ideas on what the content of the service should be. This will often result in a great deal of discussion. Already issues relating to worship are being unearthed and examined. Make sure you record all the ideas and suggestions that are made.

*Group planning*

Now appoint a small group (or committee) to do the detailed planning and to look at the suggestions that the other young people have made. They must decide whether the service is to be of an evangelistic or teaching nature and if it is to be aimed especially at young people, children or the whole family of the church. (If it is to be evangelistic, it is a good idea to think about the possibility of linking it with another event such as a concert the night before.) Then a theme for the service must be chosen. Having made these decisions, look together at the elements that make up a worship service, taking into account all the suggestions of the larger group. Explain to the planning group exactly why public worship has these elements, making sure you are open to their suggestions rather than just forcing your will on the group and decide on what elements you are going to put into the service. You will probably want to include:

Hymns
Worship songs
Songs (performed)
Prayers (open or led)
Interviews (testimonies)
Drama/Mime/Dance
Offering
Sermon
Communion
Other elements

Explain that the material for the service needs to be chosen with two principles in mind: (See Rom 14 and 1 Cor 8).

(a) Is this honouring to God?
(b) Does this help or hinder the faith of others? Certain elements may be honouring to God but, because of existing prejudices or fear, may not be conducive to harmonious relationships within your fellowship.

*Sharing responsibility*

Now appoint group members to be responsible for the different elements which will make up the service. First you need somebody to co-ordinate the whole thing and lead the worship. A good idea is to draw together a worship band for the youth group if this is possible, and appoint a co-ordinator/leader. The same can be done with drama, mime and dance.

You may feel that it is right to invite an outside speaker to come in to preach. Many good youth speakers are booked well in advance, so plan well ahead. If you are having an outside speaker, who will pay his expenses? Will it be the youth group, or does the church see this as their responsibility?

*Music and drama*

If a music or drama group are taking part in leading worship they must be thoroughly rehearsed and of a good standard. Worship is not a performance but this is no reason for lack of preparation.

If you are forming a worship band for the occasion make sure they are not too loud! It is particularly important that the members of the band understand that they are not there to 'do' the worship but rather to lead others into worship (which is impossible if their volume distracts and even deafens the congregation!).

Drama is often rehearsed in the church hall but it needs to be run through in the main auditorium. Is there a balcony? If there is, can what is being performed down at the front be seen? Perhaps the balcony could be closed for the service?

*A dress rehearsal*

On the day of the service it's good to call together all those taking part in leading the service for a last minute run. This will help them feel more relaxed later on. There are those who labour the point that worship should be Spirit led and not 'engineered' in this kind of way, but to see careful preparation as necessarily blocking God's Spirit from working is misguided.

# 17
# YOUTH CAMPS, CONFERENCES AND HOUSEPARTIES

Fruit picking on the Saturday afternoon, an evening barbeque and learning what the Bible had to say about boy/girlfriend relationships (which was very exciting though unfortunately rather theoretical because Mary Hooper had just refused to go out with me!). Those are some of the memories of my first ever youth weekend spent at Ashburnham Place, near Bexhill in Sussex, at the age of thirteen.

In this chapter we will look specifically at a weekend conference, although the principles discussed can also easily be applied to longer camps and houseparties.

**The value of the youth weekend/conference**

A youth weekend provides a great opportunity for working with teenagers because:

(1) Within this context there may be up to six teaching sessions as well as numerous other workshops and discussion groups, besides all the informal chat that such circumstances allow. This amount of input is probably more than

you would get from several months of Sunday meetings and services.

(2) The teaching can be made far more relevant to the teenagers' particular needs than it ever could be in the context of a Sunday service. Rather than having to relate generally to all age groups it can be directly geared to their view of home, school and the world. It can also deal with questions which would be totally inappropriate in the presence of older church members.

(3) It enables the leaders of a group to get to know their young people at a much deeper level as they see them at close quarters, thus developing a deeper understanding of their personalities and relationship to God.

(4) Within the atmosphere of a weekend spent together, friendships can be more closely developed both among the teenagers themselves and with the leaders. Somehow the leaders seem to be more human and approachable than before! It is often in the informal chat over coffee or last thing at night that some of the most valuable work of developing relationships is done.

(5) Often, an honesty develops that is not found in other settings. As the weekend progresses and the group gradually begins to feel relaxed and secure, barriers fall, real questions are asked and a degree of participation that is not normally possible results. I have been on weekends where even those who have appeared the hardest and most insular at the beginning of our time together have opened up by the end of the conference and wanted to talk – often more than others.

**At home or away**

The first decision you have to make is whether this weekend conference is going to be at home (held within the buildings of your local church) or a getaway weekend, at a conference centre or other venue.

The main advantages of staying at home are:

(1) The budget price. It's much cheaper because you don't have to pay for a centre or for travel. The youth group simply turn up at the church building on Friday evening with their camp beds and sleeping bags and you are in business!

(2) Those young people with Saturday jobs or other commitments can still benefit from at least some of the teaching and activity of the weekend rather than feeling excluded and left behind altogether.

On the other hand the advantages of going away are:

(1) Going away for a weekend often serves to knit the group together in a much more powerful way.

(2) Because you are away from home there are not so many distractions. If you stay at home your young people are given the opportunity to attend the sessions during the day but find excuses to opt out during the evening to go to a friend's party etc. (Warning, such to-ing and fro-ing can also occur when a weekend is held at a conference centre only a few miles from home.)

## Staying at home

### *(1) Sleeping accommodation*

Is there adequate room for sleeping the number of young people that you are expecting? The dormitory accommodation for the two sexes should be well separated. This is important not only from the point of view of standards among the young people themselves, but because of exaggerated stories that are otherwise bound to get back to parents and others in the community.

*(2) Cooking facilities*

Are the cooking facilities good enough and, of course, who will do the cooking? Perhaps some of the ladies within the church can be persuaded to help out in this way?

**Going away**

If you are going away, decisions must be made as to where you will stay:

*(1) A church building*

Many churches allow their buildings to be used from time to time for youth conferences. This is especially true of churches with larger premises and those that are situated on the coast or in other picturesque parts of the country. Again, questions regarding cooking and sleeping arrangements need to be carefully looked at. The chief benefit of this option is that while getting the young people away from home it is much cheaper than going to a conference centre. Many of the churches that are used more regularly in this way will have a standard charge for the use of their premises but if not, the question of finance needs to be dealt with early.

*(2) A conference centre*

This is moving slightly up market and therefore is going to cost that bit more, although there is a considerable variation in price and facilities offered. Certain major factors should be immediately considered:

(a) How much will the weekend cost per head? Remember to add on your travelling costs.

(b) How many people does the centre take?

(c) What kind of sleeping accommodation is available? This may be dormitory, bunk beds or single and double rooms. Do you have to take sleeping bags or is bedding available?

(d) Is the weekend self-catering or are meals included in the price?

Conference centre names and addresses can be obtained through the Christian press or from Dovetail Trust.

*(3) Camping*

During the summer months a camping weekend under canvas is a possibility. Some conference centres run camp sites which are set up permanently throughout the summer months. Another option is to use a farmer's field and set up your own camp, with the young people taking along their own two or three sleeper tents and using a barn or marquee for meals and teaching sessions and for the main meetings.

If you camp on a site which offers no facilities you will need to provide:

Tents
Toilets
A marquee for meetings and eating
A cooking area and equipment
Lighting equipment
Tables and chairs
A team to erect this equipment!

**Two questions**

It is important to work carefully through the questions raised in the first chapter of this section, by which time you should know the answers to the following two questions:

*(1) Is the weekend basically for Christians or non-Christians?*

Are you working with young people on the fringe of the church or perhaps from a school Christian Union or other setting who either know very little about Christianity, or who have some understanding of the faith but have never made any real commitment to Christ themselves? On the other hand, is the weekend basically of a teaching nature, aiming to encourage and challenge those who are already Christians? It may be that the weekend is a combination of these two aims.

*(2) Is there a particular age range (within the youth group) that you are aiming at?*

If you are aiming at a specific age group, how are you going to ensure that they are the ones that have the first opportunity of taking up the invitation to be present? (Many centres only take thirty or forty young people and if you fill your places up on a first come first served basis, you may discover that you've missed out almost altogether on the people that the event was originally planned for.)

**Theme**

A youth weekend presents you with the opportunity to examine how Christian faith relates to the world in which teenagers live and work with a frankness and honesty that could not be expressed quite as openly in the context of a church service or even perhaps a weekly youth meeting. To make the most of this, it is important to choose the right theme carefully. There are a number of ways of approaching a subject:

(1) To study a book of the Bible.

(2) To look at a particular biblical personality.

(3) To take a contemporary subject such as 'Understanding culture', 'Relationships' or 'Communicating your faith in today's world' etc.

The important thing is that the teaching given is made practical and relevant as it is continually applied by the speaker or speakers to everyday life.

You may feel that you want to approach a speaker first and then talk with him about his choice of subject for the weekend and the use of time. On the other hand, you may feel that you want to choose a subject that is especially pertinent to your youth group and ask him to address it.

**Personnel**

To make life easier for yourself, build up a team with whom you can share the workload. This team should meet together several times during the planning stage of your weekend, the first occasion being as soon as possible after the idea is initially agreed upon.

You need to appoint:

(1) *An administrator* – to hold the various elements of the planning together.

(2) *A treasurer* – to sign the cheques!

(3) *A programme organiser* – to work out the timetable for the weekend (see below).

(4) *A speaker* – it is obviously most important to choose the right speaker(s). If you do not personally know of people who can help you it is best to contact an organisation such as British Youth For Christ or Scripture Union who have many workers and associates especially gifted in this kind of work among teenagers. The Christian press is also a good resource for spotting the names of potential speakers. The well trained youth leader is always on the look out for possible speakers as well as other resources for future use. A good idea is to keep a notebook in which ideas, names of speakers, addresses etc can be recorded.

(5) *A cook* – who will probably want to appoint several assistants. (Only applicable if self-catering.)

(6) *A front man* – the figurehead for the weekend, who is seen to hold the whole thing together, make announcements, lead worship etc (although others may be involved in these responsibilities).

**Timetable**

Below is outlined a typical timetable for a getaway weekend.

This, of course, can be adapted in any way that is desired.

*Friday Evening*

8.00 – arrive
8.15 – evening meal
9.00 – introductory session (consisting of worship, meet the speaker, introduction to the theme of the weekend)
11.00 – bed

*Saturday Morning*

8.00 – rise
8.30 – breakfast
9.15 – a time of quiet (giving the opportunity to spend time alone if they choose to!)
10.00 – session one (consisting of worship, teaching, activity groups)
11.00 – coffee
11.30 – session two
12.30 – discussion groups
1.00 – lunch

*Afternoon* – free for sporting activities, ramble, outing to local ten pin bowling centre, etc.

5.30 – evening meal
6.30 – session three
8.00 – concert/talent show/barbeque etc
10.00 – late night extra (a chance to put questions to the speaker? A late night ramble?)
11.00 – bed

*Sunday*

8.00 – rise
8.30 – breakfast
9.15 – time of quiet
10.00 – session four

12.00 – free time
1.00 – lunch
2.30 – session five (and communion?)
4.30 – tea
5.30 – depart for home (sometimes the group will travel back for the evening service in their own home church where the visiting preacher will speak. This will form the last official session of the weekend).

If the weekend getaway is planned over a bank holiday then, obviously, an extra day is available!

If this timetable is expanded out into a week long programme the teaching sessions will probably take place in the morning and evening with afternoons left free each day.

## Travelling

In the case of a getaway weekend the decision has to be made whether to travel by:

(1) Coach

(2) A fleet of cars belonging to older members of the youth group, youth leaders and perhaps one or two kindly church members or the dads of young people. In many situations (depending on how far away from home you are going) this works out to be a far cheaper method of travel (especially if the drivers don't claim for their petrol!) and also has the advantage of leaving some transport with those on the youth weekend for use in emergency or for any visits off the site.

## Finance

The finances need to be dealt with at an early stage, as outlined in the first chapter of this section of the book. In this particular case the major items that need to be budgeted for are:

(1) The cost of the centre or other accommodation

(2) Speaker's fee and travelling expenses

(3) Food (if the weekend is to be self-catering)

(4) Transport costs

(5) Any outing that may take place on the Saturday afternoon or other times (such as bowling or ice skating)

(6) Publicity – brochures and programmes

The cost of the centre will obviously account for a large part of the budget and needs to be looked at carefully. Many centres issue a contract which quite fairly states that if you pull out of the weekend within a given time period you are liable to pay a percentage of the booking fee. Many of these schemes work on a sliding scale so that as the proposed date comes nearer the cancellation fee you are liable to pay rises. With some larger centres (accommodating more than one group at a time) you book a certain number of beds and are under obligation to pay for them all, even if in the event you do not use them all. Obviously, such factors considerably affect whether or not you break even on your weekend, so clear and careful thought is necessary.

To set a realistic cost for each teenager attending you should simply add up your total expenditure, calculate the number of young people you are expecting, take 75% of that figure and divide your overall budget by the result. You then have the real cost of a place on your weekend. If more than 75% of those you are optimistically expecting to attend actually come, you will have an operating surplus which can be ploughed back into your work for another project. Alternatively, you may have the backing and support of your church who will either subsidise each place or agree to underwrite the whole weekend so that you are able to budget on 100% attendance of the number you estimate and, therefore, keep the cost of the weekend for each young person down to an absolute minimum.

## Booking forms

Between six and four months before the event you should produce a booking form which gives some information about the weekend for your young people to take home to their parents. Such a form should include a few details about the accommodation, the theme, the speaker and other activities. It must carry the dates, the cost and a tear-off booking slip to be returned by a given date. This should ask the young person to fill in his name, address and age. It must also be signed by one of the parents of those under the age of eighteen (this not only ensures that the parents have been informed, but that they have seen the leaflet and have given their consent to their teenager spending a weekend away under your care – big responsibility!). It is a good idea to ask for a deposit with each completed booking form. This helps prevent a situation where a weekend is a 'sell out' at the stage when the booking forms are returned, only to have a lot of people drop out, so that few of the provisional bookings eventually result in attendance. All this does is block up the system and stop others going who would like to go.

## Brochure

Once you know who is going to be on the weekend, prepare a brochure that will be issued to each young person about a month before the weekend takes place. This should give more details of the venue, who the speaker is, and what the programme contains, including all the leisure time activities available. It should also explain what the young people need to bring, for instance, waterproof shoes and coat, and at least two pairs of jeans (in case one gets soaked!). It should list everything that the young people are likely to leave at home if not reminded, including a Bible, notebook and pen, guitars, other instruments and bedding (if necessary). Forms should also be available for parents to sign giving their young people permission for swimming, boating, rock climbing or other activities that include an element of danger.

**A lock-in**

A lock-in is actually a variation on the theme of a youth weekend. The young people arrive on the church premises at about 7.30 or 8.00 pm on a Friday evening prepared to stay for the night. After everybody has arrived the doors are locked, hence the expression 'lock-in'. The programme of activities is arranged to run right through the night, the event ending with breakfast the next morning, after which everybody creeps home to bed for the rest of the day! The lock-in should have a varied programme consisting of films on video (anything from *Superman* to *Born Again*), short teaching sessions, worship sessions and occasional drinks and light snacks. A feature that proved very successful in Tonbridge was roller skating. So was born the 'Roller Lock-In'. It's possible to hire sets of roller skates from secular companies at reasonable rates (so long as you discover the size of your young people's feet beforehand).

That particular programme ran something like this:

7.30 – arrive and register
8.00 – first roller skate session
9.00 – first teaching and worship session
9.45 – supper
10.30 – second roller skating session
11.00 – second teaching session
12.00 – film: *Superman*
2.00 – roller skating session
2.45 – short teaching session with singing
3.15 – roller skating session
4.00 – film: *Born Again*
5.00 – a snack
5.15 – roller skating session
6.15 – cartoon time
7.15 – final roller skating session
8.00 – worship session and breakfast

9.00 – home to bed!

I know that to most youth leaders this must sound an absolutely horrendous way to spend an evening. To put their minds at rest, I can assure them it is! But it's also great fun if you are young and can spend the next day in bed, and it increases the sense of unity and belonging that young people have.

**A lock-out**

A variation on the theme of a lock-in is a lock-out. Again, the young people arrive at the church building to be picked up by coach and travel, for instance, down to the coast. This kind of activity can only be undertaken during the warmer months of the year, perhaps in the summer holidays. The coach drops the young people who spend a night on a ramble together along by the seashore, stopping for the occasional snack or drink (making sure that they are well out of earshot of any local housing!). Finally they arrive on a deserted beach in the early morning for a cooked breakfast and time of worship around a bonfire, which has previously been prepared by some of your very dedicated co-workers or one or two of the church leaders (perhaps including the minister or vicar!). After this the coach returns everybody back to the church building where once again all the young people go home and spend the rest of the day in bed!

# 18
# A CONCERT

The hall is packed and the music is great! The audience, many of whom are not Christians, are thoroughly enjoying an exciting set from a terrific band. A number of counsellors have been trained and are standing by and a more than ample supply of follow up literature has been purchased from the local Christian bookshop. A small group of older people are praying throughout the concert. All that remains is for the band to 'deliver the goods', present the gospel and act as the human agents who will bring the sheep into the fold!

Unfortunately, this is where everything goes sadly wrong! From the organisers' point of view, the group do nothing more than make a few subjective remarks about the situations which led to the writing of their songs and the way in which they felt God was speaking to them at the time. As for the band, they wish that a preacher had been booked to speak after their set because they don't feel able to live up to what they know is expected of them. By anybody's account there is no cohesive presentation of the gospel and all concerned are left with a sense of failure and disappointment.

This is a far too common situation but one which you can easily avoid if your concert is carefully planned. For the purpose of this chapter we will concentrate on how to organise a specifically evangelistic concert although most of the principles outlined will have reference to any context.

**Choosing a band**

Before finally booking a band for a concert you should always ask them the following questions:

*(1) How do they see their role?*

Not every Christian musician considers himself to be an evangelist and the non-evangelist will feel uncomfortable in a situation where he is required to preach or, still worse, give an appeal. Many bands will always choose to work with an evangelist if given the opportunity. There are also those who see the first purpose of their work as being to encourage and build up Christians rather than working in directly evangelistic situations which their songs are not really suited to. Others would say that they are not in the business of directly confronting people and appealing to them to become Christians because their work is primarily art. They consider their work to be a creative expression of the gift God has given them and only evangelistic in the sense that because they are Christians their music reflects Christian thinking.

*(2) What age group do they prefer working with?*

Some artists are obviously better suited to a university or college type audience while others are much more at home with the local kids straight off the council estate. Check to make sure the band you are booking are happy with the situation you have planned and that their musical style is appropriate to your audience. It is important that they are doing more than looking for work and you are doing more than looking for a big name to make your event a success!

**Local or national artists**

The names of 'famous' Christian groups and solo performers will not mean anything to non-churched teenagers (unless you've booked Cliff Richard!). Therefore finance can often be saved by using good local bands rather than national ones. However, it may be felt that using nationally known artists will inspire the confidence of the young Christians who will therefore feel more able to bring along their non-Christian friends, or that the ministry of a particular band would be best suited to the particular situation.

**Visiting artists and finance**

View seriously your financial responsibilities towards those coming in to take part: 'The labourer is worthy of his hire!' Even if you are using amateur or part-time artists and speakers you should see that their travelling expenses are fully met (around thirty to thirty-five pence per mile, depending on the size of their vehicle, is currently [1992] a realistic level) and provide them with a gift in recognition of their ministry and its future development. Expenses for meals and other incidentals should also be met.

If you are employing professional Christian workers it is your responsibility not only to meet all their expenses but also to pay them generously, recognising that they are often totally dependent on the income they receive for the work they do. Failure to act responsibly in this way can inflict great hardship on them and their families and cause considerable unhappiness and bitterness. Often a travelling worker has found himself in the unenviable position of actually subsidising Christian youth work across the country with his time and talents at the rate of perhaps hundreds of pounds per month because of their irresponsibility and/or bad budgeting!

Many artists or travelling speakers will now advise you about the realistic cost of their work per night or week. If you don't feel that you can meet this figure it is important to talk to them about the situation before they come. There are very few workers who would not be involved in a project that is well planned with a clear aim and meeting a genuine need even though there is a lack of finance to cover all their costs. It is a different situation when they feel that they have been taken for granted, not consulted and forced to subsidise badly planned events.

Things to check with the band:

*(1) General*

Make sure they know:

(a) Date of event
(b) Their contact's name and address
(c) The organiser's name, address, home and work telephone numbers
(d) The starting time, how long you want them to play for and the finishing time
(e) The numbers and the age group that you expect
(f) Your aim
(g) Map of venue and directions to it
(h) The nearest parking place to the stage door

*(2) Equipment*

Ask:

(i) Have you agreed a time of access for unloading and setting up their equipment?
(j) Are they supplying their own PA system?
(k) Are they supplying their own lighting, equipment, piano etc?
(l) Do they supply their own sound and lighting engineers?
(m) How many power sockets do they need?
(n) How big a stage area do they need?

*(3) Publicity and sales*

(o) Do they have any particular publicity that you can make use of?
(p) Do they want to sell LPs, tapes, T-shirts, badges etc?

*(4) Fees*

(q) Do they charge a fee and can they indicate how much their expenses will be?
(r) Do they want to be paid in cash or by cheque, on the night or by post?

*(5) Hospitality*

(s) How many people will they be bringing with them?
(t) Do they need a meal on arrival or after the performance?
(u) How many dressing rooms will they need?
(v) Do they need overnight accommodation?
(w) How many are single, how many are married couples?

*(6) Helpers*

(x) How many humpers and helpers do they need?

*(7) Counselling*

(y) Do they know about the counselling arrangements you have made for the evening and how they fit into these?

Many bands will send you their own booking form (normally two copies – one to return and one to keep yourself) which will include many (or all) of these details, though you should never take any of them for granted. Always work through this list, checking it against their booking form in case there are additional things that you need to clarify with them. If the group or artist does not supply a booking form make sure to write to them setting out all the relevant information and asking for a confirmation of their booking in writing for your files.

**Planning the evening**

*(1) Choosing a date*

Concert dates have an uncanny knack of clashing with one another. I cannot remember the number of times that I have been to give a concert only to be warned that the audience will be much smaller than originally planned because the date clashes with another Christian event in the town. Clashing dates can only be avoided if concerts are planned well ahead and diaries checked with the surrounding churches. This, of course, is only necessary if the event is designed to cater for a townwide audience. Often a concert will be set up just for the young people from one school, college or particular area of the town, so that the fact that there is another event organised at another location in the town is of no real importance.

Remember that if the name of a well-known singer or band is advertised around the local churches or in the Christian press the concert hall is bound to be crammed full with Christians who have turned out to see their heroes in action. This leaves any non-Christians who attend and who will probably arrive a little later with poor seats or worse still, no seats! What was designed as an evangelistic event becomes little more than an evening of Christian entertainment.

*(2) The venue*

It is often said that evangelistic concerts should always take place on neutral territory away from church buildings. But though it may be easier for non-churched young people to attend a concert if it is held in their school, the local town hall or some other familiar venue, this does not in any way remove the problem of how to get them over the doormat of your own buildings next time. Often a young person makes a decision to follow Christ at a concert in a school hall but is never able to make the transition from that environment to the local church building or indeed even to an informal house group. It is often right to hold a particular evangelistic event in a secular venue, but in that case questions as to how those converted are to make the transition to the geography of normal church life must be carefully answered beforehand. (See chapter 22 on follow up.)

Check that the proposed venue is suitable for the concert:

(a) Does it have enough electrical power points? (I remember
(b) Stage area – is it big enough for the band and any drama that may take place?
(c) Is the hall big enough to accommodate the number of people expected?
(d) Does the venue provide a dressing room, counselling room, kitchen area and room for record and book displays?

*(3) Booking a secular venue*

When booking a secular venue it is very important to plan well ahead as many concert and community halls are booked as far as a year in advance. Besides the questions that have already been raised, the following points should be covered:

(a) Ask for a sheet explaining the terms of hire, and read them carefully. You may be required to take out a public liability insurance to comply with the regulations.
(b) Make sure you understand exactly how much the hire of the hall will cost and that you are aware of any extra costs for the use of dressing rooms etc.
(c) Check on what time it will be possible to have access before the event and until what time afterwards.
(d) Check on whether you are allowed to sell refreshments and other items (in some centres the right to sell such items is held by the management only).
(e) Make your official booking in writing, listing all your requirements and stating how much you believe this will cost. Ask for written confirmation of the booking and these other details with a statement of the hire charge.

*(4) Personnel*

Now find those from your church or within the youth group itself who are willing and able to carry the responsibilities listed below:

(a) Administrator
(b) Stage manager
(c) Prayer secretary

(d) Publicity man
(e) Press officer
(f) Counsellors (including a chief counsellor who may double as follow up officer)
(g) Humpers and helpers
(h) Box office manager
(i) Lighting and PA public address men
(j) Stewards
(k) Hosts for overnight hospitality and accommodation (comfortable beds please!)
(l) Piano tuner

*(5) Equipment*

Check that you have arranged for the following list of equipment to be available:

(a) Adequate public address system – check on the group's specifications – they may well provide their own system. If you have two bands playing, will they use the same system? Who will provide this?
(b) Lighting system – as for PA – is it possible to black out the hall?
(c) Chairs
(d) Bookstall – it's possible to come to a sale or return arrangement with most Christian bookshops.
(e) Refreshments
(f) Tables for bookstall and PA equipment
(g) Counselling cards, pens and other literature (you may find it useful to issue counsellors with badges)

**Publicity**

'Money spent on publicity is money well spent.' True? Well almost, so long as it's money spent on the right kind of publicity. Depending on the kind of project you are organising, publicity will be of greater or lesser importance. Obviously, if it is an event to which you are inviting outsiders it is important to spend considerably more time and finance in this area than if you are running an internal event where the best publicity will be word of mouth. Estimates of the percentage of an overall budget that should be spent on publicity for an 'outreach' event range from 15 to 25%. What is obvious is the importance which should be attached to good publicity.

Listed below are some of the more common publicity methods that you may choose to use (though not all are applicable to every kind of event). For more information see chapter 30.

| | |
|---|---|
| Posters* | Programmes |
| Handbills* | Press release* |
| Advertisements* | Local press |
| Mailshots* | Local radio |
| Tickets* | Television |

* including details of ticket sources and a telephone number for information.

### Tickets

Often an entrance fee is charged to give the event 'value'. This fee may not bear any realistic relationship to the overall cost of staging an event which is subsidised through direct giving from other sources. There can be no doubt that certain audiences will show far greater respect for an event which has cost them something to get into.

If you decide to sell tickets on a realistic financial basis aiming to cover the cost of the event through their sale, the way in which their price should be calculated is as follows. Make as accurate as possible an estimate of the audience that you are expecting and work out what 60% of that figure is. Divide the projected cost of the event by that number and you have the price of your tickets. You will now break even on 60% of the audience numbers you expect. If more attend you will make a profit which can then either be ploughed back into further work or given away.

### Who will attend?

In my experience one of the biggest problems is the many evangelistic concerts that are planned where, in spite of the organisers' best efforts, few or no non-Christians actually attend. In some way or other your advance preparation needs to ensure that they will be there. Often a youth group has attracted a number of non-Christians into its life and its leaders now want to use an evangelistic concert as a means of helping the newcomers make a decision about Christ. But non-Christians cannot be expected just to turn up out of the blue at a concert, so if previous contacts have not been made, the concert must be planned in conjunction with schools work or some other means of outreach. Unless a youth group are very highly motivated, few of them will bring non-Christian friends along to an evangelistic concert but when there is schools work during the week or few days leading up to a concert the result is very different, with many non-churched non-Christians being present.

### Follow-up

It is essential to have good counselling on the evening and then well organised follow-up. Many concerts will produce large numbers of converts but if follow up is not well planned and thought through, the majority of those who make decisions to follow Christ will be lost. (See chapter 22 on this subject.)

# 19
# SCHOOLS WORK

'A modern day Jekyll and Hyde', that's what one was called recently by a friend of mine. The alarming thing is that they are everywhere. Who exactly are they? Well, let's take a look at one of them.

Roger has been a Christian for about a year and has recently been learning a lot about the Bible. Last month he went on his church's youth weekend which helped him a great deal and he's now beginning to take real responsibility within the group. In fact, he took part in planning and leading a youth service just last week. The church is very pleased with his obvious spirituality and growing maturity and his mum and dad, who are both Christians, are grateful that their son has 'turned out so well'. The only problem is that outside his church and family nobody really knows that Roger is a Christian at all; in fact, quite frankly some of his school friends would be amazed. What Roger has not yet learned to do is connect what he knows about God with the way in which he lives. He leads a double life. He is a real Doctor Jekyll and Mr Hyde.

**Why do we need to do 'schools work'?**

As we have already seen, many churches take pride in what they regard as a healthy youth group, without paying much attention, if any at all, to the way in which its members live beyond it. But the young people in your youth group spend so much of their time in school that school obviously plays a very important role in their lives and the development of their Christian witness. It is also true that during adolescent years the young person is formulating the basic ideas and opinions that will determine the course of the rest of his life. Recently I was told by a church leader that working with schools was not really the responsibility of their minister, who should be doing 'more important' things with his time. But while it may well have been true that their pastor was not the right person for the job, it was short-sighted to regard such work as unimportant.

There are three main reasons for local church involvement in schools:

(1) To support and encourage young Christians in their everyday working environment. The church has a responsibility to help young Christians 'go public' about their faith among their non-Christian friends. If we do not teach young people to be bold in their teenage years, we may very well be permitting a timidity to put down roots within them that will last a lifetime.

(2) The best evangelists among teenagers are young people themselves. If we are to make an impact on the schools in our community, the most effective way of doing this is to enable existing Christians in the local schools to feel confident in their witness. Visiting speakers are abusing their position if they seek to evangelise, and teachers also have to be very careful not to fall into the trap where they too would be accused of indoctrinating the pupils, but it is quite natural for the students themselves to share with their friends what they have discovered about Jesus Christ.

(3) If it is not easy to be a Christian student in school, neither is

> it easy to be a committed Christian teacher. Christian teachers, especially those running Christian Unions or with responsibility for assemblies, need the support of the local churches. They often feel themselves to be in a very responsible, yet at the same time vulnerable position, out on a limb, beyond the church's attention and prayers.

It can be seen that it is very important that whenever possible local churches work with the schools in their area. The best way of doing this is to support the work of the Christian Union where one exists, or to help establish one where it does not. The school Christian Union is often a lifeline for Christian pupils, providing them with the support, fellowship, teaching and confidence necessary to maintain a healthy personal witness. Christian Unions are also a good base for planned evangelism. Most churches pray for and financially support missionary work in countries far distant, but as somebody recently wrote, our schools are 'the forgotten mission field'. If our churches can be helped to grasp the difficult, often very hostile and spiritually ignorant, cross-cultural environment in which many school Christian Unions operate they should be more ready to support this missionary work.

In chapter 21 there is also a discussion of intensive schools work in relation to a special mission which includes assemblies, concerts and lessons.

## Ways in which the local church can help an existing Christian Union

### *(1) By taking up or creating opportunities to speak in local schools*

From time to time Christian teachers may invite local ministers and other Christians into their school to take assemblies or religious studies lessons, or to speak at the Christian Union. When such opportunities arise it is important that they are accepted, both to provide the help that the member of staff is calling for, and to encourage the development of an ongoing relationship with the Christian Union. If those invited cannot attend or for some reason do not feel that it is right for them personally to become involved, rather than just turning down the opportunity they should always phone or write to the school, suggesting names of others who would be suitable to help, or offering other dates on which they are available. Local churches should also be prepared sensitively to take the initiative if necessary. When I arrived in Tonbridge, one of the first things that I did was to ring all the local schools and ask for an appointment to see the head of religious studies or, in some cases, the head teacher. At that meeting I simply introduced myself as the new Baptist minister and asked if there were any ways in which I could be of service to the school. I made it clear that I would always be available to help with assemblies, the Christian Union or lessons if needed. Several times the offer was snapped up there and then.

*(2) By offering ongoing help to those responsible*

Often young Christians will make the complaint, 'I don't go near the Christian Union because it's so boring.' Though sometimes this is just an excuse for not having the courage to attend, it may well have some truth in it. Often one solitary Christian member of staff battles on with the task of trying to run the Christian Union without any external support or encouragement. It is the local churches' responsibility to help the teacher(s) involved by sensitively offering practical help and advice –which may also include spending time and money on implementing these ideas. For instance, there may be something the church or youth group could buy, such as audio visual equipment or books, or it may be right for you to sit down and talk about the possibility of a school mission, jointly sponsored and organised by the church and the Christian Union.

*(3) By encouraging your young people to attend*

Often in a school where there is a Christian Union many of the young Christians do not have the courage to attend it, and therefore cannot link themselves into the support that can be received through its activities and teaching. So it is the task of your youth group to provide encouragement. The popular comment that the Christian Union is boring and that those who do go are 'wallies', should be carefully listened to but met with the positive response that Jesus constantly identified with those who were weak. By the power of his personality and involvement he was able to change individual lives and ultimately the face of history. To be Christlike is to get involved. If those with energy and enthusiasm do not do so, the Christian Union will remain weak and boring which, it should be pointed out, reflects on all Christians not just the CU members!

*(4) By talking about school in your youth group*

Sit down and talk to your young people about school. Through casual and informal conversations with individuals it is possible to learn all sorts of things about attitudes and feelings regarding this part of their lives. You can help a great deal by relating your weekly Bible teaching, as far as possible, to the school situation. Get the kids to talk about what is happening in their school and in their CU. It will encourage those who are involved and challenge the others. You should often include a time of prayer with the specific opportunity for those who wish to pray for their schools, for Christian teachers and for the life of the Christian Union.

*(5) Keep your church informed about school*

A good idea is to arrange a special 'Schools Sunday' for your church. In the afternoon the youth group may put on a tea for the whole church after which each of the local CUs can report on what is happening in their school and give their prayer needs. Then those present can form small groups to pray about what they have heard. Later some of the young people may take part in the evening service. The effect of this is that the adults in the church have their eyes opened to what is actually going on in the schools and, therefore, begin to pray with a new enthusiasm.

## Starting or re-launching a Christian Union

Where a Christian Union does not exist at all, how can a local church or youth group help start one? There are three lines of approach which we will list in order of preference.

(1) Always work through known Christian teachers if possible. Never undertake schools work without first consulting them. It is important that you understand the atmosphere within the school and the views of the staff before plunging in too deeply. If you do not do this, they will probably feel that the ground is being cut from under their feet, and may also consider that you are being insensitive to the situation that exists within the school. (What's worse, they will almost certainly be right!) If you work with teachers in the school and win their confidence they will be able to advise and help you so that you don't tread on any toes. Of course, if the head teacher or deputy is a Christian this is the place to start.

(2) If you do not have a natural 'opening' into the school through a Christian teacher, make contact with the religious studies department. In some cases you may have doubts about whether the head of RS is a Christian, but it is still important that you do not seek to work behind his back, or to undermine any of the work that he has been doing. Failure on your part within these guidelines can result in exclusion from the school, not only for yourself and any that you might seek to bring in but for all other churches and Christian speakers.

(3) Lastly, if you cannot make contact with any other sympathetic helpful members of staff, you should contact the head teacher. Your initial contact with him is vitally important: your task is to dispel any doubts and suspicions he may have about who you are and what you want to do, thus putting his mind at

rest. The minister of your church is probably the best person to make this first contact on your behalf.

### The aims of a Christian Union

Often CUs are started for no better reason than it seems good to get the Christians in a school together, though nobody is very sure why. To prevent it from generating into nothing more than a 'holy huddle', a Christian Union should have two very clear aims:

(1) To provide its members with the support and help they need to live as Christians in the school environment. It's easier to be a Christian if you are one in a group.

(2) To act as a base for evangelistic outreach in the school.

Each CU should see the school in which it is set as a mission field.

### The role of the Inter-School Christian Fellowship

The ISCF exists to encourage work in schools. It is a part of Scripture Union and has a team of regional and local staff, together with a large number of voluntary workers who are able to advise and encourage Christians in schools all over the country. Through their literature and other resources they can help you with organising a CU and establishing a programme. A representative would not only be willing to visit local schools to talk with interested staff and pupils, but also to come along to your youth group and talk about setting up and running a Christian Union (a good idea, even if the schools in your area already have CUs). The addresses for ISCF are given at the back of this book.

# 20
# OPEN AIR AND STREETWORK

It was a bank holiday Monday in an English village to which I had been invited by one of the local churches to take part in their outreach. Traditionally this day had been given over to open air work. Even the younger members of the congregation, by which I mean people in their thirties, told me what a wonderful experience the annual open air was. I had been given a great privilege, for I was to be the preacher! The plan was that we should all meet at the church building just after lunch and from there proceed on our mission.

It was a boiling hot day with the sun blazing down from the sky. There was no breeze, the streets were deserted and the village was absolutely silent because everybody who could move had gone out for the day. On arrival at the church the person who was obviously in charge led us in a prayer and then gave us the running order for the afternoon. Basically we had a half hour service which we would do three times at three different locations around the village. After several hymns and a reading I would be asked to step forward and preach 'the word'. After the afternoon's outreach we would all return to the church building for a tea, which was already laid out on the trestle tables and consisted of cucumber sandwiches, fish paste and some of the other traditional church delicacies! The organ, which was portable, was to be played by an old lady who was somewhere between eighty and ninety years of age. Despite the fact that we were in the middle of a heat wave, she found it necessary to be wrapped in a winter coat with a scarf, and to protect her delicate hands as she played the keyboard, she wore a pair of fingerless woolly hand knitted gloves.

We proceeded to the first venue which happened to be the middle of a deserted village green. We set up the rather antiquated looking organ, which the poor lady had to pump hard with both feet while attempting to play at the same time (a difficult task for anybody even at the prime of life), and passed round a set of *Golden Bells* hymn books. The first hymn was announced and we began to sing; an interesting feature of the afternoon proved to be that the lady playing the organ found it impossible to read the words at the same time as reading the music and so, instead of singing along with us she lahed and hummed the tune with the organ, obviously feeling that she must give it a hand with its job. As there were only about ten of us anyway the considerable power of the bellowing organ, aided and abetted by its player, completely drowned the singers.

A reading, a prayer and another two hymns later it was announced that 'our brother from London will now bring God's word to us' at which point I was nudged forward by the group and told to preach. I dared not ask exactly who I was supposed to be bringing God's word to. Actually, even if somebody had been evading my gaze by hiding behind a car or lamp post, I was separated from him by at least fifty yards and it would therefore have proved quite impossible for him to hear what I was about to say. Being the obedient young man that I was at that stage I stood and for the next ten minutes preached my heart out in one of the most evangelistic sermons this planet has probably ever heard. (I knew it was good because at the end they all patted me on the back and somebody even suggested that I may well be chosen as the preacher for next year as well!)

We repeated this little scenario twice more that afternoon before returning in triumphant mood to the chapel for tea. The church was ecstatic, things had gone so well. I was told it was just like the old days; the gospel had been powerfully preached and, as I was reminded, God's word would not return to him void. So ended one of the funniest and yet most tragic afternoons in my life. But what happened in that small village that afternoon was typical of what goes on year in year out in open air meetings all over our country.

It is a fantastic privilege to live in a country that gives us freedom to stand on the street and openly proclaim the truth about Jesus Christ, but the sad thing is that it is often abused or simply wasted. Enthusiasm, commitment and drive have not always been matched by common sense and as a result many Christians have a low opinion of outdoor work, regarding it as embarrassing and a thing of the past, something which they would never be involved in. In fact, open air work can be a very powerful tool in the hands of those who know what they are doing, and is especially powerful when used among young people.

The witness of the congregation mentioned above on that bank holiday Monday was not just ineffectual but also counterproductive. The one person we did meet that afternoon happened to be mending his car as we came along the road. We planned to hold our third service opposite his Ford Cortina but as soon as he saw us he hurriedly put down the bonnet and rushed indoors. Half an hour later, as we retreated back up the same street, I glanced back to see him returning from the shelter of his council house to get on with fixing his car. It was not just that we had failed to communicate but, rather more seriously, that we had communicated almost the exact opposite of what had been planned. Our witness left this amateur car mechanic more suspicious and cautious of the local church than he had been in the first place.

**The dos and don'ts of an open air meeting**

For purposes of clarity let us make a distinction between 'an open air' and 'streetwork'. By 'an open air' we will refer to an organised meeting with a programme designed to attract an audience. 'Streetwork' refers to the broader task of meeting, entering into conversation with, and presenting Christ to, the public on the streets. First, let's look at the open air meeting.

*(1) Choosing a site*

Running a successful open air is not simply a case of finding somewhere to stand and preach or sing and hoping for the best. A lot of thought must go into choosing the correct kind of site. Below are some of the criteria that should govern your choice of site:

(a) Do use a place where people gather or congregate and constantly move by. This may be the middle of a shopping centre or some swings in the middle of a housing estate, or a piece of green opposite a row of shops etc. It's no good performing in the middle of a village green, you won't be heard and you'll look somewhat strange huddled together a great distance from anybody else. The green will act as a barrier between you and others and people will not cross it to see what you're doing even if they're interested because it looks 'nosey' and they will draw too much attention to themselves.

(b) Do not block the pavement. Make sure that in choosing your site it is possible to leave plenty of room for shoppers and others to pass by.

(c) Do not block shop doorways or window space. This is most inconsiderate and is likely to lead to bad feeling, arguments and even official complaints.

(d) Do not use loud amplification. The invention of the public address system has been seen by some as the foolproof way of forcing people to hear the gospel: 'If people won't stop and listen we'll get them anyway!' This is insensitive and uncaring. Think of yourself in the local park on a sunny summer's afternoon relaxing in the quietness, when all of a sudden a fourteen year old lad with a ghetto blaster mounted on his shoulders strides by and stops a few yards away with it playing at full volume. To him the music is simply wonderful, he cannot understand why everybody does not want to listen. To you it is a pounding noise that is destroying your peace and you take offence at this invasion of your privacy. We must be careful not to inflict ourselves on people during our open air work. If a public address system is used at all, it should clarify speech for those standing around, not penetrate the plate glass of the surrounding shops. We wish to draw attention to ourselves by the colour and attractiveness of our presentation, so that the public wants to stop and listen and watch. We must not force our views upon them.

(e) Do not stop passers-by. This follows on from the last point. I myself have been stopped almost forcibly on several occasions while innocently wandering past an open air meeting. I remember well an experience that I had as a teenager in my home town of Croydon, when not only was I stopped and preached at but when I protested that I was already a Christian, was given a knowing look that said, 'So you think you'll get off the hook that way do you, sonny?' I was then subjected to another ten minute dose of the gospel. I finally managed to break into the conversation to explain that I really did have to go, and managed to make a getaway, but a handful of tracts was still shoved into my hand and several Bible verses hurled in my direction as I hurried away.

**Open airs and the law**

*Do we need a licence?*

It is our legal right in Great Britain to hold open air religious meetings in any public thoroughfare and also to make use of means other than speaking – for example, music or drama – as long as they pertain to the religious message. But though you do not need a licence or permission, it is courteous and in the interests of good relationships to:

*(1) Inform the legal department of the local council*

The best way of doing this is to make an appointment and then go along and explain exactly what you are intending to do, or, if you don't have much time, to phone and talk to somebody responsible. The benefit of an appointment or of phoning rather than writing is that as you explain what you are going to do they have the opportunity of asking questions that immediately arise which you can answer there and then. This saves an exchange of letters which could take some weeks. A letter on its own is not only rather cold and impersonal but, of course, may not be dealt with for weeks.

*(2) Inform your local police*

Let them know the date, time and venue of the event as well as your intentions, making it especially clear that you do not plan to sell anything or collect money. In the event of any complaints from other people, the fact that you have consulted them will help you considerably! The police have the job of maintaining law and order so they will wish to ensure that:

(a) You do not cause a disturbance. Legally it is the job of the police force to see that any public event is peaceful and, therefore, they are also bound to investigate any complaints made against you. The third time they have to move you on, they are empowered to arrest you.
(b) You do not cause an obstruction. Though, as we have said, you are free to hold an open air meeting, the law states that technically obstruction results when the same air space is held by a person for more than sixty seconds. Therefore the police are empowered to arrest you under this law if complaints are received.

*(3) Inform nearby shopkeepers*

Again, this helps build a good relationship, which will make it easier for you to return.

**The programme**

*(1) Forming a crowd*

The picture we all have of the traditional open air consists of a speaker on a small wooden box with a ring of Christians tightly packed round him or, even worse than this, a row of Christians lined up behind the speaker glaring at passers-by. It is important to support those taking part in the presentation but it is a big mistake to follow either of the patterns outlined above. The ring of Christians around the speaker creates a barrier which, instead of welcoming others in, barricades them out. A row of Christians lined up behind the speaker can resemble an American football team waiting to pounce. Any audience become the opposition side!

It is vital that for open air work you have a small crowd (a team of fifteen to twenty people is excellent) who simply stand around and watch the performance, so helping to give anonymity to others who gather round and watch. This will help to prevent the crowd that gathers from feeling threatened or exposed and will probably result in their staying longer.

*(2) Only performers at the front*

Some of the Christians standing round in the crowd have the work of just being there, maybe praying for some of the time while others are appointed to chat to those who seem interested and give them any relevant literature. Those who form part of the crowd are as important to the success of the programme as those who 'perform', and those who are responsible for handing out literature and getting into conversation with the public should receive training on exactly how to carry out their task. The team involved should be well briefed on where to meet, what is going to happen, when it's going to happen and their particular role. They should not be asked to fulfil roles for which they have not been prepared.

*(3) Presentation*

This can consist of drama, music, preaching, mime, conjuring, sketch board work, and so on. There are one or two principles to be remembered.

(a) *Be colourful* Music should be loud and rhythmic, drama should be filled with action and costumes should be good. The general principle is plenty of movement, action and colour.
(b) *Be brief* Short talks and short sketches are far more telling than long ones. A short programme has a greater impact than a long one. A typical programme should last between ten and fifteen minutes only and, after a break (when the cast can chat with the crowd) should be repeated. Normally people will not stand around for longer than this and will not pick up the main message of your presentation if it goes on longer. Keep it short and sharp!
(c) *Be relevant* The programme needs to be put together well in advance so that each element fits the theme and adds to what has already been said. This is especially true of chat and testimonies which must be to the point. It is sometimes good to vet items beforehand. For instance, get those who are presenting their testimony to sit down with somebody else whom they can trust to edit it, thus producing a tool which is short and punchy.
(d) *Be prepared* Open air work is front line evangelism. Because it is not within the confines of a church building where, generally speaking, the audience is conditioned to sit and keep quiet even if they are bored, you will sometimes get very lively responses from the audience! Be prepared for this to happen. Do not become angry with those who are negative and do not take their comments as a personal insult. Remember that in the New Testament the apostles were quite used to open debate and abuse!

*(4) Using literature*

Streetwork is probably best when linked with some other evangelistic event, perhaps a coffee bar or a concert. Colourful publicity can be handed out to those who are interested in knowing more. Gospels and other evangelistic literature such as *Journey into Life* should also be on hand. It is also useful to have something about your local church and what goes on there, along with a map of how to find it.

## How to organise 'streetwork'

*Handing out literature*

This may simply consist of pairs of young people going out on a busy Saturday morning or afternoon and standing chatting to other teenagers while handing out invitations or tickets to an evangelistic concert that evening. Though much more informal than the open air, to be effective it still requires planning and a great deal of preparation.

*A street questionnaire*

Another approach is to produce a street questionnaire which the young people in your group can be trained to use. This provides them with an easy way into conversation and creates the opportunity to present Christ to those interested. The questionnaire needs to be designed for your particular situation, but should start with general questions and then move specifically to Christian belief. The last question should make it easy for the interviewer either to end the conversation without embarrassment, or talk more about Christianity.

*Sample questionnaire*

1. How long have you lived in Tonbridge?
2. Are you at school, work or unemployed?
3. In your opinion, is Tonbridge a good place to live?
4. Are there enough facilities for young people in the town?
5. If not, what more could be provided?
6. Do you think the church can help young people? How?
7. Do you go to church? Never? Seldom? Often?
8. Do you believe in God?
9. If you could get to know him personally would you be interested?

If the answer to question 9 is 'Yes' the interviewer can then go on to ask, 'Would you like me to explain how I think you can do that?' In this way an open door has been created for the presentation of the gospel. If the answer is 'No' he can simply say, 'Thank you for your help, that's the end of the survey.'

# 21
# AN EVANGELISTIC MISSION

The early Christians had a burning desire to tell others of Jesus; they could do nothing other than share their faith. We, on the other hand, have to be continually coaxed into outreach with neat pre-packaged formulae which we are assured will bring success!

## Taking a closer look

The early church's enthusiasm for evangelism was overwhelming. The way in which eleven men set out to take the world by storm, and within three hundred years had 'turned it upside down' (Acts 17:6, AV) to the point where the Roman Empire itself had a Christian emperor is remarkable! But the claim that evangelism in the New Testament was simply spontaneous rather than organised is somewhat misleading. In Acts we read of how Paul had to argue the case for evangelising the Gentiles and allowing them access to the church. There was a great deal of heated discussion over exactly how Gentile converts should be treated and what should be expected of them. We also have the story of how the apostles appointed seven deacons to take care of the practical needs of the widows in Jerusalem so that they could be released to get on with the work of preaching and teaching. All of this has much more of the flavour of debate, decision making, planning, organisation and method to it than it is popular to recognise. Though it's heart-stirring stuff to hear about how the early church got on with the job of evangelism almost without thinking about it, such teaching not only fails to represent the facts fully but also guarantees those who grow up on it a continuous sense of guilt and failure. Though it is true that we need to rediscover the sense of compulsion that drove the early church to share its faith, it should also be remembered that, like us, they found it necessary to plan and organise their outreach and mission.

**Planning a mission**

(1) If you are thinking of planning a local youth mission the first thing to do is to sit down and ask yourself the questions outlined in chapter 15.

(2) Now talk the whole idea through with the leadership of your local church. There is no point at all in proceeding against their wishes or without their full knowledge, backing and support; in fact, such a course of action might prove to be very counter-productive. The aim of any mission must be eventually to integrate converts into the body of the church, which means that evangelism undertaken outside this context will ultimately prove to be of little or no lasting value.

(3) Having got the go ahead from your church or group of churches (see chapter 29) you are now ready to do the detailed planning for the mission. Many of the elements that make up a youth mission, such as schools work, streetwork, coffee bars, concerts, are dealt with in detail in other chapters, but below are some additional guidelines which you may find useful.

*Artists and speakers*

There are several professional bands, drama companies, solo singers, dance groups and speakers who spend a lot of their time working on church based missions around the country. Details of some of those who are available can be obtained from organisations such as British Youth For Christ and Scripture Union (both addresses are given at the back of this book), but you will probably have seen some in action and will already know which ones you have confidence in. You will normally need to book between six and twelve months in advance (in some cases much more). Make sure that those you are proposing to book know exactly what is being asked of them and that they feel happy working within this context; also look carefully at your financial responsibility towards them (see chapter 18).

Besides inviting in professionals, it is often good to give local talent the opportunity to participate. Many local Christian bands and drama companies have good material, but give them plenty of warning and don't stretch them beyond their resources and ability.

*Timetable*

It is mentally, spiritually and physically demanding to be involved in frontline evangelism, so do remember that those you are bringing into your town to work on the mission need to rest and sleep and that it is counter-productive to drive them so hard that they end up looking like the living dead! Of course, you want to make the most of their time with you but this must allow them to relax and think. A good principle to work on is the two-thirds day. For instance, if a visiting band are working morning and evening they should be given the afternoon to relax and prepare. It is important that you talk this through with those involved in your particular mission.

## Schools work

### *Getting it right*

If you are planning for schools work to be a major part of your mission you must do a lot more than simply approach head teachers of senior schools asking for the opportunity to take assemblies and lessons. I have been involved in several schools missions where we have been aiming at the fourteen plus age group but where I have spent most of my time taking assemblies and lessons for second or even first years (twelve and eleven year olds)! For details of how to build contacts in a local school see chapter 19.

A typical mission of this kind consists of work throughout the week in local senior schools with one or more evening evangelistic events towards the end of the week. Those taking part in full-time work on a mission would normally go into schools for assemblies, lessons and lunch-time concerts in which their job would be to:

(a) Present facts about Christianity
(b) Dispel distorted and misleading images of what a Christian is
(c) Advertise evening evangelistic events
(d) Help build an ongoing relationship with the staff, thus creating the opportunity for future visits

### *Assemblies*

These are of great value because they present the opportunity of speaking to a large number of young people at one time. Many schools no longer have an assembly for the whole school but, instead, each pupil attends one or two assemblies a week with their year or house group. However, such gatherings still offer the opportunity of speaking to several hundred young people at one time.

### *Lunch-time concerts*

Personally I not only enjoy performing at lunch-time concerts but also feel that they are of enormous value. I believe that a good package is to take an assembly or series of assemblies which, besides standing on their own, advertise the lunch-time concert. Word will soon get around and even those who were not at the assembly will be there at lunch-time. This concert should build on the message of the morning assembly and give an opportunity for pupils to meet the band, drama group etc. A renewed invitation can also be given to the evening event(s) taking place that night and/or later that week. Organisers should talk to the band or singer booked to discover their attitude towards talking individually to people.

*Lessons*

Often it is possible to take Religious Studies or other lessons. This gives the opportunity of spending a considerable period of time with a smaller number of young people; often a class of thirty or several classes together. Once again, it is good if the teaching content of these lessons can build on the theme developed in the assembly, although of course sometimes those you meet in the classroom will not have had the opportunity to attend.

*Intensive or extensive*

You may choose to work intensively, concentrating on one or two schools throughout the mission, or extensively, visiting as many as possible for a 'one off' package ideally consisting of an assembly and lunch-time concert together with some lessons.

*Time planning*

If you are using a group who need to set up public address equipment for assemblies or concerts, time needs to be given to this and access needs to be gained to the school hall perhaps an hour to an hour and a half before morning assembly or a lunch-time concert. Time must also be allowed for packing away equipment and this will affect the number of lessons the group are able to take. It is very useful to have a couple of local 'humpers' who are free to travel with the group throughout the mission and help them with setting up and packing up equipment. These helpers can double up as guides to make sure the group get to the right place at the right time.

### *Education or indoctrination*

It should also be remembered that school is a place of education not indoctrination and that therefore the content of all Christian work there should be truly educational. Sometimes there will be teachers who are not particularly well disposed towards Christians coming into the school to teach. If they have reason to believe that the pupils are coming under pressure to accept the Christian faith and 'give their lives to Jesus' they will be antagonised still further. Such a situation makes life very difficult for Christian staff members and has, unfortunately, also been the cause of many schools being permanently closed to Christian work. The place for direct evangelism is not in the classroom but at an evening evangelistic event which young people have attended of their own free will knowing exactly what it is they are coming to.

## Streetwork

If you are aiming for older teens then it may be right to think beyond schools work. What about the sixteen and eighteen plus age group who have left school? Perhaps an important factor in your mission should be streetwork, when you can make contacts and advertise evening evangelistic events (see chapter 20).

## Evening evangelistic events

### *How many events?*

Concerts may take place at different venues throughout the week(s) or at one central location at the end of the mission.

You could plan a 'Video Show' and put on a series of three, four, five or even six different presentations on consecutive evenings (see chapter 28). The value of this is that young people are given the opportunity to come along several nights running and then to go away and talk through what they have heard with their friends before returning to hear more the following night. The more opportunity teenagers have to think about and assess the gospel, the more equipped they are to make a reasoned decision about becoming a Christian. If we are not careful we ask young people to make the most life-changing decision that they could ever contemplate on the basis of no more than a ten or fifteen minute chat at the end of a concert.

*Venues for evening events*

A venue for the evening event(s) may be a secular one or one that is owned by the church (see the discussion of this question in chapter 18). The important factor to consider is ease of access to the venue by public transport. I have known missions where I have spent most of the week working in an area which is five or six miles from the venue for evening events. The public transport service is often non-existent or inconvenient and the last bus runs before the end of the event that you have advertised. You cannot rely on parents being willing to run their teenagers in and out of your event in the family car so the venue must be easily accessible to the audience you want to reach.

*Honesty*

Organisers should always be honest about the purpose of an evening event. In assemblies, lessons and lunch-time concerts it is right to mention that, besides the music, drama, videos, etc, the evening will explain more about Jesus Christ and what a Christian is. You may feel that this is bound to put teenagers off coming altogether, but I've found it makes little difference to the numbers attending and, on the positive side, you know that the audience is open to hearing about Jesus Christ and how he relates to them.

*Head hunting*

A common danger that arises in the context of 'event' evangelism is the danger of being too numbers orientated. If the appeal produces a certain number of conversions it is regarded as a great success; if not, it is seen as a failure. Though I believe it is the evangelist's responsibility to make an appeal and so offer those who have heard the gospel the opportunity to respond to it publicly, this response will only ever be a rough indication of what God has been doing on any particular night. There will be those who stand or come forward who perhaps shouldn't and those who should have but didn't, added to which there will be some whom God speaks to in a very real way but who then need to go away and think before making any decision. It has been said that those who make a first time commitment at such events should only really be counted as converts after one year of sticking to their decision.

About a year ago I was involved in a mission that was written about in the national Christian press. Over the course of four nights some one hundred and thirty young people made decisions for Christ. This disclosure greatly improved my reputation but gave entirely the wrong impression, because today only about thirty, or forty at the most, of those converts continue with their faith. The church that enters into an evangelistic mission of any kind, especially among the young people, without recognising that there will very often be a high fall off rate is a church that is blinkered. Jesus himself spoke of the seed that fell on stony, shallow and thorny ground, and for those reasons never reached maturity.

*Worship*

If it is at all possible, build the concept of worship/celebration into a mission. Very often a youth mission will finish with a Sunday evening worship service to which all the young people who attended the evangelistic events, especially those who made some public response, will be invited. In this way not only are new converts introduced to the concept of worship but a start is made towards bridging the gap between frontline evangelism and ongoing teaching and discipleship through the regular ministry of a local church. The presence of the visiting evangelist(s) and others who have been a focal point throughout the mission is always a great help because it provides the continuity which is much needed at this early stage in bridge building.

*Counselling and nurture groups*

Both of these issues must be carefully considered at an early stage of planning. They are dealt with in detail in the next chapter.

## Publicity

This should be handled in the same way as for a concert. Plenty of handbills are necessary not only for streetwork but also to accompany the school workers as they go into assemblies and lessons. Each young person should be able to have a copy of a handbill, because very often they will think of the handbills as tickets and those who do not possess one will not consider themselves able to attend your event. The handbill should clearly show:

(1) The name of the event

(2) The date(s) of the event

(3) The venue

(4) A map of how to get there

(5) The opening time of the doors and the starting time of the presentation

(6) The finishing time (this is very important in teenage work as parents will often want to know what time their children will be back home)

(7) The cost of admission. If it is free this should be clearly stated (I tend to think that evangelistic presentations should be free but there are arguments both ways)

(8) The age group the presentation is aimed at

**Prayer**

In 1984, Mission to London and Mission England very successfully used the principle of prayer triplets. In this scheme three people would get together and pray for three other people who were good friends of theirs and whom they hoped to invite along to evangelistic events. In many cases those who were prayed for became Christians long before the missions themselves actually took place. A number of central prayer and information meetings should be held from an early date and prayer sheets, cards and 'updates' should be provided. When people feel involved and kept up to date, they will pray more effectively and also give more realistically.

# 22
# FOLLOW-UP
## *Evangelistic counselling and nurture of new Christians*

Laurel and Hardy, Tom and Jerry, Jack and Jill, Rolls and Royce, salt and pepper...evangelism and follow-up. This last pair are as inseparable as the others. There is little point in organising evangelistic events if you are not prepared to care for those who respond to the message. Mass evangelism must always go hand in hand with individual pastoral care and attention because where the former is divorced from the latter disaster will follow. In fact, evangelism without follow-up can even provide the inoculation against Christianity which later prevents the patient from getting the real thing! Follow-up begins with good clear counselling at conversion and then involves the careful ongoing nurture of each convert. Without this care, new Christians are soon confused and often lost, which in turn may create the kind of negative attitude that says, 'I've heard it all before, but it doesn't work.'

### Evangelistic counselling

A few weeks before one evangelistic concert at which I was due to sing, I rang the organiser to enquire, among other things, about the number of counsellors who would be available. I was quickly informed that it was not expected that much would happen and so it was 'really not worth' organising counsellors! I also learned that there were no plans to have any evangelistic literature available, no nurture groups had been arranged and there was no way of making a record of any young people who responded. I pointed out that it was reasonable to assume that there may be those who would make some response to the gospel, and almost grudgingly the organiser agreed to see what he could do.

On the night of the event I was told that at a push the organisers could probably rustle up betwen ten and fifteen counsellors if needed, but at the close of the evening about fifty people responded to the gospel in one way or another and needed counselling. Those in charge were in a state of shock and in the confusion there were at least a few who, though they wanted to talk, did not receive the opportunity. In fact, no one was quite sure about who the counsellors were and who wanted counselling!

If a message is going to be presented at the end of an evangelistic event with the opportunity to respond, the facility must exist for those who do, to sit down and talk through their decision. The need for evangelistic counselling and the role that belongs to the counsellor need to be taken seriously and looked at well in advance of the event itself.

### Training

Each local church should have a number of people, both young and old, who have been trained in evangelistic counselling. There is no space within the confines of this book to present such a training course but many are available from good Christian bookshops. It is important, however, to make several general comments that may not be found elsewhere.

*(1) Age and experience*

Some claim that the role of counsellor does not belong to teenagers themselves but to older Christians with more experience and maturity, in whom those seeking advice will place a greater degree of confidence. Others argue that it is right that Christian teenagers be given the responsibility of counselling, thus providing them with the opportunity to gain experience. The most convincing counsellors, it is claimed, will come from the same age group as those being counselled. In fact there is no black and white answer to this question. It will be different in differing situations because it is dependent upon exactly who the young people are in your group, how old they are, and how mature they are as Christians. Other counsellors at youth events should include youth leaders and others who are 'in tune' with the young. It is not age that drives the gap between the generations but lack of understanding. The important quality of a counsellor is the ability to relate to the world of those with whom he speaks so that they can identify with and understand him.

*(2) Sex*

Wherever possible, counselling should be male to male and female to female. We all know of the kind of teenage girl who only ever seems to have problems when a particular male youth leader is there to help sort them out! Or the boy who, while being counselled by an older girl, is actually paying a lot more attention to her shape than to what she is saying!

*(3) Don't keep those being counselled for too long*

It's easy for the counsellor to fall into the trap of believing that he has to pack a whole discipleship course into one initial counselling session in order to ensure the continued spiritual life of a new Christian! This is obviously not true and can actually be quite harmful, for several reasons:

(a) The person who has just become a Christian will not normally be able to grasp very much of what the counsellor has to say, but what he really needs to get hold of is that he has been forgiven for all that is wrong in his life by God because of what Jesus Christ did when he died on the cross and that now he has been given the Spirit to enable him to live a new life. The only other thing that the counsellor needs to explain is when the follow-up classes will actually take place. If that comes across loud and clear, the counsellor has done a good job. If the counsellor tries to say much more it all becomes confusing rather than helpful and the main points will have been lost.

(b) The problem is often not just that the counsellor says a lot which is unnecessary but that he takes far too long to do so. The gospel is harmed when the publicity for the evening gives the finishing time as 10.00 pm but at 10.15 the counsellee is still being kept and his father is still waiting outside in the car with the engine running or his friends are still waiting inside the hall with very worried looks on their faces because they've just missed the last bus home! We must respect those whom we counsel. If we have told them in our publicity that they will be away from the building at 10.00 we must keep our word. The programme should finish at 9.45 so that fifteen minutes can be devoted to counselling. Unfortunately I have witnessed many incidents where a young Christian's first encounter with the non-Christian world is in the shape of his father who storms into the building to drag him away from a bewildered counsellor, while swearing and uttering threats to all concerned because he has been kept waiting: 'You're never coming here again...I'm not having you mixed up with religious nuts...I'm going to sue you lot...you wait,' are all expressions that I've heard in such circumstances. Let's be careful not to make a young person's first night of being a Christian a night that he, and we, have to try and forget.

*(4) Counselling cards*

It is very important that counselling cards should be available so that a record can be made of each young person who responds in any way. You need to have a record of:

(a) Home address

(b) School

(c) Any church connection

(d) Particular response to the appeal

Often I have witnessed a situation where somebody stands up at the end of an evangelistic evening to hand out sheets of blank paper and pens, and shout orders across a crowded counselling room to those who are actually doing the counselling. This is a policy guaranteed to make those who are being counselled feel as though they are being processed. Apart from the embarrassment of such a situation, it rarely works anyway because the counsellors will invariably forget to take down one of the most important details, so making effective follow-up difficult. It is essential that the counselling card be ready well before the event and that the training course include the opportunity for the counsellors to become familiar with it. It must also be made clear that completed cards should be handed back to the organiser at the end of the evening, and under no circumstances be taken home by the counsellor, which is another common problem – one that is as unhelpful as forgetting to fill it in to start with!

Young people should never be asked to fill in the counselling card themselves. This can happen when, for instance, the counsellor asks the counsellee's name but fails to hear it properly or feels unable to spell it. Because he is embarrassed to ask for clarification he decides that the easiest way out of the situation is to ask the young person to fill in the form. The problem arises when the teenager goes straight home and enthusiastically reports to his parents that he has just become a Christian and signed a form to that effect down at the church. This is guaranteed to ring alarm bells with the unsympathetic parent: 'What has my son signed up for?' 'What has he been forced into?'

'What kind of pressure has been used?' To most non-Christian parents this has the taste of 'one of those cults', the kind they have read about in the Sunday press. Make sure that your counsellors explain exactly what the card is for – that it is simply to -give you a record of their decision so that you can help them as they grow in their Christian faith. The counsellor should not demand the information but should ask the young person if he minds giving details of his name and address, etc, and should allow the opportunity to refuse. Only then should the form be filled in. As many of the details as possible concerning the nature of the commitment should be completed after the counsellee has left. Finally the form should be handed in. Counsellors should also, of course, have a good working knowledge of any literature that is being used and given away.

*(5) The term 'counsellor'*

Though we have used the term 'counsellor' many times in this chapter, it is not the best description for general use. The term sounds very professional and in everyday life 'counsellors' are people to be avoided except in dire circumstances. They are people you go to when you're in trouble, experts who tend to see right through you and know your every thought. At the end of an evangelistic event I simply say, 'There are some Christians here who would like to chat briefly about the decision you've just made to follow Jesus.'

*(6) Listening and asking*

It is important that the counsellor be trained to listen carefully to exactly what the counsellee has to say about why he came forward, rather than jumping to the conclusion that he necessarily wants to become a Christian. It is just as important that the counsellor should also have the ability to assess when and how to ask questions which will enable the counsellee to clarify why he has responded to the invitation. This saves you the embarrassing situation where somebody is pushed by a counsellor into 'becoming a Christian' only to have the job of sheepishly explaining at the end of the session, 'But I made a commitment to Christ three years ago...it's just that I find it so difficult to pray!'

Don't expect everybody to know why they have come forward; some come simply because they need help in explaining to others why they are Christians, some may not even be sure whether they are Christians or not. Counsellors need to be patient and should be trained never to try and force the conversation in a particular direction or to push somebody into God's kingdom. I once heard Floyd McClung say, 'Don't try to do the Holy Spirit's work for him . . . you haven't got what it takes!' Give each young person room to manoeuvre. If they are not totally sure that they want to become Christians they should be given the opportunity to go away and think it over, rather than being pushed into something that they are not ready for.

*(7) Chief counsellor*

It is good to appoint somebody suitable as chief counsellor with the responsibility of working out the practical arrangements well before the event and communicating these to the other counsellors. Each counsellor should be informed of exactly what is required of him at the end of the evening. He will want to know where the counselling room is; when he should move through to it; by what process he will be paired up with someone wishing to be counselled; where he should leave the counselling card (and pen?) afterwards, and so on. The more practical planning that is done, the more efficient the process, which not only leaves more time for counselling but also helps make everybody feel more relaxed.

*(8) Literature*

Counsellors should understand that there are three strands of follow-up for those who become Christians at evangelistic events:

(a) Local church (through nurture groups etc)

(b) School (through the Christian Union)

(c) The counsellor himself. A counsellor's responsibility to those whom he counsels does not end as he prays a prayer of commitment with them and sends them on their way with a handful of literature. At this stage he may well be the only Christian that these young people know. It is the counsellor's responsibility to pray for them and to stay in touch, at least until other relationships have been formed. The counsellor can do this quite easily by saying something like, 'And I'll meet you outside here next week for the first of the "following Jesus" meetings.'

**Nurture of new Christians**

The question of exactly how prospective converts are to be nurtured should be part of the main agenda when the planning of a mission or other evangelistic event is decided on.

I once visited a mission committee which was made up of members of several churches in a particular area. They had booked me to present an evangelistic concert on a Friday evening at which, I had been informed by letter, four hundred non-Christian teenagers would be present. At the meeting I asked them two questions:

(a) How could they be so sure so many non-Christians would be present?

(b) What plans and preparations were being made for the care and nurture of any converts afterwards?

A silence fell across the room which said much louder than words ever could that absolutely no thought had been given to either issue.

There are many excellent follow-up or nurture courses for new converts published by a number of different organisations and available through any good local Christian bookshop. Once again, it is far beyond the scope of this book to provide an alternative to these, nor is it necessary! All I will do here is outline a few basic principles which apply universally to follow-up work with teenagers but which are often not included as part of a training package.

*(1) Planning ahead*

Nurture or discipleship meetings need to be planned well before any evangelistic event takes place. This means that the venue, date and time can be announced at the event itself and that each counsellor can personally invite those he counsels: 'I'll meet you back here at 7.30 pm next Friday for the first of a series of meetings for all those who want to know more about being a Christian...Can you come?' This meeting can also be announced from the stage at the end of the evening because there may be those who would like to attend but did not make any public response to the appeal.

Why is it so important to work in this way? Simply because in the case of teenage work, especially among the unchurched, it is practically impossible to plan effective follow-up after the event. Let's examine the alternative.

Often the plan has been to collect together the counselling cards after the event, then sit down to analyse them and set up home nurture groups on the basis of geography (where the convert lives in the town) or existing church contact. Then a letter is written inviting the convert along to the meeting or a visit is made to his home. Unfortunately, this plan of action does not normally work, for several reasons.

In the summer of 1984 I was sent a considerable number of follow-up cards relating to teenagers who were counselled for conversion at Mission to London. I was asked to visit their home, to establish a link and invite them to a nurture group. The problem was that I had no natural reason to call on any of these young people. I would pluck up courage and knock at their front door only to be greeted in every case by one of their parents (teenagers tend to leave the door bell to their parents, unless they are expecting a friend). I would then have to ask to see their son or daughter, at which point they would, understandably, want to know why (that's when I'd really begin to wish I wasn't there!). I would try to explain as simply as I could that their child had become a Christian or expressed interest in the Christian faith at Mission to London. None of the parents I ever spoke to were Christians and I could tell from the look on their faces that they found this news rather disturbing; either they knew nothing about it, or did know but were not sympathetic. One father flew into a rage there and then, calling down his son from the bedroom to inform him that this was the last time he would ever set foot inside a church: 'We don't want anyone in our family mixed up with this sort of thing,' he yelled. This attitude was understandable because, of course, most people in our country believe that they probably are Christians and that 'Christian' equals 'good person' (which accounts for the popularity of the statement, 'You don't need to go to church to be a Christian'). A 'born again' Christian is 'a religious maniac'. Of all the teenage contacts who came from non-Christian homes whom I visited from Mission to London there was not one that resulted in any continued contact with the church. Home visiting is not a realistic means of follow-up for a teenager under the age of eighteen.

Letters posted through the door are just as unhelpful – few teenagers normally receive neatly typed envelopes through the door. But whether it is typed or hand written, when the letter arrives they are at school and their mother, who picks it up from the front door mat, spends the whole day wondering what it contains. When the teenager arrives home the letter is presented to him, maybe even with some excitement and they are required to report on its contents after opening it, which draws the same kind of response as the call at the door.

The chief problem that must be overcome is the deep suspicion of non-Christian parents concerning what has happened to their child. They are understandably worried as they often have a distorted and misleading idea of what the church is.

The best way of coping with this difficult situation is, therefore, to simply tell the teenager about the nurture group on the night of his conversion. For a teenager to come home and say,

'I went down the church with my friends tonight, it was good and we're going to go again next Friday,' will probably only arouse the response, 'It's a passing phase, he'll soon grow out of it.' The parents can see that this is something their child wants to do. They probably believe that it's 'taking religion too seriously' but since he's going with his friends, and is not being forced they probably shrug and say, 'It's his choice.' In time, of course, the parents will learn that their teenager has become a Christian and that he has made many new Christian friends. But all this will happen as a gradual process while the parents have the chance to discover that being a Christian (whatever that really means) has not taken their child away from the family and brainwashed him, but has, if anything, made him a better son!

*(2) One central group*

As the result of any evangelistic event or mission, whether organised by one church or townwide, there will be those who are converted who are friends of existing Christians. These young people will quite naturally become involved in the church to which their friends already belong. The problem arises over those who are contacted through schools work or by some other means who have no natural friendship with an existing Christian. For these, one central group should be set up. This is preferable to trying to divide them – whether it be geographically, into different house groups or denominationally, by sending them to a church to which their counselling card indicates they have some affiliation.

As we have recognised in Part One of this book, the gang spirit is particularly important during teenage years. Daniel and Andy are best friends and respond to the gospel together at a concert. Daniel happens to live at one end of the town while Andy lives at the other. If you work on a geographical basis you will ask them to go to two different home groups or centres, but the chances are that neither will go anywhere! There is another difference between them. Daniel was christened at St Agnes whereas Peter used to go to the Baptist Sunday School which he left six years ago. When asked by their counsellors if they have any church contact both thought it was important to put these down. However, an attempt to send them to the church they claim to have contact with is not only unrealistic but will again split their friendship.

In relation to a townwide event, the establishing of one central nurture group for those who do not have a natural connection with one particular church creates a problem because it means that the churches involved have to acknowledge the fact that everybody in this category will end up with the one fellowship who are chosen to run the group. This obviously demands a great deal of commitment and maturity from all the participating churches.

*(3) Running a nurture group*

Several points need to be made about the functioning of a nurture group.

(a) Rather than referring to the meeting as the 'Discipleship' or 'Nurture' group, both of which sound somewhat technical, come up with another name which you think will be suitable in your situation. Names that I have come across include 'Talking Shop', 'Just Looking' and 'Master Class'.

(b) The group should meet once a week on a convenient night with a programme that lasts about one and a half hours (for example, 7.30–9.00 pm). This leaves time for coffee and chat afterwards but means that those present can still be away by 9.30 (especially important if your group is to be held mid-week). Its life should be about ten weeks, though again this will vary, depending on the literature you are using.

(c) Existing Christians and especially the counsellors should attend the group on a regular basis, taking every opportunity to befriend those who have so recently made a commitment.

(d) There should be a number of leaders who can share the responsibility of running the group. This will prevent it turning into a one man show.

(e) The programme should include worship and prayer as well as teaching and discussion. It's good to use a worship band if possible. Teaching should be varied: from the front, in small groups, and through drama, videos, etc. The group should present the new convert with lively, relevant worship and teaching and thus create a natural bridge into the life of the adult church.

# 23
# STARTING A DRAMA GROUP

**Nine reasons for starting a youth drama group**

1. Drama is one of the most powerful and thought-provoking tools for presenting truth.
2. A drama group creates an excellent resource for use in your local church.
3. A drama group provides an effective tool for powerful evangelism in the local community.
4. A youth drama group which regularly takes part in the life of a local church creates a 'window', enabling others to appreciate and understand young people.
5. Through participation, drama harnesses and uses young people's energy and creativity.
6. Old Chinese proverb: 'I hear – I forget; I see – I remember; I do – I understand.'
7. Being part of a drama group creates and encourages confidence in young people.
8. Being part of a drama group and seeing God effectively use its ministry builds faith.
9. Being part of a drama group is a lot of fun.

**Ten tips for starting from scratch**

*1. Leadership*

This is a key position as the initial development of the group depends heavily on the quality of the leader. He or she needs organisational skills as well as the ability to inspire and keep the other members of the group on course. In the early days of the group a wide range of responsibilities will inevitably be carried by this person, although as time passes it will be possible and also important to shed some of the load to other members. An ideal leader would be an older member of the youth group or one of your overall church leadership team.

*2. Membership*

Ideally the size of your drama group should be somewhere between four and eight members. Though it is possible to work with a smaller number this can be limiting as far as variety of material is concerned. On the other hand, if the team is too large it becomes difficult to involve and include everybody and as a result individuals feel left out and the team spirit begins to collapse.

*3. Commitment*

It is important that group members possess the basic potential gifts needed to perform, but these do not need to be highly developed (though having one or two talented members certainly adds something).

The two essential qualities group members will need are the desire to learn and real commitment to the project. Beware of those who want to get involved 'a bit'! There are a number of ways in which you can involve people like this (for example, organising transport, publicity, diary, costume, props, correspondence, expenses, and so on) but for those who are going to be part of the group itself you are looking for 100% commitment. That is not necessarily long-distance commitment, but total involvement now.

It is best to set up your drama group on a six month trial basis, after which members have the option of leaving, jointly deciding to end the project or carrying on.

*4. Aims*

Why are you setting up a drama group? What is its purpose? Will you primarily exist for teaching, outreach or entertainment? Is your goal to take part in Sunday worship services, evangelistic events in the local community, or both?

It is essential that you sort out the answers to these questions from the start. Failure to do so will lead to disillusionment, argument and disaster. In fact you may feel that you need to tackle the issue of your aims even before you think about membership. Then those who join know what they're joining.

*5. Rehearsals*

It is essential to set aside regular rehearsal time. To be really effective this needs to be a once-a-week commitment for a couple of hours on a midweek evening or a Saturday morning. Lots of local church drama groups exist on an ad hoc basis and meet to rehearse when necessary because the vicar has asked them to perform in the family service, perhaps, but a consistent ongoing group can obviously be ten times more effective.

*6. Material*

Are you going to write your own material or use the work of others? Using other people's material at the start of your drama group's life has lots of advantages. Writing good material is demanding and takes lots of practice. By using published material you are ensuring quality which will help you get off to a good start.

But don't get sucked into someone else's rut. Get group members to start writing their own material (see tip 10 below). If you are going to use material from books, in most cases you will need to obtain a licence to perform it. Sketch books always contain details of how to obtain licences. Suggestions for recommended books appear at the end of this chapter.

*7. Name*

Choose a name. Make sure it's a good one because it will either sell you or become your worst piece of publicity. Don't choose anything which attempts to be too 'spiritual' ('The Sonworshippers', 'Sonrise', 'The Revival Players') as it will end up with a very high cringe factor rating.

*8. Communication*

Make sure to keep your church well informed about what you are doing. Work hard at getting their active backing and support. If you do, you'll find there are opportunities which begin to open up for performing in Sunday services, at family days, children's clubs, evangelistic meetings and other events.

*9. Perform*

Make sure you get your group performing soon. Don't fall into the trap of constantly putting off your first performance! Your group will mature and develop only through the experience of performance.

*10. Reading*

It is essential to get the leader of your group to read at least one of the following three books before doing anything else. Besides containing some classic sketches, all three contain loads of information on how to run your new drama group. They are available from all good Christian bookshops and will help your group avoid all kinds of common pitfalls – everything from script writing and refining, rehearsing and performing to casting, costume and publicity.

*Time to Act* by Paul Burbridge and Murray Watts (Hodder and Stoughton).
*Back to Back's Little Black Paperback Book* by the Back to

Back Theatre Company, published by Kingsway but now out of print – try to borrow a copy.
*Using the Bible in Drama* by S. and J. Stickley and J. Belben (Bible Society).

**Drama books**

The following are all excellent books of sketches and longer dramas suitable for many different occasions. Try to build up a collection of these to provide a resource for your drama group.

*Act Justly* from Christian Aid and Cafod (Collins).
*The Dame Cecily Spume Drama Notebook* by Nick Page (Minstrel).
*The Drama Recipe Book* by Alan McDonald and Steve Stickley (Minstrel).
*Ex Machina* by David Lee (Marshall Pickering).
*Footnotes* by Steve and Janet Stickley (Hodder and Stoughton).
*Laughter in Heaven* by Murray Watts (Minstrel).
*Lightning Sketches* by Paul Burbridge and Murray Watts (Hodder & Stoughton).
*Red Letter Days* by Paul Burbridge and Murray Watts (Hodder & Stoughton).
*Scene One* by Ashley Martin, Andy Kelso and others (Kingsway).

**Drama companies**

There are some excellent drama companies performing in various parts of the country. Why not book one of them to perform in your town and ask them to lead a drama workshop? It could help your group – and perhaps others in the area – to develop their own skills and expertise.

Back to Back
15 Trafalgar Road
Moseley 22
Birmingham B13 8BJ
(Tel 021 449 1609)

Footprints
St Nicholas Church Centre
Maid Marian Way
Nottingham NG1 6AE
(Tel 0602 586554)

Saltmine
PO Box 15
Dudley
W Midlands DY3 2AN
(Tel 0384 238224)

Shout
Haddon Hall
Tower Bridge Road
London SE1 4TR
(Tel 071-231 4583)

Stairs and Whispers
Flat 27 The Centre
Stoke Park Drive
Ipswich IP2 9EG
(Tel 0473 687186)

Trapdoor
21 Ashburton Avenue
Llanfumney
Cardiff CF3 9FR
(Tel 0222 777634)

# 24
# OPEN YOUTH WORK

## Nightmare on Elm Street

Here is a simple story of an ordinary local church open youth club disaster. Any resemblance the script has to your local church is completely deliberate. The storyline is not based on any one church, but on events that are happening in thousands of churches throughout the UK at this very moment.

### *Part I – The Dream*

Elm Street Evangelical Church is on the edge of the Elm Park Estate in East Wickford. East Wickford is a mixed housing area in a large city, but the Elm Park Estate consists mostly of high-rise council tower blocks with a bad record of social problems and crime. The evangelical church has a good congregation made up of members living in the various parts of East Wickford and beyond, but very few from the Elm Park area. Over the last years some have made increasing efforts to get the church to recognise and change this situation, but they have been largely unsuccessful. One whole family was converted three years ago, but they have not been very regular on Sundays (!) and generally struggle to fit in to things. The official line is that this is because they are a bit awkward.

Mary Thompson is in her early thirties. She has been a member of Elm Street since she was a teenager. Over the years she has been increasingly concerned about the lack of teenagers in the church. It's about time something was done about it. There is a very successful week-night children's club which has a regular attendance of around sixty five- to eleven-year-olds, and a Sunday school numbering about forty of the same age group. There are a handful of teenagers in the church who are Christians. There are no young people from Elm Park in the youth group.

Over the last few years Mary has constantly niggled away in church meetings about this issue. Her concern has met with a variety of responses ranging from total indifference to the very sincere 'Yes, something really ought to be done.' Finally, in desperation, though she doesn't think it's really her thing, Mary decides to take action herself and launch a Saturday night youth club to attract teenagers from around the town, but especially from the Elm Park Estate. It would be an exaggeration to say that anybody else in the church was enthusiastically committed to her plans, but on the other hand she was keen and nobody wanted to stand in her way – so long as the halls didn't get vandalised.

Some of the more pastorally sensitive members even promised to pray for her, and the elders generously assured her that she was always free to approach them for support if any major problems cropped up.

Mary formed her plans. The club would run each Saturday night from 7.30 till 10.00 pm. It would provide a place to be for the youth of East Wickford, especially of the Elm Park Estate, who otherwise hung round on street corners and in local pubs. It would be a safe place for them to relax and have fun. It would provide volley ball, football, snooker, table tennis, a disco, refreshments and the opportunity to sit down and talk. Most importantly, each evening would end with a five or ten minute epilogue, clearly presenting the gospel.

*Part II – The Nightmare*

All that was just over ten years ago, but for the last decade the reality of Elm Street's open youth club has been a living nightmare.

Saturday after Saturday, Mary has faithfully given up her time, but seen very little to encourage her. It's not that the club doesn't attract the youngsters – there are usually fifty or so around the building at any time on a typical evening. The real problem is that it doesn't seem to be getting anywhere, and Mary feels that the pressure is always all on her.

Of course there have always been those in the church who have helped out, though it has been a constant battle to get volunteers of any quality. It's just that Mary feels she constantly has to take the initiative and shoulder all the burden and responsibility without anyone else to lean on. Her helpers tend to give a year or so and then lose interest or move on to other important commitments in the church. But whatever the reason, it always amounts to the same thing. Mary is left struggling with inadequate assistance once again.

Over the years Mary has pumped quite a lot of her own money into running the club, but the problem is that this has not really been adequate, and to be honest she feels that the church has been unwilling to release the resources she has needed.

For their part, many in the church feel that the youth club has failed to achieve what it set out to do. Sadly, no young people have ever been integrated into the life of the church, and though huge numbers from the Elm Park Estate have attended the club, this has meant that other teenagers from around the town (including their own children) have either been afraid to go or for some other reason haven't wanted to be there. Very occasionally, over the ten years, there have been stories of young people who have become Christians, but their commitment has not lasted and they have never been seen in the church. On top of all this, Elm Street's premises have taken a real battering. The fabric committee have had to deal with a constant (sometimes weekly) list of broken windows, doors, chairs, tables, lights and toilet seats. The church has also had to cope with the anger of the caretaker, who is always complaining of swearing, rudeness and insults from the young people who attend. He also claims that he is going to stop even attempting to unblock the toilets in time for the Sunday morning service if any more loo rolls are stuffed down them week after week. And, as if all this wasn't enough, there has been a constant stream of equipment, money and possessions that have gone missing from the church over the years.

All in all it is not too difficult to see how these events have not exactly helped to make Mary popular with some of the other church members. Mary is burned out and very near to finally throwing in the towel for good. She feels guilty about letting the club members down, but fears she's going under. She is disillusioned with the church, which she feels has not pulled its weight, and if she is honest (though she tries very hard not to be) she is fed up with the kids and angry with God. The members of the club fight and swear and there are constant problems with drink, drugs, and even occasionally sex on the premises. The police are often called. Mary feels that the young people who come to the club lack respect for her. She finds them rude and aggressive, in fact recently she has been threatened several times, twice with a knife. She is also aware that there is a constant turnover and that most kids don't stay as members of the club for more than eighteen months before drifting off.

The epilogue has turned into a weekly disaster. People hide in the loos, go home just before it starts, or talk and laugh throughout.

When she has tried to ban kids, some parents have complained and been insulting or threatening. The Sunday school are never happy about the way the hall has been left the night before, however much Mary tries to get it right.

The other question niggling away in the back of Mary's mind is 'Why doesn't anyone ever become a Christian and stick?' Is it all her fault? Perhaps she's not spiritual enough. Or is it that the church doesn't pray and isn't concerned enough? Perhaps it's simply that Elm Street and its services are completely irrelevant to the young people she's working with? This seems to be borne out by the fact that once, after Billy Graham's mission a couple of years ago, two of the girls did come to a Sunday evening service – and walked out halfway through, refusing ever to go again.

Mary thinks back on her dream, but this is a nightmare. What can she do? Where is she going wrong? How can she get help?

Elm Street's problems are typical of those of vast numbers of churches which have experimented with open youth work and ended up getting their fingers burned. Should they give up, or are there important foundational guidelines and principles which can be learned and employed in order to make open youth clubs work?

In a recent edition of one Christian magazine a well-known leader, commenting on the evangelistic role of his particular church grouping, expressed the opinion that they feel sure it is right to stick solely to working with the middle classes because that is what they are best at. Their intention, he claimed, was to leave other, more difficult-to-reach sectors of society for somebody else to deal with. At least he was honest! But the tragedy of such statements is that they often represent a thinly disguised, unconscious attempt to justify complacency by the amazing twist of implying that it is not less than the direct result of listening to God!

Could this be the same God who, as the New Testament tells us, loves the whole world and does not intend that anyone should perish? In the light of the themes of love, justice, mercy and concern for the poor, all of which are at the very heart of the gospel; in the light of the riots involving so many bored and frustrated teenagers on housing estates around the country; in the light of the latest figures showing that half the crime in Britain is committed by those under the age of twenty, and a quarter by those under the age of seventeen; the question is, how can we communicate the gospel in relevant ways to the already vast, and for ever growing, numbers of young people totally outside our church subculture?

## Spot the errors

As you read through the story of Elm Street Estate, did you spot the fatal errors that resulted in disaster and disillusion? Of course there were lots of additional problems at Elm Street, just as at any other church, but the really big mistakes were made because the basic principles of open youth work were ignored. So what are the dos and don'ts?

*Church ownership*

DO ensure that your proposed plan for launching open youth work is 'owned' by your leadership. It must be seen as the responsibility of the church rather than of one or two individuals. The burden of youth work belongs with the whole church. This key principle is the foundation to running any successful church-based open youth work. Only when a local church fully 'owns' the open youth club that takes place on its premises will the result be the provision of vital support and other essential resources.

DON'T embark on an open youth work project without the real backing of your church. When problems arise, as they are bound to, it is the commitment of the church to the project that will get you through.

*Church strategy*

DO recognise that any open youth work project is only likely to be successful if it forms part of your church's overall strategy. It is only as the whole church begins to see how work with non-churched teenagers fits into their overall aims that vital support and resources will become available.

DON'T fall into the trap of letting the development of your

open youth work become the task of one or two enthusiastic and visionary 'lone ranger' church members. Enthusiasm rarely lasts without the supportive structure and environment which it is the job of the rest of the church to provide.

DO make sure that your church grasps that the issue of reaching non-churched teenagers is about more than running a Saturday night youth club on their premises. If your open youth club is to be successful in terms of evangelism, its existence will have implications for other areas of church life – including the format of Sunday services.

DON'T assume that teenagers who become Christians will automatically fit into existing church patterns and suddenly develop the miraculous ability to sit through your Sunday services.

DO recognise that the integration of young people from outside the Christian subculture into church life is a slow process.

DON'T view running an open youth group as an operation guaranteed to fill your church's pews quickly. You will only be disappointed.

*Appointment of leaders*

DO ensure that all youth leaders are officially appointed and recognised by your church. Far too often responsibility for youth work is conveniently dumped on the shoulders of anyone willing to accept it.

DON'T ever allow your open youth work to operate under a self-appointed, 'I'll do it my way, I don't want your advice' leadership.

DO ensure that there is always accountability back to church leaders. Make sure of this by creating regular opportunities for discussion and review of progress and direction.

DON'T leave youth leaders to operate without pastoral cover and clear lines of accountability. Remember, the church leadership should always carry the ultimate responsibility for all youth work.

DO ensure that those who serve as youth leaders bring to their

task the qualities and gifts needed to do a good job. Be careful about who is appointed to such responsible and influential role model positions.
DON'T appoint leaders simply because of their enthusiasm. There are doubtless many Christians who would be highly enthusiastic about preaching in their local church next Sunday morning, but the result would be extreme boredom and maybe even a dose of mild heresy for the congregation!

*Team building*

DO make it a top priority to start building a team of leaders. Any open youth work project which falls on the shoulders of one or two highly committed individuals without the development of supportive input and backing from others will eventually crumble.
DON'T allow your open youth work to become the responsibility of a single individual. If your church is committed to this type of youth work as part of its overall strategy, work to encourage involvement and commitment from a larger group of individuals.
DO talent spot for up-and-coming young leaders. Think very seriously about your responsibility to train and encourage leaders for the future. And remember, after you've thought about it...do something!
DON'T inadvertently create the situation where those who want to be committed to work in the youth club are faced with other, conflicting priorities and demands on their time from the church.

*Training*

DO make sure to provide opportunities, resources and information for the in-service training of all youth leaders. Always remember that open youth work is a cross-cultural mission situation which necessitates the use of acquired skills.
DON'T leave your youth leaders to sink or swim without adequate support. Never dump them and expect them to cope

without the benefit of ongoing training and input. Get wise, think long term!

*Funding*

DO ensure that your youth work is adequately funded through your church's central annual budget. A church's budget should always be a practical expression of its strategy.
DON'T take advantage of your youth leaders by expecting them to pay for the work out of their own pocket.

*Strategy*

DO take plenty of time and care to think through exactly why you want to run an open youth club. What is your overall aim and purpose in doing so? Your goals and objectives should then be set to provide a monitored and measurable way of achieving your agreed purpose.
DON'T let yourself, or anyone else, get pushed into setting up an open youth club without first thinking through a clear strategy and rationale for doing so.
DO make sure that your club's strategy clearly fits into your church's overall strategy for local outreach.
DON'T make the mistake of trying to develop your club strategy without consulting closely with your church leaders.

*Programme*

DO remember that the club's programme can only be decided on after you have carefully thought through your strategy and purpose. Your purpose determines your programme. Your programme should embody your purpose. The question why must be answered before you can accurately say how or what.
DON'T be tempted to put your programme together as if it were an end in itself. If you don't know why you've planned it in the programme, it's unlikely you will achieve very much.
DO regularly review and analyse the progress of your open youth work in the light of your purpose and aims. Be ready

constantly to adapt your programme to make it as effective as possible in meeting your overall aims.
DON'T allow yourself to slide into the trap of running your programme month after month without regular built-in reviews. If you do, it's easy to end up mistaking the means for the end and then slowly forget what the end was in the first place!

*Communication*

DO work hard to keep the church informed. Make sure that information about your youth work is regularly passed to the rest of the congregation in order for them to pray and support its ministry in an educated way.
DON'T assume that the rest of the church necessarily know or understand anything of what is going on in the club, or the pressures that are being faced, unless you actively work at keeping them informed. No information flow always equals dwindling support.

# 25
# COFFEE BAR

'Innpacked' was the name given to the evangelistic coffee bar held back in 1970 where I became a Christian. Since then I have been involved in all sorts of Christian coffee bars, night clubs and non-alcoholic bars in venues ranging from a disused pub to an old canal barge, and an empty supermarket to a double decker bus. But it's not just unusual venues that can be used in this way. With a bit of flair and imagination even the dustiest church hall can be transformed into a great coffee bar.

One of the first projects that we ran in Tonbridge was a coffee bar called 'Streetbeat', when premises formerly occupied by a supermarket became vacant in Tonbridge High Street. It was an ideal setting for an evangelistic coffee bar – right in the middle of the town and next to the River Medway. We negotiated with the owners who eventually gave us their permission to use it, though this was only obtained six days before the event was due to start! Publicity, sound and lighting equipment, tables, chairs, decorations, refreshments, counsellors, bouncers, stewards, electricity and water supplies, had to be arranged with great speed, not to mention the programme! 'Streetbeat' was a great success, although it did test our organisational abilities to the full.

The basic principles behind the organisation of a coffee bar are dealt with in chapter 28, 'Video Show,' and also in chapter 18, 'A Concert'. Here we will look at a subject which has already been raised in this chapter and which we will be raising again in several of those following.

**The short-term use of vacant commercial premises**

*How do you go about acquiring the use of empty premises?*

This seems such a daunting prospect that many simply never attempt it. Actually like most other tasks it is simply a matter of knowing what to do and when:

(1) Take a walk through your local high street with a pen and note pad, taking down the names of any suitable empty shops and their street numbers, and note down from the boards outside the particulars of the estate agents who are handling the sales.

(2) First try to contact the shop owner (rather than the estate agent). Your enthusiasm and your personal contact will very often sell an idea to the owner, whereas the same idea may fail when put forward by the non-committal estate agent.

At this stage always make phone calls rather than trusting to letters. A friendly phone call briefly explaining why you require the use of the premises and explaining that it is only for a short period of time, will often go a lot further towards winning support than a formal-sounding letter. Besides this, you can wait weeks for a reply to a letter, whereas the telephone is immediate and, if the property is not available, you will know at once. Always ask to speak to the boss if possible. You can waste a lot of time talking with those who have no real authority and who will probably only pass on a rather inaccurate and brief message to those responsible. If the boss is out, rather than leave a message, courteously ask when he will be available to speak to you and say that you will phone back.

(3) If you are unable to make direct contact with the owner, negotiate through the estate agent handling the sale.

(4) Shop premises are obviously a great financial asset and also a costly liability if they stand empty. Therefore, though it may appear to the public that for months on end a certain shop stands empty, in fact, there is almost certainly a great deal of activity going on behind the scenes. The present owner is probably doing his best to sell as quickly as possible in order to release the capital that he has tied up in the premises. Because he hopes to sell, it is usually not until two or three weeks before the proposed dates that a shop owner will definitely promise you the use of his property (and then it is likely to be for not more than a month at a time!). In spite of this, it is good to make an initial enquiry some months beforehand. Though it is very unlikely that you will be promised anything at this stage, the owner or agent may well ask you to contact them again nearer the dates you require. By establishing contact in this way, you avoid springing your project on them at the last moment. This gives those concerned plenty of time to think through your case and, therefore, increases your chances of gaining a positive response if the property is still available when you need it. There may also be other groups in the town looking for the same kind of arrangement, so it helps to introduce your name as early as possible. Basically the owner needs to know that your use of his premises will not interfere with his plans. With tact and diplomacy, it is often possible to arrange for the free or nominal hire of shops for a coffee bar or other events such as those outlined in other chapters in this book.

(5) When, and if, permission is granted for use of particular premises you need to immediately get in touch with:
   (a) The Electricity Board to arrange to have power supplied.

(b) The Gas Board (if necessary).
(c) The Water Board (you need working toilet facilities if nothing else).
(d) The local police station, to advise them when you are using the building and to inform them of the purpose. Don't be afraid that they will ban your project. As long as you have the owner's permission and you do not cause a disturbance or have any official complaints filed against you by the public, you are in the clear.
(e) The fire service. They will make a visit to the premises and as a result will ask you to comply with certain regulations. They will want to know exactly what use the building is being put to, and will then advise you as to the maximum seating capacity, the required width of gangways leading to fire exits, the way in which such exits should be lit and marked, the number and type of fire extinguishers needed and the correct level of stewarding etc.
(f) The department of health and hygiene. If you are going to be cooking and serving food as part of the project it is important to make sure your facilities are adequate and meet the required standards. (This does not apply if you are simply selling pre-packed sweets and drinks.)
(g) Insurance. Have you got the necessary cover – for premises, equipment, customers and staff?

Though all this may sound daunting, you will find that most people are pleased that something imaginative is being done in the community and will give you all the help and advice that they possibly can. After the event, make sure to write and thank all those who have given you help, giving them a short report of how the project went. If you run a similar project at a future date you will need the good will of these same people. Coverage in the paper and on local radio also ensures that the community becomes aware of what you are doing. Again, this helps with future planning.

# 26
# BEGGARS BANQUET

'Eat less...pay more.' That was our motto as we served lentil soup, very small portions of chicken curry and rice and glasses of water for as much money as the public were willing to part with at the *Beggars Banquet*, a restaurant which served Third World meals at western prices in the centre of Tonbridge High Street. It was open all day six days a week for a month leading up to Christmas in 1983, and was manned by our youth group with help during school and college hours from other church members. All the profits made were then given to Tear Fund for relief work in the Third World.

In the years since then the idea behind the *Beggars Banquet* has achieved wider prominence through *Christmas Cracker*, which has developed the concept both nationally and internationally.

**Getting involved**

The *Beggars Banquet* was a very practical way of helping those in great need, but it also served several other functions. Not only did it give our young people a goal to work for but it was of great benefit to the whole town by helping them express their concern for the Third World at Christmas, a time of year when there is a great awareness that the western world has so much while others have very little or nothing. Lastly, it provided us with a way of telling the town that the church was actively involved in the relief of world suffering.

Rather than simply contributing towards Tear Fund's finances we wanted to give specifically to a project which we could take on ourselves. We were told that there was a project in Southern India to drill wells in some of the small villages that had been very badly hit by severe famine of over five years and that the cost of drilling one well was about £1000. Our youth group thought that we might be able to raise £1000 through the shop, and so we adopted a village and a well drilling project.

**Praying for a shop**

It was early in October when I originally talked through the idea with our youth group and asked them to pray about the provision of a suitable shop. Eventually, after several disappointments, we homed in on a disused bakers'. Ideally situated in a central position in the town, it was just the kind of thing we were looking for. I phoned the owners (see chapter 25) and briefly explained our project to their property manager, only to be informed that unfortunately they couldn't help because they had a long-standing policy not to let their empty shops out on a short-term basis. He explained that they had already turned down five charities who had made similar requests in the last month. While he was talking I began to think about Elijah calling down the fire on the mountain side and Moses parting the Red Sea: they could do all that and I couldn't even get a measly shop! So I knelt down there and then in my office while the man was still speaking on the phone, and silently prayed, 'Lord, you know that we need premises if this project is to go ahead, but that can only happen if you change this man's mind.' At that very moment the voice at the other end of the phone said, 'On the other hand...' and before I knew what was happening he was promising to do his best for me. By the following afternoon we had the keys to the shop and its use right up until Christmas Eve.

Besides our rather thin lentil soup, small chicken curry and a glass of water which had a minimum price of £1.80, we served several other more English meals, including potatoes in their jackets, beans on toast and chicken supreme. Many people would pay for a £2 meal with a £5 or £10 note and refuse the change. Others bought cups of coffee for £1 or more, while some popped in simply to make a donation before rushing off again. We were overwhelmed by the enthusiastic response. TVS filmed the restaurant and interviewed us about the concept behind it for their regional news programme, while national radio coverage meant that a number of cheques arrived for the project from distant parts. Cliff Richard was contacted, but couldn't come. Instead he sent an autographed photograph which was framed and then auctioned to the highest bidder, finally going for an astonishing £651! (The buyers were another youth group who ran a sponsored event to pay for it.) By the end of the first week we had already raised over £700, so we decided that rather than aim for £1000 and one drilling project, we'd go for £2000 and two wells! The final profit we were able to give Tear Fund totalled over £4000 with which they eventually drilled five wells in five different villages.

**How to serve your own 'Beggars Banquet' or Christmas Cracker**

(1) Find your premises and contact the necessary parties (see chapter 25). Remember that, as your shop front is your best publicity, it's no good getting premises in some backstreet where no one ever goes.

(2) Contact Tear Fund or some other Christian relief agency and sort out what kind of scheme you are going to support. Remember that people are more likely to give to a specific cause than to the general kitty!

(3) Set a financial target just beyond that which you think is attainable. You now have a challenge on your hands.

(4) When you've got your shop, appoint from your youth group a:

(a) General manager
(b) Chef
(c) Kitchen team
(d) Head waiter
(e) Waitress team
(f) Accountant/cashier
(g) Publicity/press secretary
(h) Maintenance and decoration crew

(5) Now together start work at obtaining the following items:

(a) Paint
(b) Carpet
(c) Lighting
(d) Tables
(e) Chairs
(f) Cutlery
(g) Crockery
(h) Cooking utensils
(i) Cookers (we used old ones run by calor gas and borrowed from the Boys Brigade)
(j) Fridge
(k) Freezer
(l) Microwave oven
(m) Cash desk and accounts book
(n) Heating – we used fan heaters
(o) Washing-up liquid and tea towels
(p) Serviettes and trays

*Notes*

*Decoration* – people don't like eating in shabby conditions (and in any case you will have to meet health regulations). You may need to paint your premises (it's amazing what a couple of cans of emulsion can do). With some old carpet, a few plants, a bit of lighting you can have the place looking quite inviting! The *Beggars Banquet* took a week to clean and decorate before we could open the doors to the public.

*Cooking equipment* – for quick service you must be well equipped.

(6) Menu – you're not the Ritz! Be practical. Don't offer food that you can't produce quickly. Do you have a local Cash and Carry card?

(7) Publicity – personally visit your local paper. This is a front page story and they want the news as much as you need the publicity. Don't be intimidated by the mystique of the media!

(8) Put a prayer and news sheet out to all the local churches, which will not only inform them but encourage their active support.

Don't be put off by this massive list. Much of the equipment we used was donated or lent free of charge by local businesses. Local traders will want to help and just need to be approached. We had enormous help from so many people and shops in the area. All kinds of things were donated, from cash registers and microwave ovens, to fridges, paint and even dining tables and chairs. When we got permission to use the shop I was given a gift of £50 to help set it up and when we opened I still had £5 left in my pocket!

# 27
# RADIO CHRISTMAS

Following the success of running 'Eat Less, Pay More' restaurants on a national scale, the Christmas Cracker Trust has launched a brand new fund raising, youth orientated project. Throughout the month of December 1991 just over ninety 'Tune In, Pay Out' stations situated throughout Great Britain broadcast high energy FM radio to their local communities. But, once again the idea started life in Tonbridge with our local youth group. Radio Cracker's national project has been developed from what we originally called Radio Christmas. So if you want to broadcast on FM to your whole town – that's schools, shops, homes, offices, cars, factories etc, register for this year's Radio Cracker (address at the end of checklist 27) and we will give you all the advice and help you need to get launched. On the other hand, if you want to be part of this kind of Radio project without having to get a licence to transmit keep reading!

I have set out two versions here, first the project in its original form as we ran it in Tonbridge, and then a much simpler idea for running the same kind of scheme on a smaller scale.

**Radio Christmas – version one**

In July 1984 I was asked by Invicta Radio (Kent's commercial radio station) to present a weekly Sunday morning show. This helped me to see the opportunities that broadcasting presents to the church, and also gave me some insights into the practical aspects of producing and presenting radio. So was born the idea of Radio Christmas, a radio station which would broadcast for a month leading up to Christmas Eve and focus on the same principles as the *Beggars Banquet* (described in chapter 26) had done the year before.

*Getting started*

We negotiated with the Home Office regarding the possibility of obtaining a 'Community Radio' licence to broadcast around the town on medium wave or FM, though it soon became clear that any form of broadcasting would be illegal and therefore a non starter (the law has changed since then). Not wanting to give up, we hit on the idea of setting up a studio in the town centre which would actually cable a signal up and down both sides of the High Street and into each shop. Because we were not broadcasting we knew that this scheme would not require a licence. Shoppers who heard Radio Christmas as they wandered in and out of the shops in the town centre and as they passed our studio, would have the opportunity to pop in and leave a donation for relief work in the Third World (we had already decided to support a project which had been set up by World Vision to work among children at a feeding station in Southern Ethiopia). At the studio they would also be able to make a record request or dedication for a friend or for those working in a particular shop or simply just wish the whole of Tonbridge a happy Christmas.

*Cabling the High Street*

In effect our plan was to run one huge public address system around the town centre, sending a signal through an ordinary two core cable up one side of the High Street (which is about half a mile long) across the road and then down the other. We planned to run the cable along the shop faces, just above their name boards, and then when a particular shop wanted to be fed our signal we would tap into the line, run a cable through a window or other opening and down into the store. By fitting a five pin DIN plug or a phono socket to the end and connecting it up to their hi-fi or other sound gear the shop could then receive our programming through their ordinary equipment. This meant we didn't have to provide speakers and that we only had to supply the signal at line level. Our signal was then amplified by each individual shop. This gave the shop complete control not only of the volume but also of the on/off switch.

The big problem was getting hold of enough cable and then installing it. In all we needed about one and a half miles of cable which I estimated could cost as much as £1000 to buy. We prayed about this little problem and then approached several national cable making companies, whose names I found in the *Yellow Pages*, with the result that eventually one agreed to supply all we needed completely free of charge. A local store agreed to provide all the DIN plugs and phono sockets we required on the same basis. We employed a team of three young men who had previously been involved with running the radio station for Greenbelt to work in Tonbridge for a week installing the cable, tapping off points down into the individual shops, and connecting the stereos. In the end, as well as cabling the entire High Street we were able, with the help of British Telecom (who gave us free use of several land lines under the town's river and railways), to 'wire up' the local leisure centre and the two biggest supermarkets in the town which were situated elsewhere.

### *Running repairs*

A major problem we faced was that because we were running one huge public address system which linked the whole of Tonbridge High Street, any break or short in the cable had a rather drastic effect on the reception in many of the shops. On one day almost half of the shops were unable to receive any signal at all for almost three hours, during which time we frantically searched almost every inch of the cable up and down the High Street, only to discover eventually that the broken cable was in the studio where the girl serving coffee to the DJs had trodden on it with her stiletto heel! There was one other difficult day when again reception totally disappeared all down one side of the High Street. A search eventually revealed that where our cable ran along the front of a building site (a new shopping arcade was in the process of being erected) an unknowingconstruction worker had authorised the pouring of about three tons of concrete on top of it. It was completely severed! We found that we always needed to have at least one engineer on duty.

*Building up a record library*

Another local store sponsored the project by donating the top thirty each week, along with a generous supply of other Christmas records. We also wrote to the big record companies informing them about what we were doing with the result that we obtained from some of them free copies of LPs and singles which they were promoting. In this way we built up an adequate record library which was supplemented with 'Golden Oldies' given by members of the youth group and records that those who worked as DJs brought in with them for their own shows. We contacted the Performing Rights Society who gave us an exemption certificate on the payment of royalties for the records we played.

*Wiring up the shops*

We now had to obtain the support of the local shop owners as well as their willingness to participate in the scheme. To do this we first visited a meeting of the local Chamber of Trade and obtained their backing, which gave us credibility as we approached individual shopkeepers. The Chamber circulated a letter to all their members and we then visited every shop in the

High Street to introduce further the concept of Radio Christmas. We spent a lot of time explaining to owners and managers how they could be involved by allowing it to play on their premises. Whether or not a shop wished to take our signal it was important that we gain permission from the owner to run our main cable along the front of his premises. In the end well over half of the shops in Tonbridge High Street who were able to receive our signal participated in the scheme while a fair percentage of those who did not were only left out because they did not possess the necessary stereo equipment to be wired in! Throughout the project we had a waiting list of shops wanting to come on to our network.

We negotiated with the town council regarding the cable which we were proposing running against the shops up each side of the High Street and which also had to run across many side streets. They gave us permission to do this but stipulated that where we crossed a street we must provide adequate clearance (twenty feet) for articulated lorries and buses.

*Manning the studio*

We set up our studio in the front of the local United Reformed Church which, besides being ideally placed right in the centre of the High Street, is also a very attractive modern building with a glass front. This meant that the studio was very visible to the whole community and that the station was brought into the heart of the shopping area.

Our DJs were all members of the youth group at Tonbridge Baptist Church or ministers of local churches. I gave them all a crash course in how to operate the studio desk, although some presenters preferred to have an assistant to do this for them rather than 'self-op'. We also arranged for local celebrities to visit the studio, to be interviewed and record a Christmas greeting for the town which we could then play as a kind of 'jingle' from time to time. Through our contact with a local hospital radio station we also obtained a set of Christmas jingles.

As the DJs introduced records or talked about discs they

would, from time to time, chat about the meaning of Christmas or their own Christian commitment. We also advertised all that was going on in the churches over the Christmas period and had in the studio a good supply of free leaflets which gave details of events and explained what Christmas was really about and how to become a Christian.

*The Radio Christmas Schools Cassette*

We visited all of the local primary and junior schools as well as a few senior schools and recorded their choirs singing Christmas carols. Besides playing these on the air, we produced a tape for £2.50, of which we sold several hundred copies. The cost of production was just under £1 so that £1.50 went to the Ethiopian famine relief fund. For this it was necessary to contact the Performing Rights Society, supply them with the names of the authors and arrangers of the pieces of music we used.

Because we had already been granted exemption from royalties on the project we did not have to make any payment to them with regard to the production of the cassette.

*Jesus on the air waves*

We negotiated with Radio Kent (the BBC station, Invicta's rival!) who agreed to do a three hour 'outside broadcast' from Tonbridge to launch the project. This got us off to a promising start and gave us some great publicity. The station was on the air for four complete weeks leading up to Christmas Eve. We broadcast from Monday to Saturday and from 9 am to 8 pm each evening (because several of the larger shops were open until that time). We obtained the interest of local newspapers and radio as well as regional television. TVS gave us considerable air time on their six o'clock show *Coast to Coast* which follows the national news.

The four weeks spent operating Radio Christmas were very hard work indeed, but the impact on the town and surrounding towns was quite tremendous. By Christmas Eve we had raised almost £7000 for relief work in Ethiopia and successfully united the whole town in an effort to give to others. We had also shown the whole community that the church was alive and actively involved in meeting the needs of the Third World. On top of all this, Radio Christmas gave us the opportunity to present the gospel to all sorts of people who would never otherwise hear it. Several who are now mature Christians were converted during the project or as a direct result of it.

**Radio Christmas – version two**

Radio Christmas was a technically complicated and time-consuming project both to set up and run. There will be those who are drawn to the idea of running their own radio station who are intimidated by the work load involved in setting up and maintaining such a project. An exciting and simpler alternative (one that I would like to try some time) is to negotiate with a large department store in your town and then set up a station inside it. All the management need to do is give you a few feet of floor space in a corner somewhere to run your studio, and allow you to tap into their existing public address system from your mixing desk. This will then carry your signal around the store providing good Christmas music, instead of the usual muzak. Because of local press publicity, much attention and custom will be attracted to the store (two commodities which more than compensate the management for the inconvenience of having the studio on their floor space!).

Obviously, this scheme is far easier to organise than a townwide project. The only cable needed is that which connects with the shop's internal public address system; there are no negotiations with Council, British Telecom or the Chamber of Trade; nor do you have to find an empty shop or conveniently placed church building. So try Version Two this Christmas and Version One next year!

**Resources needed**

*Personnel*

(a) DJs (we operated a system with two- and three-hour shows)
(b) Tea makers (we served tea and coffee to those who popped into the studio)
(c) Receptionists (to take requests, sort out records and handle the donations)
(d) Technical staff (essential that at least one is always on duty!)

*Equipment*

(a) Studio
(b) Mixing desk (at least six channels)
(c) Microphones and microphone stands (two or three)
(d) Two record decks
(e) One cassette deck
(f) One or two CD players
(g) One reel to reel machine (helpful but not essential)
(h) Compressor (this stops too much variation in the sound level output)
(i) One accurate clock with second hand
(j) Records and tapes
(k) Jingles (again not essential)
(l) One and a half miles of cable!* (you will have to do your own measurements)
(m) Ample supply of DIN and phono sockets/plugs*
(n) Cable joining blocks* (used for running off the cable into each shop)
(o) Amplifier to act as line driver*
(p) Small amplifier and speaker to act as a studio monitor system and run a couple of speakers outside for passers-by.

* These items are only applicable to Radio Christmas version one.

# 28
# VIDEO SHOW

What have *Top of the Pops*, Breakfast TV and *Wogan* all got in common?...Give up? They, like all other television programmes, make use of fast-changing images to hold the viewer's attention. If television holds the same camera shot for thirty seconds, that is considered a very long time! Also on each of the programmes we have just mentioned no one item would normally last for more than a few minutes. Surely there is a lesson here for the church to learn about evangelism and communication in the television age?

Early in 1984, the old bus garage in Tonbridge became disused. I enquired about its availability for short-term use for a nightly youth event and though at first I was turned away, finally (some nine months of consistent campaigning later) permission was given for this purpose. At about the same time I had an interesting lunch with Steve Goddard and Tony Cummings of what used to be *Buzz* magazine where, over their egg and chips, they explained an idea for using videos on a large screen as an evangelistic tool among teenagers. Later as I drove home along the M25 I suddenly realised that the bus garage was a perfect venue for using videos in an evangelistic presentation and would give me an ideal opportunity to try out my ideas about communication. I felt that by using pre-recorded videos of Christian bands on a large screen, as well as live music, interviews and drama it should be possible to present an audience with the same kind of fast-moving menu that television offers. So was born the idea of the Bus Company Video Show.

**The content of the show**

The show eventually ran each night for a week from 7.30 to 10.00 pm. A typical show began with the venue in darkness and then as the lights came up there was a welcome from the presenter who introduced the first music video on the big screen. The lights blacked out and the video played until, during the last frames, it faded and the lights came up again. Then the presenter announced the guest band for the evening who performed two songs with lyrics and chat that fitted into the evening's theme. Two video camera operators picked out shots of the band which were beamed up onto the screen. As the band left the stage it was instantly blacked out and once more a video was projected. At the end of this, lights came up on a second stage where a drama sketch was performed. The presenter briefly chatted about the sketch, reinforcing its message. Next came the opportunity for the audience to participate as three teenagers came up on stage for 'Video Box' (their chance to comment on video clips from current chart songs and contemporary Christian material). This was followed by a couple of songs from the resident band, Tony Clay and the Ambassadors, who had spent the previous week working in the local schools advertising the show. Tony chatted and introduced the audience to a local Christian policeman (known to many of the teenagers present) and talked with him about his faith. This was followed by another video which played into a fifteen minute break (for people to get drinks, look at books and LPs and to visit the loo).

The second half of the programme followed in the same kind of style as the first, slowly expanding and explaining the message already introduced. Finally, at the end of the evening, the gospel was preached and people invited to respond to Christ.

Each video used in the Video Show was carefully chosen to play a part in the clear presentation of the gospel, though this did not mean that all the videos used were made by Christian artists. Secular artists with whom those present would be familiar and could readily relate were featured each evening. For instance, on one evening we showed a video of 'Wide Boy', a song by Nik Kershaw that had recently been in the charts. The song and video depict a young man who becomes a famous pop star but whose life is empty and leads to loneliness and depression. This song related superbly to our theme for that night: 'Is there life before death?' One young person commented, 'It was like getting the news straight from the horse's mouth.'

We decided that we would run our own free bus service to and from the show each evening for teenagers who came from surrounding villages. To this end we managed to obtain the free use of several double deckers, one of which was kindly supplied by the local bus company along with its own driver and conductor! Each evening this bus made a run through several villages in Tonbridge while another single decker did exactly the same on the other side of town. After the show, both did a return journey. We had four other double deckers permanently parked in the garage to form a back drop for the stage, and these doubled up as dressing rooms and a base for a team of people in their early twenties whose job it was to provide security each night by living on the premises.

The show had a great impact on the town and by the end of the week we were running lunch-time presentations as well as the evening ones. By the end of the week lunch-time audiences were numbering about three to four hundred, with evening attendances as high as nine hundred. In fact, on the last evening we gave admission to nine hundred and turned away about two hundred people! We estimate that about half of each evening's audience were already on the periphery of church youth groups while the other half had no Christian connection whatsoever and had been attracted by publicity in schools during the previous week and the free bus service! Several hundred teenagers were counselled during the course of the week, of whom about a hundred and twenty were actual conversions. About 50% were known to be still in the local churches after one year.

We produced a press release which was distributed to the Christian and secular market. As a result of becoming front page headlines in the local paper plus one or two phone calls, we were able to get good television coverage by TVS on their six o'clock news show *Coast to Coast*.

**Why use the video show?**

Using this Video Show format for evangelism among teenagers has several benefits:

(1) The show is fast-moving and so the audience does not get easily bored. Even if they don't like a particular element in the programme, they know that this image will soon pass and the next element of the programme will be different and exciting.

(2) There are many amateur local Christian bands, singers and drama groups who while being able to perform perhaps three or four items very well during the course of an evening, are overstretched when asked to present a whole concert. The video show format offers them the opportunity of performing and learning without pushing them beyond their capabilities.

(3) It gives the opportunity to develop a particular theme and to make sure that all the items reinforce the same message. Through the evening a foundation can be laid and slowly built on, block by block, to the point where, after a 'preach' which ties all the ends together, a response can be called for on the basis of more than the emotion of a particular moment.

(4) Whereas a traditional schools mission may include one or

two evening concerts at the end of the week, through the use of the Video Show a whole series of evangelistic presentations can be put on. Because teenagers have the opportunity to come back night after night they are able to hear, go away, think, chat with friends, ask questions and return again and again before finally making a well thought through decision to follow Christ.

**How to plan your own Video Show**

Since the Bus Company Video Show I have been involved in similar presentations at Greenbelt and Spring Harvest, and also in the development of a travelling version as part of my work in schools, colleges and churches around the country. As well as this, a number of youth leaders and ministers in this country and abroad have enquired about setting up similar shows as part of their outreach. One or two churches have been in a position to purchase the necessary equipment but many others have been able to hire and borrow it to make their own local video show a possibility. Below is a checklist that should enable you to do the same.

*(1) Resources needed*

(a) Venue
(b) PA system
(c) Lighting
(d) Video projector, screen and mixer
(e) Video recorder
(f) Two cameras
(g) Supply of videos
(h) Staging
(i) Seating
(j) Publicity

*(2) Personnel*

(a) Drama groups
(b) Bands/solo performers
(c) Interviewees
(d) Presenters
(e) Administrator
(f) Publicity agent
(g) Prayer secretary
(h) Stage manager
(i) Stewards
(j) Counsellors

(k) Sound man
(l) Lighting operator
(m) Video operator
(n) Two camera men

*(3) Follow-up*

Planning for follow-up must be done well in advance of the event itself and firm plans laid that can swing into action from the time the first convert is won. (This subject is dealt with in chapter 22.)

# 29
# INTER-CHURCH ACTIVITY

'Streetbeat', 'The Bus Company Video Show' and 'Radio Christmas' were all projects which were originally undertaken on a townwide basis in Tonbridge and involved a group of seven churches working together. All of the other projects mentioned in this book were planned and organised by Tonbridge Baptist Church. Working on an inter-denominational basis is more difficult than working alone, so why do it?

**Reasons for inter-church activity**

It's good to get involved with the churches in your town for a number of reasons:

(1) Involvement of this kind demonstrates that the church is one. We spend a lot of time painstakingly attempting to teach this principle to young people, whereas it is often very obvious that there is little real evidence to suggest it is true. To spend time working together, learning together and getting to know each other is of the greatest value to all involved. It also becomes a visible expression to the community that the churches are one. One of the greatest of the stumbling blocks which prevent people of all ages becoming

Christians is undoubtedly the problem of knowing which denomination is the true church. Only by working together can we convince others that we are one.

(2) Working together with other denominations and groups will open the eyes of your own young people to new ideas and increase their vision and concept of the church as a whole. It is too easy for them to grow up within one denominational structure, unaware that God is at work beyond their local fellowship and even their denomination. It is obviously good for our teenagers to see how other Christians work and think.

(3) By giving our young people the opportunity of meeting other Christians from across the town we help them to understand that they belong to something big, which is a very practical way of encouraging them to live for Christ at school. It is great for them to see that there are teenagers from each of the schools right across the town who share a common faith with them.

(4) Inter-denominational activity enables teenage boys to meet teenage girls and vice versa! This may sound rather unspiritual but, in reality, one of the biggest problems for many young people in our churches is that they do not have the opportunity to meet Christians of the opposite sex – or at least, suitable members of it! Many eventually become romantically involved with non-Christians and as a result often drift away from a living walk with Christ.

(5) By working together you can often plan projects on a larger scale, because you will obviously have greater resources at your disposal and be in a position to call on more support. When it comes to evangelism this means that it is possible to make a bigger impact on your town or area.

**How to go about it**

If you want to work together with other youth groups in your town, here are some practical steps to take:

(1) Write a letter to the other church youth leaders in your town explaining to them what you want to do and why. A week later, phone round them all and find out how they feel about this. If they are in favour, you are in business.

(2) Arrange a meeting. This is easiest to achieve by phone, though even then it can prove quite difficult. The best way of approaching it is to suggest a number of dates to each person you ring, asking them to indicate which ones would be most convenient. You will probably be able to draw together at least one date when the majority, if not all, of those involved can be present.

(3) At this first meeting your task is to consider carefully and then clarify the group's aims. You may think such matters are so obvious that it is not worth spending time discussing them. In Tonbridge an inter-church youth association had existed for many years and once a year they arranged a barn dance and a sports day. Nobody quite knew why these particular events were organised or why nothing else ever happened, but as I became involved with the group the answer was actually quite clear – it was simply not the stated aim to do anything else. The group had no clear, written purpose to guide their thinking and so down through the years they had become nothing more than a barn dance committee.

(4) Contact the council of churches or the ministers' fraternal. It is very important to talk to them at this stage. Explain to them your vision and aims and obtain their advice and support.

(5) Having got this far, some kind of leadership structure must be set up before you move on to the next stage of working out a strategy and planning particular projects. Your group will only ever be as good as its leadership. You need to appoint a chairman, a secretary and a treasurer with the time, energy and vision for the job. It's no good choosing

the most gifted Christian person in town if he is already over-committed to other things. Also, remember that although these are the three most important appointments, everyone who serves on the committee needs to be in a position to take on responsibility.

(6) Now get on with the job, remembering to involve as many as possible of the young people themselves in real responsibility. Your planning group should meet on a monthly basis for business, and if possible on a separate occasion for prayer.

(7) You may decide that you want to explore the possibility of becoming a Youth For Christ centre or of affiliating to some other national youth organisation. The great value of this course of action is the invaluable external support and objective advice based on a wealth of experience gained over the years that such an organisation can offer. In Tonbridge we chose to become a Youth For Christ centre because of their great emphasis on, and experience in, evangelism. If you are interested in such a course of action, contact those concerned who would be glad to send a representative to discuss the possibility further. The address of British Youth For Christ is given at the back of this book and more information can be obtained from their headquarters.

# 30
# HOW TO USE THE MEDIA

'The local press are never interested in what we do at all. In fact we think that they are probably biased against the church and Christian events.' Many Christians adopt this view because at one time or another they informed the press about what they were doing and got little or no response. Now they feel it's just not worth the effort of trying to get coverage for their events. Even when it comes to the Christian press or the Christian Sunday morning slot on the local radio, there is still the feeling, 'They won't be interested...we're just not big enough news.' Having worked as a presenter for a local radio station and also been involved with other media, I've discovered that nothing could be further from the truth!

Below are three principles that it is important to grasp concerning the media:

(1) All media are continually searching for good news material; it is their life-blood. Added to this, at a local level there are several interesting developments. Generally speaking the readership of local newspapers is falling and in an attempt to halt this slide most publishers are increasingly aware that their papers must develop good public relations. When it

comes to local radio, again the management are very keen to reflect what is happening throughout the community. If you are running something newsworthy, they are missing out on an opportunity if they do not report it. They need your news as much as you need their interest! This is especially true in the many areas of the country where there are now two local stations, one BBC and the other IBA (Independent Broadcasting Authority), where a rivalry develops in the attempt to attract the bigger audience. As a result they are very keen to know and report on what is going on in the community. The Christian press are also keen to know what you are doing. When we ran 'Streetbeat' in Tonbridge (described in chapter 27) we did not bother to issue a press release because of the hurried nature of the project. Some months later the editor of a weekly Christian newspaper gave me a telling off, pointing out that I had a responsibility to him and others in his position to keep them informed! I have since had this message reinforced by several others.

(2) All 'media people' are very busy with tight schedules and deadlines so the time and effort they can give to this quest is limited. We often imagine that local papers and radio stations and the Christian press operate with a huge staff waiting to pounce on each and every relevant story that breaks. This is not true! Every local paper, local radio station, Christian magazine or denominational newspaper that I know of is run by a small, highly committed staff who work as hard and fast as they possibly can to meet their deadlines and simply do not have the time to hunt for material. While presenting a Sunday morning show for local radio, I was for ever longing that local Christians would write in informing me of what they are doing but this very rarely happened, although I sometimes got complaints that I should be giving more coverage to what they were doing! It was somehow expected that I would miraculously know what was going on across the country and approach them. Unfortunately, I had no means of knowing this at all, except what I could

read in the local papers or the Christian press or stumble upon during my travels! As I was also working as assistant pastor of a church with a congregation of over four hundred, a time-consuming task in itself, I did not have the time or energy to do much hunting. Although there are about a hundred local radio stations in this country, I only know of two or three that have a full-time religious producer or presenter.

(3) All 'media people' are continually bombarded with badly presented information and publicity for almost every sort of event imaginable, and simply don't have the time to work their way carefully through it all. Therefore, any material that you present must stand out from the crowd.

**How to prepare and use a press release**

In some situations adverts are well worth taking out but the best coverage always comes free, when a newspaper or magazine writes up your event in its editorial space. So exactly how do you get the local and even national media to cover your event? Though there is no watertight answer to this question, and nothing you do can ever guarantee coverage, a good press release can be a most effective tool.

*What is a press release?*

A press release should give the facts about your event in a snappy and exciting manner, using short phrases, sentences and paragraphs, and with clear headings for easy scanning. The first paragraph should contain the most significant news (in case someone reads no further!) and should be presented in a way that will capture attention. People will pay attention to something that is humorous, heart-warming or out of the ordinary, so let this be your first sentence.

The press release should be typed with double spacing on one side only of A4 paper, with at least a two inch margin down one side. At the bottom put the day-time telephone number of at least one person from whom further information can be obtained by a reporter.

*How to use a press release*

1. Look through the *Yellow Pages* to obtain the addresses and telephone numbers of local newspapers and radio stations. Any numbers you cannot find can be obtained from Directory Enquiries.

2. Ring all these contact numbers. Very briefly explain your story to the receptionist and ask who you should contact about it. Make sure to have a pencil and pad ready to write down their name and position. If you don't have the address of some of these contacts, make sure you get that too as personally addressed mail is far more likely to be dealt with.

   For those with plenty of money, Pimms of 4 St John's Place, St John's Square, London EC1 4AH publish a monthly media directory covering everything from radio and television to the national, local specialist and Christian press. The directory has a listing of every news publication of any sort produced in Great Britain, including the names of sub-editors for the national press (and those responsible for church news). It lists every radio and television programme both nationally and regionally and gives the name of the appropriate producer, as well as the address at which to contact him, along with a telephone number. Those without the money and wishing to look at this directory should try the reference section of their nearest main library.

3. Two or three weeks before your event, post your press release to the people whose names you've been given. As you continue to put on events you will slowly build up your own contact list. Record names, telephone numbers and addresses in a notebook. These contacts will gradually come to trust and respect you, knowing that if you are involved in an event it is worth covering because it will be well organised.

4. Very many press releases arrive on the desk of editors and producers so make sure your press release is followed up with a phone call several days later.

5. Don't give up. None of this will guarantee success, and even if you do get a story in a local paper or the national press, you may sometimes be disappointed with the finished product. While I worked with the youth group in Tonbridge, though we had many stories which had good coverage locally and some which were covered nationally by newspapers as well as radio and television, we also had more failures at this level than I can remember! In fact, there may be no apparent objective reason why one story is taken and another ignored. Just keep on going.

# Part Five

# PANIC!

# 31
# IDEAS FOR USE IN EMERGENCY

Nothing can take the place of a well-planned, well-prepared programme for your youth group. However, we all know that occasionally things go wrong and you are faced with coping single-handed and no time to prepare. Here are a few ideas that will help you rise to the occasion.

**Black, white or grey**

This requires no preparation beforehand, other than having a pen and a slip of paper for each group member, and a plastic bucket, or some other container, available.

Give each group member a piece of paper and a pen. Ask them to write down a question about anything they find hard to deal with or difficult to understand about Christianity or the Bible: 'Can a Christian go out with a non-Christian?' 'Can someone who once made a commitment to Christ backslide and then go to hell?' Give everyone a few minutes to think about the issues they want to raise, then ask them to fold their slips of paper with their questions on and place them in the bucket.

Now ask everyone to form a straight line down the middle of

the room. Explain that one side of the room has been designated 'black and white' (ie the issue is perfectly straightforward), and the other side has been designated 'grey' (ie the issue is not clear).

Pull a question out of the bucket and then read it out. Ask everyone to move to the side of the room which represents the way they view the question. When they have done this, invite them to comment on why they see the issues as they do. Allow the discussion to develop, with group members questioning each other about the stances they have taken up. Things get very interesting, especially when sometimes those on the 'black and white' side of the room realise that they are there for opposing reasons.

Repeat the process for each question until they have all been dealt with or you have run out of time.

**Double Your Money – a fundraising idea**

Tell your youth group that you are going to give each member two pounds, but point out that there is one very important condition attached. Each member has exactly seven days in which to multiply the money as many times as possible, with all profits going to your designated charity or project. Everyone has complete freedom as to how they go about their task, as long as their plan is completely honest and morally upright! A good time to do this would be the half term holiday.

The leaders of one group that did this were amazed at the response. Not only did the young people take up the idea, but some of the projects and results they came up with were highly creative. One member invested his money in a sponge and some detergent and spent a day washing cars. A few young people clubbed together, bought cake ingredients, spent the morning baking and the afternoon selling their produce at great profit to neighbours and friends. They then reinvested their earnings and started again, but this time on a bigger scale! One member organised a custard pie throwing competition where he featured as the target!

Perhaps your youth group could come up with some even more imaginative ideas. It gives the parable of the talents a whole new meaning.

**Unhappy Families**

Divide your group into four equal parts. Set your meeting room out in four triangular areas with four chairs closely facing each other (as shown in the diagram).

1 2 3 4

Each group will take on a character in a role play. Give them information about their character (see below). *Don't allow the groups to see the details of another character.*

Once the role play starts, anyone in a group can speak on behalf of their character on condition that they are sitting on the chair at the head of the triangle at the time. If someone wants to speak they must tap the shoulder of the person in the chair, who must give it up immediately. The game starts when the team that plays Beth rings the door bell.

Allow the role play conversation to develop naturally for about fifteen minutes. Spend the next thirty minutes talking through what happened. This is the time when most learning will take place. Let the young people talk openly and honestly over the way they felt about their role, the way other people in their group spoke, and about the other characters in the situation.

If discussion is slow in getting started, you can encourage and direct it by asking questions such as:

- What did you think of Beth's behaviour?
- Are Beth's parents justified in their attitude?
- Did Kate help Beth or make things worse?
- How can better relationships be built?
- Did the youth leader help or hinder?
- How many of you have been in a similar situation to Beth? How did you feel?
- Has the Bible got anything helpful to say about this?

As the youth group talk, make notes of what they say and your observations about their attitudes – you will then be able to feed these back in at a later stage. Conclude the evening by looking at the biblical principles relating to family life.

*Character 1* – YOUTH LEADER

Your church youth group meets each Wednesday evening, and Beth (aged fifteen) is an occasional attender. When she does come she is difficult to get on with, but you are keen for her to feel welcome and involved. Her older sister Kate (aged seventeen), a regular member, has told you that Beth hasn't been getting on too well at home. You decide to pop round and see Beth. As you arrive you meet her on the doorstep...

*Character 2* – PARENT

You think you are a good, keen Christian parent. You have two teenage daughters – Kate, seventeen, and Beth, fifteen. Kate has always been a sensible, reliable and responsible girl, but Beth is a rebel whom you find difficult to handle. She is disobedient, irresponsible and impossible to communicate with. She arrives home late, wears outrageous clothes and mixes with bad company, especially boys. Three days ago you had a huge argument when she arrived home late yet again. As a result Beth stormed out and ran away from home. You've informed the local police. You still haven't heard anything when suddenly the door bell rings...

*Character 3* – KATE

Aged seventeen and the older of two teenage sisters, you are responsible and respectful of your parents, unlike your younger sister Beth (aged fifteen). This annoys you, especially as her unreasonableness often seems to earn her privileges you never had. You sometimes feel sorry for her because your parents tend to expect her to be a carbon copy of you. You think she's irresponsible because they treat her like a child. The other night your parents and Beth had a huge row, and as a result she ran away. It's been quiet without her around, but now you're getting very worried about her safety. Your parents have informed the police of her disappearance. The door bell rings...

*Character 4* – BETH

You are fifteen years old, love your parents but wonder if they love you. They seem to be continually arguing with you. You can never do anything right in their eyes. Your older sister Kate (aged seventeen) seems to be their favourite. She never does anything wrong in their view. Your parents treat you like a ten-year-old. For instance, they make you come home long before your friends are expected to be in at night, and they always insist on knowing where you are and who you are with. They just don't trust you. They don't like your hair, your choice of clothes, and they disapprove of most of your friends, especially the boys.

A few days ago you arrived home fifteen minutes late, and as a result got into the biggest row you've ever had with them. You packed a bag, ran away, and have been staying with a friend you met at a disco a few weeks ago whom your parents don't know about. After three days without making any contact you decide to give things another chance and return home. You ring the doorbell...

**Newsnight**

How many times have you introduced a time of open prayer with your youth group by explaining nervously, 'I'll start and leave you to pray aloud as God leads...' only to be faced with that almost inevitable very long period of utter silence. And the truth is that although you would like to convince yourself that the quietness indicates your group have chosen to wrestle silently in prayer, you have the distinct feeling that there are other less holy explanations for what you can't hear! After five minutes of painful silence, your nerve finally cracks and you round things off with a closing prayer by thanking God that he has heard the silent requests and longings of the group!

Try using the following idea to breathe new life and energy into your youth group's prayer life.

On the night of your youth meeting record the evening news, either from television on to video tape, or from a radio station on to an audio cassette.

As part of the meeting play the tape or video back to your group. After each item of news, switch off and get everyone to spend a few minutes talking, then praying about the issues raised and the people involved.

Ring the changes by varying the way in which you do this. For the first item get the whole group praying together; for the next get them to break into small groups to pray; for the next item get everyone to pray silently on their own for two minutes, and so on. Pray for all those involved in or affected by each news item, and remember to give thanks to God for any good news! (When you get to the football, rugby or cricket results, this will test everyone's inventiveness!)

It's highly likely that at least one item in the news could form the basis of a major discussion for the evening which allows you to look at an important contemporary issue in the light of the Bible's teaching.

**Lights, Camera, Action**

Get your youth group to read through the story of the Good Samaritan in Luke 10:25–37. Now cast members of the group as the characters in the story and get them to act it out without any rehearsal. Be sure not to force anyone into a rule unwillingly.

After the presentation the cast stay in character while the other members of the group interview them about the story, the way they behaved, the attitudes they took and their reasons for doing so. Group members may choose to disagree and argue with the attitudes taken by the cast who then have to defend their actions and viewpoints.

Not only does the evening provide loads of fun, but as the conversation gets going you create a relaxed and open learning environment where even you are likely to be surprised by the depth of some of the insight and understanding about what Jesus was teaching.

On other occasions you might try *Lights, Camera, Action* with another parable or a story from the Old or New Testament. Don't overdo it, but once in a while this interactive learning method really does get the brain cells going!

**Scrabble**

This one is great for helping familiarise your group with the books of the Bible. Divide the young people into teams of two or three and give them this brain-teasing crowdbreaker to tackle. You may choose to allow them to use Bibles to give them a bit of help. You could also make up your own using books from the Old Testament.

*Instructions* Rearrange the following sets of letters to spell books from the New Testament. (Example: KEUL = LUKE.)

| | | |
|---|---|---|
| KEUL | HILANOSNASSET | ACILNOOSSS |
| AALSGTINA | ACHINNORSTI | LIAHIPPPSIN |
| AEEILNORTV | CTSA | EHILMNOP |

| | | |
|---|---|---|
| ANORMS | TREEP | UITTS |
| AEJMS | SHNESPIAE | BEHRSWE |
| KAMR | YITMHTO | TAEHTMW |
| DEJU | HJNO | |

Answers: Luke, Galatians, Revelation, Romans, James, Mark, Jude, Thessalonians, Corinthians, Acts, Peter, Ephesians, Timothy, John, Colossians, Philippians, Philemon, Titus, Hebrews, Matthew)

**Into the Unknown**

For this you will need a box, six pens and two pads of paper. Label the box 'Everything you always wanted to know but never dared ask!' Start the evening by encouraging your group to think of questions about issues that worry, confuse or concern them. Tell them that there will be an opportunity to put them anonymously into the box and that later in the evening you are going to take an honest, down-to-earth look at the issues raised.

Follow your introduction with another activity and a coffee break to allow group members to think of, write out and place questions in the box. It is best if you leave the room during the break to allow group members to think freely. Take the questions out one by one and let the group talk the issues through, trying to apply what the Bible has to say. End each question by summing things up.

If you are ever looking for a time filler on a future occasion, use one or two of the questions you didn't manage to get through on the original evening.

**Oscar, Oscar**

Instead of watching a video with your youth group, why don't you make one? It will probably be possible for you to borrow a camcorder for the evening. Split the group into two, and tell each group that they have thirty minutes to prepare a video, and fifteen minutes to record it. Give them three objects which must be included somewhere, and a Bible verse which must be used at the end to sum it all up.

For example, give one group a ladle, a hat and a fluffy toy duck, and set them the verse from Ecclesiastes 10:18: 'If any man is lazy, his rafters shall sag.' The other group could have a boot, a spider plant and a colander, with the Bible verse from Matthew 5:40: 'If any man asks for your coat, give him your cloak as well.'

End the evening by sitting everyone down to watch through both videos and comment. Once people start using their imagination this can be great fun, and everyone can get involved, acting, filming or directing.

*Variations*

- If your group is on the small side, get them all working together
- Run over two weeks – planning the first week and filming the second week
- Try filming on location at the local park or the shops
- Invite church members to stay to lunch one Sunday and show them what you have achieved (if you think they could cope!).
- Use your video in house groups as a discussion starter.

### The Name of the Game

This is a great one to use with a newly formed group whose members don't know each other very well. It provides them with a great opportunity to learn each other's names and relax together.

It can also be used as an icebreaker to relax and open up a group who do know each other if you are looking for their uninhibited vocal input later in the evening.

If the group is more than fifteen strong divide into two or more groups as appropriate. Get each group to stand in a circle and number themselves. Person number one in each group has to announce his or her name to the others as part of a rhyme: 'My name's Steve, I wear my heart on my sleeve.' Number two in the group then has to repeat the first rhyme and then add their own: 'My name's Jane, but I don't take the blame.' The third member of the group has to repeat rhymes one and two before giving one for their name...and so on. Group member number fifteen has the task of repeating, without error, all fifteen names and rhymes.

By the time the game is complete you can be pretty sure that everyone in the group knows everyone else's name and is feeling relaxed for the start of the rest of the evening's programme.

# Epilogue
# WALKING ON WATER

'One of the greatest failures of all time.' That's the way Peter's attempt to walk on water is most generally remembered. At Spring Harvest in 1986 Peter Meadows preached a sermon at the closing Communion in Prestatyn which I remember very clearly. He spoke about the time when Peter saw Jesus walking on the water and at once climbed out of the fishing boat he was in and took a few steps across the choppy lake towards his Master. As soon as he took his eyes off Jesus and looked at the wind and waves he rapidly began to sink. It was only the hand of Jesus that saved him from certain death. The other much wiser disciples decided sensibly to leave Jesus to do any walking on the water that had to be done while they kept their feet firmly inside the boat.

But how many people do you know who have walked on water? Besides Jesus himself, Peter is the only man in the history of the world ever to achieve such a great accomplishment. It was truly *Guinness Book of Records* material! Peter's few steps across the water, far from being one of the greatest defeats or failures of all time, was one of history's most outstanding achievements.

I can remember being told some years ago that if you came

up with a really good idea and presented it to an Englishman, by the time you had finished telling him about it he would have thought of three reasons why it would never work. On the other hand, if you gave the same idea to an American, by the time you had finished explaining it to him he would have thought of three ways in which it could be put into practice.

**Get out of the boat**

Some time ago I attended a management course where the lecturer stated that he felt all British people tend to be pessimistic in their outlook. If you take this basic outlook on life and mix it with a good dose of Christian teaching about personal responsibility and sin you are often left with people who feel totally inadequate, insignificant and unworthy – people who do not believe in themselves or in God's ability to use them in any significant way at all.

We are told of all sorts of reasons why the church in this country is not growing: it needs to work harder at this or that, it needs to plan more effectively and efficiently, to give more generously, to pray more consistently, to reappraise its priorities and increase its vision. While I am sure that many of these things are in part true there is a far more fundamental problem than all of this, which these other answers often serve to increase rather than help solve. There is the need to believe in ourselves because God believes in us and has chosen to use us. This is not humanism. In fact it is the very opposite! Our assessment of our worth is not based on human considerations but on God's ability to take hold of us and use us beyond our wildest dreams. The church needs to be positive and optimistic, to follow Peter, and get out of the boat! Yes, there was failure mixed with his great success, but don't forget that Peter took several steps more across the water than any other human being has ever done before or since! He started to sink only when he began to think about the situation he was in and his limitations rather than looking at Jesus who had already told him to come.

**Think big...plan realistically**

In our youth work we need Peter's obedience and enthusiasm, but most of all we need his trust. How often has a really good idea been squashed because of an 'It's impossible, we've tried before, it didn't work then and it won't work now' attitude? As a well-known poster states, 'Most people who say things are impossible are proved wrong by those who do them.' It is said of the people in Dallas, Texas, that they think big and build bigger. God wants Christian youth leaders who will think big, plan realistically and then build! We are to have large vision but also the energy to do the hard work that brings the vision into being. It's easy to talk in grand terms; it's difficult to translate these into reality. But it can be done when people are prepared to stick at a task even when at first it seems impossible.

CHECKLIST TO CHAPTER 16

# The Youth Service

| | | Allocated to | Done |
|---|---|---|---|
| *6 months* | Decide aim and target group (see chapter 15).<br>Talk idea through with minister/church leaders.<br>Book date or series of dates.<br>Discuss finance of possible outside speakers etc with church leaders.<br>Book speaker (confirm in writing). | | |
| *4 months* | Inform youth group.<br>Brainstorming session.<br>Decide theme.<br>Appoint planning group. | | |
| *3 months* | Hold planning group meeting.<br>Allocate jobs.<br>Book publicity/invitation cards. | | |
| *2 months* | Rehearse drama/music etc. | | |
| *1 month* | Fix date and time of dress rehearsal.<br>Contact speaker, inform him of arrangements.<br>Ask for readings, songs, hymns etc.<br>Encourage youth to invite friends.<br>Arrange hospitality for speaker. | | |
| *2 weeks* | Remind participants of date and time for dress rehearsals.<br>Clear music arrangements with church organist! | | |

| | | Allocated to | Done |
|---|---|---|---|
| *1 week* | Remind participants of date and time of dress rehearsal!<br>Check last minute details with speaker. | | |
| *On the day* | Meet speaker.<br>Dress rehearsal.<br>All participants to arrive by stated time.<br>Prayer meetings.<br>Pay speaker. | | |
| *After the event* | De-briefing meeting.<br>Encourage those who took part.<br>Start planning for next date.<br>Letter of thanks to speaker. | | |

CHECKLIST TO CHAPTER 17

# *Youth Camps, Conferences and Houseparties*

| | | Allocated to | Done |
|---|---|---|---|
| *1 year–6 months* | Decide on aim and target group (see chapter 15.)<br>Check idea and proposed date with church leaders.<br>Appoint planning group.<br>Book speaker(s) and confirm in writing.<br>Decide whether to stay at home or go away.<br>How many places do you need?<br>Within what radius must the venue be?<br>Decide on 3 possible venues.<br>Option 1 2 3 Decide theme, consult with the speaker.<br>Plan timetable (consult with speaker).<br>Book films and other resources (confirm in writing).<br>Set departure and return times.<br>Book coach for transport and confirm in writing.<br>Prepare budget.<br>Will the camp be subsidised by central funds?<br>Prepare and distribute publicity sheet/ booking form.<br>Book all necessary equipment. | | |
| *3 months* | Book Saturday afternoon outing/bowling centre etc and confirm in writing.<br>Prepare menu (if self-catering). | | |

| | | Allocated to | Done |
|---|---|---|---|
| *2 months* | Check with centre for rules and regulations concerning meals and curfews etc.<br>Prepare brochure for those attending.<br>If planning to attend a local church on the Sunday morning, write and inform them. | | |
| *1 month* | Distribute brochure.<br>How many volunteer drivers do you need for transport to and from the church?<br>Ask for volunteer drivers. | | |
| *2 weeks–1 week* | Buy food.<br>Check with coach for last minute details.<br>Check with speaker for last minute details.<br>Check with venue.<br>Check all other participants.<br>Hold briefing/prayer meeting for leaders. | | |
| *At event* | Pay speaker<br>Pay centre | | |
| *After event* | De-briefing meeting.<br>Pay coach company etc.<br>Write thank yous to speaker, centre and any other participants. | | |

CHECKLIST TO CHAPTER 18

# *A Concert*

| | | Allocated to | Done |
|---|---|---|---|
| *1 year–6 months* | Decide on aim and target group of concert (see chapter 15)<br>Check ideas with church leaders.<br>Appoint planning group.<br>Contact artists, speakers etc.<br>Decide on mutually convenient date.<br>Book artist and confirm in writing.<br>Book hall and confirm in writing.<br>Check details.<br>Prepare budget.<br>Fix ticket price.<br>Circulate information around local organisations, churches and supporters. | | |
| *4–3 months* | Book schools visits.<br>Appoint required personnel.<br>Order publicity (is this obtainable from the artist?)<br>Order tickets.<br>Book sound and lighting equipment (if necessary)<br>Book piano tuner (?).<br>Confirm all bookings in writing. | | |
| *8 weeks* | Prepare counselling cards.<br>Plan counselling arrangements.<br>Plan counselling training.<br>Order counselling literature.<br>Brief bookstall manager/local Christian bookshop. | | |

| | | Allocated to | Done |
|---|---|---|---|
| | Distribute tickets to sales outlets.<br>Fix accommodation for guests (if needed). | | |
| *6–4 weeks* | Prepare press release.<br>Put tickets on sale.<br>Distribute posters etc. | | |
| *4–3 weeks* | Distribute press release (see chapter 30).<br>Work out final programme and timing of evening. | | |
| *2 weeks* | Hold production meeting (see personnel list).<br>Check through all details of bookings with band, hall, equipment etc. | | |
| *1 week* | Contact band.<br>Check on counselling arrangements.<br>Hold prayer/briefing meetings.<br>Buy refreshments. | | |
| *On the day* | Meet band at hall with humpers.<br>Brief refreshment and bookstall helpers and stewards.<br>Meal for band.<br>Prayer meeting.<br>Counsellors' meeting.<br>Pay artists.<br>Introduce guests to overnight hosts. | | |
| *After the event* | De-briefing meeting.<br>Follow-up (see chapter 22).<br>Letters of thanks. | | |

CHECKLIST TO CHAPTER 20

# *Open Airs and Streetwork*

| | | Allocated to | Done |
|---|---|---|---|
| *3 months* | Decide on aim and target group (see chapter 15).<br>Appoint planning group. | | |
| *2 months* | Choose site.<br>Arrange amplification (if appropriate).<br>How will this be powered? Battery, generator or supply from nearby shop?<br>Inform local council.<br>Plan programme.<br>Inform youth group and church. | | |
| *1 month* | Prepare or obtain literature to be distributed.<br>Prepare questionnaire.<br>Commence rehearsals for drama/music etc. | | |
| *2–1 week* | Inform police.<br>Inform local shopkeepers.<br>Check availability of material with all performers.<br>Prayer/briefing meeting.<br>Publish programme.<br>Confirm meeting time for open air. | | |
| *On the day* | Prayer meeting.<br>Briefing. | | |

## CHECKLIST TO CHAPTER 21

# *An Evangelistic Mission*

| | | Allocated to | Done |
|---|---|---|---|
| *1 year–*<br>*6 months* | Decide aim and target group (see chapter 15).<br>Discuss idea with church leadership.<br>Discuss with other local churches if appropriate (see chapter 29).<br>Appoint steering group:<br>(a) Administrator<br>(b) Treasurer<br>(c) Prayer secretary<br>(d) Press/publicity officer<br>(e) Chief counsellor<br>(f) Representatives of all youth groups in the area or of the different activities within the local church.<br>Book visiting evangelist(s), bands etc.<br>Arrange initial planning meeting with them.<br>Plan counselling and nurture arrangements.<br>Plan training sessions for counsellors and nurture group leaders (see chapter 22 and checklist).<br>Prepare budget.<br>Inform other local churches.<br>Initiate planning for separate concerts etc (see separate checklists). | | |
| *4 months* | Produce prayer, news and information sheet for churches.<br>Approach possible local participants.<br>Meet with visiting participants (discuss their ideas)<br>Draw up provisional programme. | | |

| | | Allocated to | Done |
|---|---|---|---|
| *3 months* | Order publicity.<br>Order tickets.<br>Prayer and news update to churches.<br>Approach schools (booking schools work).<br>Start prayer groups.<br>Order evangelistic literature. | | |
| *2 months* | Update churches.<br>Arrange hospitality for visiting bands, speakers (comfortable beds, doubles for married couples, singles for singles!).<br>Prepare press release (see chapter 30).<br>Check programme with participants.<br>Prepare counselling cards.<br>Start counselling and nurture training sessions. | | |
| *1 month* | Distribute publicity posters etc.<br>Update churches. | | |
| *2 weeks* | Check all bookings for last minute details. | | |
| *1 week* | Update churches.<br>Final briefing/prayer meeting for counsellors. | | |
| *After the event* | De-briefing meeting.<br>Letter of thanks. | | |

## CHECKLIST TO CHAPTER 22

# *Follow-up*

| | | Allocated to | Done |
|---|---|---|---|
| *1 year–6 months* | Plan follow-up classes.<br>Appoint chief counsellor.<br>Decide on follow-up/nurture materials.<br>Plan venue or venues for nurture groups, dates, times, duration of course.<br>Order materials.<br>Decide on evangelistic literature.<br>Order material.<br>Plan training course for counsellors (training day).<br>Plan training course for nurture group leaders (training day).<br>Appoint nurture group leaders.<br>Approach possible counsellors. | | |
| *4–3 months* | Get samples of nurture literature for group leaders.<br>Run nurture group training course.<br>Prepare counselling card. | | |
| *2–1 month* | Run counsellors' training course or day.<br>Collect evangelistic literature.<br>Collect nurture group material. | | |
| *1 week* | Briefing/prayer meeting for counsellors.<br>Briefing/prayer meeting for nurture group leaders. | | |

| | | Allocated to | Done |
|---|---|---|---|
| *On the day* | Final briefing for counsellors.<br>Issue badges etc.<br>Announce central nurture group meetings at event.<br>Collect completed counselling forms. | | |
| *After event* | Process counselling cards.<br>Issue copies to:<br>(a) local churches<br>(b) schools<br>(c) nurture group leaders.<br>Check on progress of nurture groups after 1 week.<br>Check on progress after 1 month. | | |

## CHECKLIST TO CHAPTER 25

# *Coffee Bar*

| | | Allocated to | Done |
|---|---|---|---|
| *1 year–6 months* | Decide on idea, aim and target group (see chapter 15).<br>Talk through idea with church leadership. | | |
| *4–3 months* | Make list of suitable vacant shops etc in locality.<br>Contact owners (by phone if possible) registering interest in the temporary use of their premises.<br>If favourable, ask for date when confirmation could be given.<br>If it is not possible to contact owner, contact estate agent handling sale.<br>Keep a look out for new empty shops coming on the market. | | |
| *1 month* | Contact the list of owners again.<br>If the use of a particular shop is agreed, confirm booking in writing.<br>*Now immediately:*<br>Appoint planning group.<br>Contact relevant authorities:<br>(a) electricity board<br>(b) gas board<br>(c) water authorities<br>(d) local police | | |

| | | Allocated to | Done |
|---|---|---|---|
| | (e) health and hygiene<br>(f) fire services<br>Check on insurance cover.<br>Prepare and order publicity etc.<br>Book schools work (?)<br>Book bands (?)<br>Book speaker (?)<br>Others (?)<br>Arrange renovation and decoration of premises.<br>Issue prayer/information sheet to churches.<br>Prepare press release.<br>Distribute press release.<br>Arrange tables/chairs and all other necessary equipment. | | |
| *1 week* | Prayer meeting/briefing session for all involved. | | |
| *After the event* | Leave premises clean and tidy.<br>Write letter of thanks to owner and others involved. | | |

## COFFEE BARS/NON-ALCOHOLIC BARS

For coffee bars, non-alcoholic bars, etc, work through relevant checklists:
(1) Evangelistic mission
(2) Planning a concert
(3) Temporary use of vacant premises.

## CHECKLIST TO CHAPTER 26

# *Beggars Banquet*

| | | Allocated to | Done |
|---|---|---|---|
| *1 year–6 months* | Decide on aim and target group (see chapter 15).<br>Discuss idea with church leaders.<br>*Work through 'Using Vacant Shops' checklist.* | | |
| *4 months* | Contact relief agency.<br>Decide on relevant project to support. | | |
| *1 month* | When you've got your shop, appoint personnel.<br>Obtain equipment.<br>Order and obtain publicity/prayer sheet.<br>Prepare press release.<br>Prepare menu. | | |
| *2–1 week* | Order food.<br>Decorate shop. | | |

For more information about Christmas Cracker Restaurants contact:

Christmas Cracker
Oasis Trust
Haddon Hall
22 Tower Bridge Road
London SE1 4TR
Tel: 071–231 4583

## CHECKLIST TO CHAPTER 27

# *Radio Christmas*

**Version One**

| | | Allocated to | Done |
|---|---|---|---|
| *1 year–6 months* | Decide on idea and aim (see chapter 15).<br>Do you want to work with Radio Christmas Version One or Version Two? (if Two, see under 'Version Two').<br>Discuss idea with church leaders.<br>Appoint planning group:<br>(a) administrator<br>(b) treasurer<br>(c) technical manager<br>(d) press and publicity officer.<br>If planning on an inter-church basis, see chapter 29.<br>If planning to use a vacant premises as a studio, see chapter 25 and relevant checklist.<br>Decide on the exact area which you wish to cable (High Street, shopping centre, shopping mall etc).<br>Measure this area, calculate where you will cross roads etc.<br>Contact large national cable manufacturers and ask for their help, tell them about your project and its aim, obtain required length of cheap or free 2-core cable (if this proves impossible you may then consider Version Two).<br>Approach British Telecom if needed.<br>Contact relief agency and decide on relevant project to support. | | |

| | | Allocated to | Done |
|---|---|---|---|
| *4 months* | Approach the local branch of the Chamber of Trade, ask for their support and backing of your project.<br>Contact highways department of local council (obtain permission to cross side streets with cable etc).<br>Write to Performing Rights Society asking for exemption from royalties on charitable basis. | | |
| *3 months* | Send a letter to all the shops in the High Street (if possible this should be done jointly in the name of the church and the chamber of trade). This letter should:<br>(a) Inform them about Radio Christmas<br>(b) Ask for their permission to cable above their shop face.<br>(c) Ask for their involvement, playing the station on their premises.<br>Include a tear-off slip for their reply on which they can also request a personal visit to talk through further details.<br>Appoint a team of shop visitors. Familiarise them with the overall concept and then visit each shop giving more details, offering Radio Christmas and explaining how it would work and be fitted.<br>Check that each shop has suitable equipment for receiving your signal.<br>Send out a prayer and information letter to all the local churches. In this, ask for volunteers to act as receptionists, tea makers and members of a crew for laying cables.<br>Appoint a team of engineers under technical manager.<br>Approach local shops for supplies of sockets and plugs, records etc.<br>Get technical team working on the setting up and operation of a studio. For this, they will need the list of equipment printed on page 288. Write to record companies telling them of your project and asking for singles and LPs which may be available.<br>Write to local celebrities asking for their involvement.<br>Negotiate with local radio station for outside broadcast coverage of your project. | | |

| | | Allocated to | done |
|---|---|---|---|
| | Write to schools about taking part in the production of a cassette for sale.<br>Update to churches (asking for golden oldy records and any others to add to your record library).<br>Write to local churches for information concerning Christmas services to be included in your publicity.<br>Write to the relief agency you are working with asking for publicity concerning the project you are supporting. | | |
| *2 months* | Appoint team for the installation of cables.<br>Decide on hours of broadcasting.<br>Work out timetable for shows.<br>Appoint DJs, studio receptionists, tea makers.<br>Install cable (this job will probably have to be done slowly over the course of the next 2 months on Saturdays and other convenient times).<br>You will need several good sets of ladders.<br>Design and print dedication forms. | | |
| *1 month* | Design and print leaflet including information of what is on and happening over the Christmas period in the churches.<br>Finalise station timetable. | | |
| *6 weeks* | Record cassette in schools.<br>Have it copied by a recording company such as ICC or Springtide.<br>Inform the Performing Rights Society of this.<br>Print cover and inserts. | | |
| *2 weeks* | Prayer and information update to churches. | | |
| *1 week* | Install radio.<br>Hold prayer/briefing meeting for all involved. | | |
| *After the event* | Thank you letters to all involved.<br>Disconnect shops.<br>Take down cable and all other apparatus. | | |
| **Version Two** | | | |
| *1 year –* | Decide on idea and aim. | | |

| | | Allocated to | Done |
|---|---|---|---|
| *6 months* | Discuss idea with local church leaders.<br>Appoint planning group as Version One.<br>If inter-church, see chapter 29.<br>Approach local department store with your idea.<br>If they are interested, proceed with arrangements as for Version One although, of course, cables and permission from local council are not necessary. | | |

For more information about registering to be part of Radio Cracker contact:

Christmas Cracker
Oasis Trust
Haddon Hall
22 Tower Bridge Road
London SE1 4TR
Tel: 071–231 4583

CHECKLIST TO CHAPTER 28

# *Video Show*

| | | Allocated to | Done |
|---|---|---|---|
| *1 year – 6 months* | Decide on idea, aim and target group (see chapter 15).<br>Discuss and agree the idea with church leaders.<br>*If you're looking for an equivalent of your local bus station, work through chapter 25 and checklist.*<br>Appoint planning group.<br>*Now work through checklists 21 and 18* | | |
| *4–3 months* | Book video projector, screen and mixer, video recorder, two cameras.<br>Secure a video supply.<br>Book personnel, local drama, mime, interviews etc. | | |

# Resources Directory

A directory of specialist youth organisations, denominational agencies, funding ideas and other invaluable addresses – on hand when you need them.

**Evangelism and training organisations**

*Agape* (schools work), 4 Temple Row, Birmingham, West Midlands B2 5HG  Phone: 021 233 3677.
*Brainstormers* (training days and weekends for leaders), Elm House, 37 Elm Road, New Malden, Surrey KT3 3HB  Phone: 081-949 6858.
*British Youth For Christ* (schools work, evangelism, missions), Cleobury Place, Cleobury Mortimer, Kidderminster DY14 8JG  Phone: 0299 270260.
*Crusaders* (planting and development of local Christian youth groups), 2 Romeland Hill, St Albans, Herts AL3 4ET  Phone: 0727 55422.
*Frontier Youth Trust* (The 'open' and 'detached' youth work specialists, resources, training, support), 130 City Road, London EC1V 2NJ  Phone: 071-250 1966.
*Oasis Trust* (schools work, evangelism, missions) Haddon

Hall, 22 Tower Bridge Road, London SE1 4TR Phone: 071-231 4583.
*Saltmine* (schools work, evangelism, missions), PO Box 15, Dudley, West Midlands DY3 2AN Phone: 0902 881080.
*Scripture Union* (England) (schools work, missions, training), 130 City Road, London EC1V 2NJ Phone: 071-782 0013.
*Scripture Union* (Ireland) (schools work, missions, training), 157/159 Albert Bridge Road, Belfast BT5 4PS Phone: 0232 454806.
*Scripture Union* (Scotland) (schools work, missions, training), 9 Canal Street, Glasgow G4 OAB Phone: 041 332 1162.
*Youth With A Mission* (evangelism, missions, training), 13 Highfield Oval, Ambrose Lane, Harpenden, Herts AL5 4BX Phone: 05827 65481.
*Operation Mobilisation* (missions, training), The Quinta, Weston Rhyn, Oswestry, Shropshire SY10 7LT Phone: 0691 773388.

**Denominational youth departments**

*Anglican Young People's Association,* Chi Rho House, 53 Cedar Drive, Keynsham, Bristol BS18 2TX Phone: 0275 64306.
*Assemblies of God Youth Department*, 106–114 Talbot Street, Nottingham NC1 5GH Phone: 0602 474525.
*Baptist Youth Ministries*, Baptist Church House, 129 Broadway, Didcot, Oxon OX11 8RT Phone: 0235 512077.
*British Council of Churches*, Youth Unit, 2 Eaton Gate, London SW1W 9BL Phone: 071-730 9611.
*Catholic Youth Services*, 39 Fitzjohn's Avenue, London NW3 5JT Phone: 071-435 3596.
*Church of England Young People's Assembly*, Board of Education, Church House, Dean's Yard, London SW1P 3NZ Phone: 071-222 9011.
*Church Youth Fellowship Association* (Anglican), CPAS, Athena Drive, Tachbrook Park, Warwick CV34 6NG Phone: 0926 334242.

*Methodist Association of Youth Clubs*, Methodist Division of Education and Youth, Chester House, 2 Pages Lane, Muswell Hill, London N10 1PR Phone: 081-444 9845.
*Pathfinders* (Anglican), (specialists in 11–14 age group), CPAS, Athena Drive, Tachbrook Park, Warwick CV34 6NG Phone: 0926 334242.
*Salvation Army Youth Office*, 101 Queen Victoria Street, London EC4P 4EP Phone: 071-236 5222.
*United Reformed Church Youth Office*, 86 Tavistock Place, London WC1H 9RT Phone: 071-837 7661.

**Secular youth organisations and agencies**

*British Youth Council*, 57 Charlton Street, London NW1 1HU Phone: 071-387 7559/5882.
*Childline* (freephone helpline, confidential advice and counselling given) Phone: 0800 1111.
*National Association of Boys' Clubs*, 369 Kennington Lane, London SE11 5QY Phone: 071-793 0787.
*National Association of Young People's Counselling and Advisory Services and National Youth Bureau*, 15–23 Albion Street, Leicester LE1 6GD Phone: 0533 554775.
*National Association of Youth Clubs*, 30 Peacock Lane, Leicester LE1 5NY Phone: 0533 29514.
*National Council for Voluntary Youth Services*, Wellington House, 29 Albion Street, Leicester LE1 6GD Phone: 0533 554910.
*National Youth Assembly*, St Martin's College, Lancaster LA1 3JD Phone: 0524 338360.

**Specialist help** (* = Christian based group)

**Addictions (alcohol, drugs, gambling, etc)**

*Ash* (Action on Smoking and Health), 5–11 Mortimer Street, London W1N 7RH.

*Advisory Council on Alcohol/Drug Education*, 1 Hulme Place, The Crescent, Salford MM5 4QA Phone: 061 834 9777.
*Alcoholics Anonymous*, PO Box 1, Stonebow House, Stonebow, York YO1 2NJ Phone: 0904 644026.
*Alateen* (part of AA working especially with teenagers affected by someone else's drinking), 61 Gt Dover Street, London SE1 4YF Phone: 071-403 0888.
*Anorexia Aid*, 11 Priory Road, High Wycombe, Bucks.
*Credit Action*, Jubilee House, 3 Hooper Street, Cambridge CB1 2NZ Phone: 0223 31196.
*Families Anonymous* (support for families/friends of addicts), 88 Caledonian Road, London N7 Phone: 081-278 8805.
*Gamblers Anonymous*, 17/23 Blantyre Street, London SW10 Phone: 071-352 3060.
*Narcotics Anonymous* (drug abuse), PO Box 246, 47 Milman Street, London SW10.
*National Campaign Against Solvent Abuse*, 245a Coldharbour Lane, Brixton, London SW9 8RR Phone: 081-733 7330.
*SCODA* (Standing Conference on Drug Abuse), 1/4 Hatton Place, London EC1N 8ND Phone: 071-430 2341.
**UK Band of Hope Trust*, (alcohol, drugs, tobacco, solvents), 25F Copperfield Street, London SE1 OEN Phone: 071-928 0848.
*United Council for Alcohol and Other Drugs*, 112 Albany Road, Cardiff CF2 3RU Phone: 0222 493895.
**Yeldall Manor* (Drug rehabilitation centre), Blakes Lane, Hare Hatch, Reading, Berks RG10 9XR Phone: 073522 2287.

**Homeless and housing**

**Adullam Homes*, 11 Park Avenue, Hockley, Birmingham B18 5ND Phone: 021 551 5030.
*CHAR*, Room 22, 5–15 Cromer Street, London WC1H 8LS.
**Church Action on Poverty*, Central Buildings, Oldham Street, Manchester M1 1JT.

**Cornerstone*, 5 Ethel Street, Birmingham B2 4BG Phone: 021 643 1984.
**Missing Persons Bureau*, Salvation Army, 105/109 Judd Street, London WC1H 9TS Phone: 071-383 4230.
**Oasis Homeless Department*, Haddon Hall, 22 Tower Bridge Road, London SE1 4TR Phone: 071-231 4583.
**Shaftesbury Society*, 2a Amity Grove, Raynes Park, London SW20 OLH Phone: 081-542 5550.
*Shelter*, 88 Old Street, London EC1V 9HU Phone: 071-253 0202.

**Sexual issues (Sexually Transmitted Diseases [STDs], AIDS, abuse, rape, etc)**

**ACET*, (AIDS Care Education Training), PO Box 1323, London W5 5TF Phone: 081-840 7879.
*AVERT*, (AIDS education and research) PO Box 91, Horsham, West Sussex RH13 7YR Phone: 0403 864010.
**Care for the Family*, 53 Romney Street, London SW1P 3RF Phone: 071-233 0455.
*Family Planning Association*, 27–35 Mortimer Street, London W1A 4QW Phone: 071-636 7866.
*National AIDS Helpline* (information on AIDS or advice from a trained counsellor; calls are free, confidential and available 24 hours a day, 7 days a week) Phone: 0800 567123.
**True Freedom Trust* (homosexuality), PO Box 3, Upton, Wirral, Merseyside LA9 6NY.

**Unemployment, job training etc**

*Youthaid and Unemployment Unit*, 9 Poland Street, London W1V 3DG Phone: 071-439 8523.

**Offenders**

*National Association of Young People in Care*, 20 Compton Street, London N1 2UN.

• *Prison Chaplaincy Service,* Cleveland House, Page Street, London SW1P 4LN.

• *Christian Prison Fellowship*, PO Box 945, Chelmsford, Essex CM2 7PX Phone: 0245 490249.

**On file**

The addresses given above are national ones. Why not slowly build up a list of local agencies and addresses from the phone book and information available from your GP etc? Your list should include:

- agencies dealing with alcohol/drug or substance abuse
- agencies and statutory departments dealing with housing and homelessness
- Citizen's Advice Bureaux
- Unemployment office and Job Centre
- Department of Health and Social Security
- Careers Office
- Youth and Employment Training
- Social Services
- Probation Service
- Other contacts for family breakdown, racism, rape, sexuality, etc

**Funding ideas**

Funding is often available for equipment, training and sometimes even staffing. Here are three ways in which to explore opportunities.

*Register your youth group*

Registering your youth club with the Local Education Authority or Youth Service could give you access to funding, training and other useful resources. Make it a priority to find out whether your Local Education Authority makes grants to help youth clubs in their work. Get their address from the phone book.

*Grant making trusts*

Look through the Directory of Grant Making Trusts which you will find in the reference section of your local library. Identify any who would be in sympathy with your aims or objectives, especially those who are locally or regionally based. Your library will also have plenty of helpful information on how to go about applying for these grants to the bodies concerned.

*Others*

Other sources of possible funding include the Children in Need appeal, the Urban Church Fund, and so on. Don't be afraid to have a go. As the saying goes, 'Nothing ventured, nothing gained'!

**Residential facilities**

Weekends away are an important part of any youth work. The following are some of the many residential centres around the country which are available. Choose your centre well and ensure that the management is sympathetic to the needs of the teenagers you are working with. It makes sense not to go too upmarket. You can save a lot of money and unnecessary headaches by keeping it basic!
Activity centres operated by the Northampton Association of Youth Clubs include:

*Cleobury Place*, Cleobury Mortimer, Kidderminster DY14 8JG Phone: 0299 270260.

*Frontier Camp*, Welfrod Ave, Irthlingdorough NN9 5XA Phone: 0933 651718.

*Ranch Adventure*, The Wharf, Pensarn Harbour, Llanbedr LL45 2HS Phone: 034 123 358.

*Boy's Brigade Training Centre*, Broomley Grange, Stocksfield, Northumbria NE43 7RX Phone: 0661 842299.

*Carroty Wood*, Higham Lane, Tonbridge TN11 9QX Phone: 0732 354690.

*Cockney Spirit Sailing Trust*, The Sail Loft, Woodroffe Road, Tollesbury, Maldon CM9 8SE Phone: 0621 868839.

*Fellowship Afloat*, Tollegsbury, Essex Phone: 0618 68113.

*Gaines Christian Youth Centre*, Gaines Road, Whitbourne, Worcester WR6 5RD Phone: 0886 21212.

*Hollowford Centre* (Lindley Educational Trust) Hope Valley, Castleton S30 2WB Phone: 0433 20377.

*Hothorpe Hall*, Theddingworth, Market Harborough, Leics LE17 6QX Phone: 0858 880527.

*Marrik Priory,* Richmond, North Yorks DL11 7LP Phone: 0748 84434.

*Pickenham Activities Centre*, Pickenham Centre, Swaffham PE37 8LG Phone: 0760 440427.

*Quinta Christian Centre*, Weston Rhyn, Oswestry SY10 7LR Phone: 0691 773696.

*Sizewell Hall Ltd*, Leiston, Suffolk IP16 4TX Phone: 0728 830273.

*St Ninian's Centre*, Crieff, Perthshire PH7 4BG Phone: 0764 3766.

*Whitaugh Park*, Newcastleton, Roxburghshire TD9 OTY Phone: 03873 75394.

*YMCA National Centre*, Newby Bridge, Cumbria Phone: 05395 3758.

*Accessibility* (computerised access to details of centres to meet specific needs), 8b 1st Floor, Cash's Business Centre, Coventry CV1 4PB Phone: 0203 559099.

**Training for youth leaders**

Training is always a good investment. The options include:

*Basic training for volunteer workers*

This is provided by a variety of agencies including Frontier Youth Trust, Scripture Union, Brainstormers, most of the denominational agencies and Local Education Authorities. (For further information contact them at the addresses given above.) A number of denominations have worked together to produce an excellent package called *Spectrum* which is available from: Southwell House Youth Project, 39 Fitzjohn's Avenue, London NW3 5JT Phone: 071-435 8534.

*Part-time training*

There is a growing number of short term or distance learning courses run by organisations including:
YMCA National College, Newby Bridge, Cumbria Phone: 05395 3758.
Youth With A Mission (address as above)
St John's College, Bramcote, Nottingham NG9 3DS.

*Full-time training*

The format of this training includes varying levels of theology, youth and community study and local church ministry.

YMCA National College – leads to a recognised youth and community work qualification (address as above).

The Oasis Trust – leads to recognised youth and community work and theological qualifications (address as above).

Moorlands Bible College, Sopley, Christchurch, Dorset BH23 7AT Phone: 0425 72369.

Oxford Youth Works, Old Mission Hall, 57b St Clements, Oxford OX4 1AG Phone: 0865 722050.

# NOTES

**Chapter one**

1. Quoted in *Jesus is Alive* (Falcon, 1972), p. 15.
2. *ibid*.
3. James Dobson, *Preparing for Adolescence* (Kingsway Publications, 1982), p. 9.
4. Anne Townsend, *Families Without Pretending* (Scripture Union, 1976), pp. 103–4.
5. James Dobson, *op. cit.* p. 9.
6. F. Musgrove, *Youth and the Social Order* (Bloomington, 1965), p. 33.
7. Malcolm Doney, *Summer in the City* (Lion Publishing, 1978), p. 2.
8. *ibid*, p. 1.
9. Quoted by Graham Cray, 'Rock: power and illusion', in T. Morton (ed.), *Solid Rock* (Pickering and Inglis, 1980), p. 4.
10. Quoted by Malcolm Doney, *op. cit*, p. 3.
11. Quoted by John Allan, 'Christian Rock Today', *op. cit,* p. 6.
12. Malcolm Doney, *op. cit*, p. 4.
13. Quoted by Graham Cray, *op. cit*, p. 4.
14. John Allan, *Youth Workers Manual* Vol 1:1 (The National Youth Council of Assemblies of God in Great Britain and Ireland, 1984), p. 1.

15. Clifford Hill, *Towards the Dawn* (Fount, 1980), p. 52.
16. Larry Norman, 'Why don't you look into Jesus' from the album *Only Visiting this Planet* (Word, 1972).

**Chapter two**

1. J. A. Hadfield, *Childhood and Adolescence* (Penguin, 1962), p. 185.
2. Pete Gilbert, *This Generation Youth Evangelism File 4:4* (British Youth For Christ, 1985), p. 2.
3. Trevor Partridge, *Youth Workers Manual*, Vol 1:3 (The National Youth Council of Assemblies of God in Great Britain and Ireland, 1984), p. 1.
4. Quoted by J. A. Hadfield, *op. cit*, p. 24.
5. *ibid*, p. 240.
6. *ibid*.
7. *ibid*, p. 241.
8. *ibid*.
9. James Dobson, *Preparing for Adolescence* (Kingsway Publications, 1982), p. 105.
10. Mark Ashton, *Christian Youth Work* (Kingsway Publications, 1986), p. 55.

**Chapter three**

1. Quoted by Clive Calver, *Youth Workers Manual*, Vol 2:1 (The National Youth Council of Assemblies of God in Great Britain and Ireland, 1985), p. 2.
2. Quoted by Trevor Partridge, *Youth Workers Manual*, Vol 1:3 (The National Youth Council of Assemblies of God in Great Britain and Ireland, 1984), p. 4.
3. *ibid*, p. 4
4. Paul Hardcastle, *Nineteen* (Chrysalis, 1985).
5. Roy Joslin, *Urban Harvest* (Evangelical Press, 1982), pp. 129–138.

**Chapter four**

1. John Mott, quoted in *Guidelines B2* (British Youth For Christ, 1978), p. 1.

**Chapter six**

1. Leslie J. Francis, *Teenagers and the Church* (Collins, 1984), p. 29.
2. Lawrence O. Richards, *Youth Ministry* (Zondervan, 1972), p. 128.
3. Mark Ashton, *Christian Youth Work* (Kingsway Publications, 1986), p. 114.

**Chapter seven**

1. Clive Calver, *Youth Workers Manual*, Vol 2:1 (The National Youth Council of Assemblies of God in Great Britain and Ireland, 1985), p. 1.
2. Tony Dann, *This Generation Youth Evangelism File 4:5* (British Youth For Christ, 1985), p. 1.
3. Leslie J. Francis, *Teenagers and the Church* (Collins, 1984), p. 49.
4. Quoted by Trevor Partridge, *Youth Workers Manual*, Vol 1:3 (The National Youth Council of Assemblies of God in Great Britain and Ireland, 1984) p. 1.
5. Rob White, *Youth Workers Manual*, Vol 1:10 (The National Youth Council of Assemblies of God in Great Britain and Ireland, 1984), p. 2.
6. Nationwide Initiative For Evangelism, Special Interest Group E Report, *Young People in Pop Culture* (1981).
7. David Watson, *I Believe in Evangelism* (Hodder and Stoughton, 1976), p. 35.

FRONTLINE
TEAMS